Kamala Harris and the Rise of Indian Americans

Kamala Harris and the Rise of Indian Americans

Editor

Tarun Basu

wisdom tree

Editor's photo on the jacket courtesy Amit Bose

The opinions expressed herein are of the individual contributors and do not necessarily represent the views of the editor and the publisher of the book.

ISBN: 978-81-8328-571-1

Published by
Wisdom Tree
4779/23, Ansari Road
Darya Ganj, New Delhi-110 002
Ph.: 011-23247966/68
wisdomtreebooks@gmail.com

Printed in India

Contents

Preface vii

Kamala Harris: "She Can Be President Someday Herself" xvii
Aziz Haniffa

Kamala Harris and the Great Indian-American Diaspora 1
Shashi Tharoor

Indian-Americans as "Ambassadors" of India 19
TP Sreenivasan

A Community Zooms into Political Spotlight 35
Maina Chawla Singh

From Struggling Immigrants to Political Influencers: How a Community Came of Age 53
Tarun Basu

An Accidental Capitalist: How Indian-Americans Made Their Mark in Silicon Valley 75
MR Rangaswami

Professors and Academic Administrators: Conspicuous Presence in Temples of Learning 99
Pradeep K Khosla and Suman Guha Mozumder

Success Drivers of Indian-American CEOs: Fostering a New Wave of Corporate Leadership 119
RAJ L GUPTA

Leading Meaningful Change: Building a Culture of Philanthropy among Indian-Americans 133
DEEPAK RAJ AND ASHISH SHAH

All the Presidents' People: Trust in the Corridors of Power 147
ARUN KUMAR

At the Center of Excellence: Seminal Contributions in the World of Science 163
MAYANK CHHAYA

Physicians of Indian Heritage: America's Healers 181
AJAY GHOSH

From Stereotypes to Household Names: A Cultural Shift and New Role Models 201
VIKRUM MATHUR

Three Generations of Hoteliers: How Indian-Americans Reinvented the Hotel Industry 221
BIJAL PATEL

Millennials: Straddling Two Cultures Halfway Around the World 237
LAXMI PARTHASARATHY

"Success" Through Lens of Women: Celebrating an Alternative Model of the Marginalized 255
SUJATA WARRIER AND SHAMITA DAS DASGUPTA

Epilogue 279
ARUN K SINGH

Contributors 283

Index 289

Preface

The word "epiphany" is etymologically referred to as insight from the divine. Today, the word has come to mean a moment of sudden and great revelation or realization. And this epiphanous moment dawned on me in mid-August when Kamala Harris, a biracial politician who had demonstratively extolled her Indian cultural and social roots, was nominated on August 11, 2020 as Democratic Party candidate for vice president of the United States. The move was somewhat dramatically described by American media as making the senator and former attorney general of California a "heartbeat away" from being the president of the United States.

"I may be the first, but I will not be the last. It's on those of us leading the way to leave the door more open than it was when we walked in," an exultant Kamala Harris tweeted on December 14 after the electoral college officially affirmed the victory of Joe Biden in the 2020 presidential election. It not only confirmed her ascent to vice president on January 20, 2021 but made her a putative candidate for the 2024 presidency.

The nomination—and subsequent election—of the US-born Indian-origin Kamala Harris put the media spotlight on America—and around the world—on the small, but respected and high-achieving Indian-American community. It is a fascinating and inspiring story of how an immigrant population from a developing country, with low education levels, became the most educated, highest-earning ethnic community in the world's most advanced nation in almost a single generation.

Immigrants from India, as well as their children born and raised in America, have made their mark in almost every conceivable field in the US—science and engineering, medicine, business and entrepreneurship, academia, media and the arts, philanthropy, and now, increasingly, in administration and public service.

Physicians (doctors) of Indian origin have very high visibility, and are among the most respected, as they make up the largest non-Caucasian segment of the American medical community. The American Association of Physicians of Indian Origin (AAPI), a professional body of Indian-American physicians, claims an 80,000-strong membership. These doctors have been hailed for their dedication, particularly during the Covid-19 pandemic. Likewise, in the hospitality industry, Indian-Americans have made a name for themselves by virtually reinventing the hotel industry. The Asian American Hotel Owners Association (AAHOA) counts a majority of its nearly 20,000 members as being of Indian origin, notably Patels from Gujarat.

Numbering over four million, and fast heading to be five by 2022, people of Indian origin make up about 1 percent of the US population and are expected to rise to 2 percent by 2030. And yet they have made their mark with a culture of hard work, inclusive attitude, risk-taking, and passion for excellence in whatever they do.

In their seminal work of 2016, *The Other One Percent: Indians in America*, professors Sanjoy Chakravorty, Devesh Kapur, and Nirvikar Singh observed that immigrants from India have a unique position in the US, not comparable to other ethnic groups, not even to the natives of India. Indian-Americans are by far the best-educated group in the country with roughly three times more India-born residents with college degrees than the general population; and Indian-American households have the highest income level among any group in the country, more than twice as high as the general US population, as many of this anthology's authors have noted.

Sethuraman Panchanathan, who was appointed as director of the National Science Foundation in June 2020 by President Donald Trump, believes that Indians, especially the subset of people from the subcontinent who come to the US, are imbued with a passion to achieve more in the country of their adoption.

The fact that many come to the US with just a few dollars in their pockets but with big dreams and ambitions itself is a testimony to their risk-taking mentality and entrepreneurial spirit.

Dipak Jain, co-president and global advisor of China Europe International Business School, who did not know English very well before coming to the US for a PhD from Assam, gives a lot of credit to US meritocracy. "The Indians who have come here have all strived for excellence and not mediocrity, and people in the US can see through this quality of Indians because America values meritocracy," Jain told our authors Pradeep Khosla and Suman Guha Mozumder.

In recent years, the Indian-American community has been hailed variously by many American politicians and public figures as a "model minority", as a "community that has arrived" and has taken its place in American history—even though there are also critics of this "success" story itself.

And although Harris's identity has been so far more identifiably black than Indian, it is her Indian identity—through her Chennai-born cancer-specialist mother who had migrated to the US for higher studies and made her daughters, Kamala and Maya, not only dream big but to be the change agents and confident of who they were. Kamala Harris's articulated beliefs and value systems, that she said she culturally inherited, got her a lot of American media attention and made her a community aspirational model, especially among the second generation.

She is called biracial because of her estranged Jamaican father, and she rarely talked publicly about her Indian heritage till her vice-presidential nomination, as being a politician she presumably preferred a broader "South Asian" or "African" identity label to appeal to a larger panoply of voters.

"My mother, grandparents, aunts, and uncle instilled us with pride in our South Asian roots…we were raised with a strong awareness of and appreciation for Indian culture," she writes in her memoir *The Truths We Hold: An American Journey*.

It is perhaps a lesser-known fact that her pride in her Indian roots made her fly down privately to Chennai to immerse the ashes of her mother—who died in February 2009 of cancer—in the Bay of Bengal where the Ganga river, held sacred by Hindus, merges.

Diaspora Tracking

With nearly three decades of association with and tracking of the Indian diaspora, particularly of the Indian-American community, through my various media responsibilities—starting with the opening of the India office of the New York-based *India Abroad* paper in 1987; creating its news agency manifestation in the India Abroad News Service in 2000; which became Indo-Asian News Service, or the present-day IANS—I had often wondered if I would be able to put all that diasporic "resource" and connections to some use one day. After all, IANS at one time had nearly a score of foreign correspondents covering India and Indian-interest news from around the world.

Some of us had even toyed with the idea of creating a global digital platform to connect the Indian diaspora, which Gopal Raju, the visionary founder-editor of the New York-based *India Abroad*, had always dreamed about in the pre-digital era of the last century. His idea was to have multi-country editions of the weekly newspaper—*India Abroad* then had multi-city editions in North America and Europe—as a global voice of the Indian diasporic community and an information and communication bridge with India.

It was Raju, with whom I worked and remained closely associated for over two decades until his death in 2008, who introduced me to the unraveling Indian-American story. It was Raju's dream to "inspire, encourage, and introduce Indian-Americans to public service" and greater "civic and political engagement with a view to influencing public policy" to benefit the community and better US–India ties. This was at a time when few Indian-Americans wanted to get out of their professional comfort zone and "muddy" their hands in politics.

Senator (now President) Joe Biden was a close friend of Raju and often sought his and his newspaper's help in having a better understanding of key issues between the two countries, especially on sensitive issues like Kashmir.

Digitization killed this iconic paper a few years ago. But it had, no doubt, been instrumental for nearly five decades in amplifying the word about the community and its growing achievements, their expanding public profile and political influence.

An event that reflected the understanding of the importance and influence of the Indian-American community needs mention. In the wake of Operation Blue Star in June 1984, when the Indian Army stormed the Golden Temple—the holiest of Sikh shrines in Amritsar—that had become a sanctuary for heavily-armed Sikh separatists, some of its sacred sites, including the Akal Takht, were damaged in the shelling. Keen to project to the influential Sikh community in North America that the main shrine was unscathed—contrary to rumors that it had been destroyed—the Indian government relied on the *India Abroad* newspaper (in the pre-digital era) to spread the "right message" to the Indian-American community in the US and Canada. And I was flown to Amritsar to see things for myself and convey that message to Indians in North America.

Later, as the chief editor of IANS, I had the occasion to visit the US several times as part of the Indian prime minister's media delegation. Invariably, each prime minister would engage the diaspora and reserve an evening for that engagement. The interest and the levels of engagement increased with each prime minister—PV Narasimha Rao, who was the first to recognize the Indian diaspora as an asset to the country; Atal Bihari Vajpayee, who first fashioned a structured policy toward the diaspora; and Manmohan Singh, whose government set up a full-fledged Ministry of Overseas Indian Affairs with a cabinet minister in charge. Narendra Modi took the diaspora engagements to a jamboree level, but by that time, I was not part of the media industry anymore, though I retained my interest and associations with the diaspora, particularly the accomplishments of the Indian-American community, in different ways.

The Book

It dawned on me that if I really wanted to put to use my decades of professional knowledge and contacts with the Indian diaspora, there couldn't be a better time to chronicle that in a book—something which my wife, daughter, and several colleagues and well-wishers had been egging me to do for quite some time.

A publisher friend had suggested a quick paperback to be published within days of the US election results in early November. But I did not want to be rushed into a literary quickie. If there were to be a book, it had to tell the story of the community in all its rich and multifaceted dimensions. That was how the present edited compilation took shape and is now in your hands.

Accepting the challenge of chronicling the history and accomplishments of a community on the basis of received wisdom is one thing; finding storytellers was a completely different proposition.

It was a daunting task, especially in scouting for the right authors for this anthology, and they in turn having the time and the interest in this seminal project. One of those who quickly recognized the book's potential was MR Rangaswami—or MR as he is better known—the San Francisco-based IT entrepreneur, investor, philanthropist, and founder of Indiaspora, an influential network of global Indian-origin leaders from diverse backgrounds and professions that seeks to "transform the success of the Indian diaspora into meaningful impact worldwide".

He and his colleague, Indiaspora executive director Sanjeev Joshipura, helped identify the right people for some of the chapters and got them hooked into the project, despite its impositions on their tight schedules.

Also very solicitous and supportive of the project was the veteran community activist Thomas Abraham, the New York-based chairman emeritus of the Global Organization of the People of Indian Origin (GOPIO), the earliest of community mobilizers, that is also a global network.

This book is neither an attempt to document the community's saga, nor is it a compendium intended to glorify the community or put a shining light on their achievements alone.

It is an eclectic amalgam of perspectives on the emerging Indian-American story as seen through the eyes of public intellectuals and former diplomats like Shashi Tharoor, TP Sreenivasan, and Arun K Singh; community and professional leaders like MR Rangaswami, Deepak Raj, and Raj Gupta; industry representatives/observers like Ajay Ghosh, Vikrum Mathur, and Bijal Patel; diaspora scholars/academics like Pradeep Khosla, Maina Chawla Singh, Sujata Warrier, and Shamita Das Dasgupta; journalists like Aziz Haniffa, Arun Kumar, Mayank Chhaya, Suman Guha Mozumder, Laxmi Parthasarathy, and myself, who have lived and tracked the Indian-American story over decades.

So the narratives are, in many ways, personalized and subjective views of the author(s), through their own lived or viewed experiences, or a snapshot of a professional realm in which Indian-Americans have made a name for themselves.

It also must be borne in mind that the "success story" of the community has not touched all. Some activists, like our authors Sujata Warrier and Shamita Das Dasgupta, see the "model minority" label as self-serving and elitist and have propounded an "alternative model of success" among the marginalized sections, including socially non-conforming groups and women.

As an Indian-American entrepreneur and civic leader, Frank Islam notes in a recent article, "While the community's many successes and accomplishments have been well-documented, a less-publicized fact is the plight of hundreds of thousands of Indian nationals in the United States."

Indians constitute 4 percent of all the undocumented immigrants in the United States—about 630,000 people—a significant number considering that Indian-Americans form just 1 percent of the US population. This would mean every eighth person of Indian origin in the United States is an undocumented immigrant.

The Community in Spotlight

The Indian-American community was much wooed by both Democrats and Republicans prior to the 2020 election like never before. Of the roughly 4 million Indian-Americans, around 2.4 million were eligible voters. And of those, 1.4 million lived in nine battleground states.

As a Trump campaign official said, no doubt to please the community: "The powerful Indian-Americans are a force to reckon with today. You have not realized your own power, but President Trump understands your power."

The Democrats, more knowledgeable about Indian diversity, released campaign ads in 14 Indian languages and with Biden taking pains to greet the community on their important religious festivals like Ganesh Chaturthi and Diwali.

After the November 2020 elections saw a clutch of Indian-Americans, including many US-born, rising to political prominence at national, state, and local levels, one young activist proudly proclaimed, "Our time has come."

With one of their own seen as the nation's second-most powerful figure, Indian-Americans are quite comfortable in their minds with their blended identities—culturally Indian yet emotionally American—and see no contradiction in that.

Kamala Harris had told the *Washington Post* in 2019 that politicians should not have to fit into compartments because of their color or background. "My point was: I am who I am. I'm good with it. You might need to figure it out, but I'm fine with it," she said.

It is a line that will echo with most Indian-Americans today.

"For the US-born children, Harris's journey is that of an immigrant child who navigated cultural 'otherness' and stands today as the confident high-achiever immigrant American, who has not disavowed her ethnic or racial identity," as author Maina Chawla Singh puts it.

Although books on the community have been published in the US, in my understanding it is the first time that such a book on the community is being published from India.

Putting this together in less than five months—between its conception, sometime in mid-August, and the book's launch soon after Kamala Harris was anointed as the vice president of USA—has been a literary and publishing challenge.

Acknowledgments

I have already acknowledged the role played by MR Rangaswami and his deputy, Sanjeev Joshipura, in scouting for the right authors, given the limited time I had. I also need to acknowledge the role of my old IANS/*India Abroad* colleagues in it—Aziz Haniffa, a Washington "institution" for the last 28 years with instant name recognition in South Asian community and diplomatic circles as also the administration, who I got out of self-imposed "retirement" in Florida to pen the fascinating Prologue; as well as Mayank Chhaya and Suman Guha Mozumder, both US-based journalists who I had to cajole into writing under challenging deadlines despite their other schedules; Arul Louis, a New York-based veteran journalist, who has worked with ethnic, mainstream, and Indian media and who was instrumental in forging my association in the eighties with *India Abroad* and the evolving Indian-American story, and who has remained a friend and professional sounding board since. Another old *India Abroad* colleague, Ela Dutt, now editor of *News India Times*, also helped in author scouting, endorsements, and vital background information.

I must thank all my esteemed authors for agreeing to be part of this literary "adventure" and giving their valuable time—including over Christmas and the year-end holidays—to this project. I must particularly thank Maryann Thompson, a San Francisco-based writer, for her supportive research and writing work in several of the chapters.

Others who readily agreed to speak and share their experiences, despite time barriers, were Swadesh Chatterjee of North Carolina, Ashok Mago of Texas, Shekar Narasimhan of Virginia, and former Indian Ambassador Ronen Sen, who put me in touch with many community veterans and readily shared perspectives.

Ajit S Nagra, a schoolmate, now a practicing physician in the US, helped with his inputs for the doctors' chapter.

And, finally, my wife Ranjita, the family rock and anchor, whose gentle goading and pep talk when I despaired—which was often—got me through the finishing line in pretty record time. And my daughter Tonu, a public policy professional, and son-in-law Gautam, a scientist—in spite of their own professional preoccupations and in different time zones—who readily agreed to critique my chapter and give feedback on some of the others which proved immensely useful.

I cannot but thank my publisher, Shobit Arya, an old friend, for enthusiastically taking up this challenging job in such a short time despite all the professional and logistical constraints imposed by the pandemic, and also patiently walking me through the mire of track-change editing software that was completely Greek to me!

I dedicate this book to my parents, my parents-in-law, and my many mentors in the profession, who honed my skills, gave me the opportunities, and broadened my horizons to the "big picture" of a fast-changing globalscape where Indians are increasingly recognized for their talent, temperament, and culture.

Kamala Harris: "She Can Be President Someday Herself"

Aziz Haniffa

Just over a decade ago, Jeff Zucker, the then powerful president and CEO of NBC Universal, did something he confessed he had never done before—hosting a power breakfast at the NBC headquarters at 30, Rockefeller Plaza in Manhattan for the movers and shakers on the East Coast. His guest: an aspiring politician and a rising star who was already a West Coast sensation.

Apparently, Zucker, who is currently the president of CNN, and who had made and unmade TV stars and shaped the public images of politicians and television anchors while presiding over some marquee television programming, had some kind of a sixth sense that the personality he was introducing at this event would be an iconic political figure in the twenty-first century.

I had managed to cadge an invitation to attend this power breakfast for Kamala Devi Harris, then San Francisco district attorney who was running for the post of attorney general of California in 2010 and who, in the first six months of 2009, had raised $1,204,606—more than any other Democratic or Republican candidate for the position.

"I believe Kamala is not just important for the city of San Francisco, the state of California, but for the entire country," Zucker told his surprised guests, while throwing in a disclaimer: "This is not something that I ever do. This is in fact the first time I have ever done one of these, and that's because I have a very, very strict policy because of my job. I have taken a position that I completely stay out of supporting candidates of any party and try to stay out of politics entirely."

But he said the incident that influenced him to make an exception for Harris, which he had not made even for old friends and classmates, was a dinner he and his wife, Karen, attended in San Francisco four years ago. "We met someone who really knocked our socks off. For better or worse, I get to meet a lot of people and so it takes a lot to do that."

Referring to that first meeting with Harris, Zucker said, "I found her to be unbelievably special, and we have maintained a friendship for the last four years, and we talk by phone occasionally and I see her occasionally when she comes into New York. So, I got to know her quite well and, through that time, really came to understand what she's about both personally and professionally."

Zucker spoke of how Harris had told him, a year ago, that she was planning a run for attorney general of California. "I told her that this was the one time that I was going to break my rules—she was that impressive to me and that important, that special, and just that incredibly exciting," and adding that when he learned Harris was going to be in New York, he decided to put the breakfast meet together so the candidate could get to know people who matter.

"She is the district attorney of San Francisco," Zucker said while introducing Harris. "She is San Francisco's first African-American female elected district attorney, first African-American district attorney, first Indian-American district attorney."

He added, "She is California's first African-American female elected district attorney and she will be California's first female attorney general, first African-American attorney general, and yes, first Indian-American attorney general of California."

Then added helpfully, "By the way, this was something that I really liked, this really caught my eye, when the *New York Times* recently said that Kamala was among the 17 most likely women to become the first female president of the United States. I guess that's a good list to be on."

Harris then took to the podium and simply wowed the audience, regaling the New York power elite with an hour-long pitch to promote her run for the top elected law enforcement official in the country's most populous state—an attempt, analysts said at the time, could be a stepping-stone for a run for governor before she turned 50.

Harris, then 44 in 2009, spoke of how she grew up, one of two daughters of parents who were graduate students at UC Berkeley in the 1960s. "They met when they were both very actively involved in the civil rights movement, and so, as a child, I grew up with all these folks who were full-time shouting and marching about this thing called justice.

"I would like to say, I was there marching too in a stroller, but marching nonetheless, and for me frankly in that environment, the heroes were the architects of the civil rights movements, and they of course, were the lawyers—Thurgood Marshall, Charles Hamilton Houston. They were taking the skill of their profession to translate that passionately in what was happening in the streets and to bring it to the courtrooms of the United States where we were able to remind folks, who needed to be reminded, of that promise that we articulated in 1776. They were able to do that thing of bringing justice through the law to the street."

All of this, Harris said, inspired her desire to be a lawyer, and informed her time as prosecutor: "Law enforcement has such a profound impact on the most vulnerable among us. And it has as its essential duty the responsibility to be the voice for the vulnerable, and to give them dignity in the process."

Harris also spoke of her relationship with President Barack Obama, and pointed out that she was the first elected official to endorse him in California, and tied her campaign in with Obama's messianic message of change.

In the interaction that followed, Harris displayed the oratory and wonky and geeky grasp of issues that at the time had led sections of the media to dub her "the female Obama". Questioned, for instance, on the controversial Proposition 8 at the time, that sought to ban gay marriages, Harris spoke of her vehement opposition to it.

Ever the progressive, even then, she said, "I campaigned against it. The reality is, in this country it goes against our very basic principles to allow us to take rights from people. We can debate all day whether somebody should get rights, but once they have been given a right, it is just fundamentally, morally wrong to take that right from them."

For that reason, she said, the proposition—which states that marriage should only be between a man and a woman—"should never have been passed, and I will join with every effort we need to take to repeal it."

Later in the morning, I sat down for an exclusive interview with Harris—her first with a South Asian publication. And, for *India Abroad*, landing this interview with a rising star, who was then only a West Coast phenomenon but had the potential to be a national one, the fact that she was only half Indian-American, hardly mattered.

The interview, scheduled for 15–20 minutes, extended for nearly an hour and she was everything she was cracked up to be—tough, yet vivacious; supremely confident yet unassuming, but laser-focused on where she wanted to go in the world of public service in order to make a difference. And, added to this mix, someone with a mischievous yet non-malicious sense of humor who loved to laugh uproariously.

As the excerpts from that interview (at the end of the chapter) show—much of which Harris expanded on in her memoir nearly 10 years later—the influence of her mother was all-encompassing and the "foundational knowledge" she had dispensed to her (Harris) as she set forth on her political career was "focus on what's in front of you and the rest will follow", and "you may be the first, but make sure you're not the last".

On January 20, 2021, when Kamala Devi Harris, 56, was sworn in as the 49th vice president of the United States of America on the West Front of the Capitol by Justice Sonia Sotomayor—the first Latina member of the US Supreme Court—she created history on many fronts.

Besides being the first woman to be elected as vice president in the 244-year history of the United States, Harris—the Oakland, California-born daughter of Indian and Jamaican parents, who had met in the early 1960s, when both were students at the University of California, Berkeley, and bonded in the bassinet of the civil rights movement on campus—was the first black, the first Indian-American, the first biracial, and first child of immigrants, to hold the second-highest office in the country.

Although Harris was no stranger to historical firsts, vis-à-vis her career in public service and elected office, there was no denying that this was an unprecedented mother of all firsts, and hence the euphoria among minorities, women, and immigrant groups, most of all the Indian-American community—who have traditionally voted Democrat—was palpable. These even included some of the Indian-American Republicans, particularly the Never Trumpers, who marveled at her shattering not just the glass, but the bamboo ceiling, as she was now, as the cliché goes, "a heartbeat away from the presidency" as President Joe Biden's second-in-command.

For the Indian-American community, that has been punching way beyond its weight despite being just a little over 1 percent of the US population, excelling in a whole host of endeavors, from medicine to information technology, from business and industry—including small business and hospitality—to academia, and from law to the arts, making its presence felt even in Hollywood, and boasting of the highest per capita affluence and erudition in the country, Harris had catapulted into its consciousness only in the last decade.

The community had come of age politically more than 30 years ago, with the election of Democrat Kumar Barve in 1990 to the Maryland state legislature—who is now the longest serving Indian-American legislator—followed by the election of fellow Democrats Swati Dandekar and Satveer Chaudhary to the Iowa and Minnesota state legislatures in the 1990s.

Also, Republicans Piyush "Bobby" Jindal and Nimrata "Nikki" Randhawa Haley had been elected and reelected governors in Louisiana and South Carolina in the deep south, respectively, in 2007 and 2011—Jindal having the distinction of becoming the first Indian-American governor and Haley, the first female governor of South Carolina, who later went on to be the US ambassador to the United Nations from 2017 to 2018 in the Trump administration, and the first Indian-American to hold a cabinet rank.

At the time of their gubernatorial debut, Jindal, born to Hindu immigrant parents, Amar and Raj Jindal, and Haley to Sikh immigrant parents, Ajit Singh Randhawa and Raj Kaur Randhawa, had converted to Catholicism and the Methodist faith, respectively. Nevertheless, the Hindu-American and Sikh-American communities did not let their conversions to an Abrahamic faith inhibit or prejudice their acceptance by the Indian-American community, despite some of their xenophobic and intolerant stands on immigration and other social issues that their Republican Party espoused.

Meanwhile, Harris, who at the time was a rising star, serving as San Francisco district attorney, after being elected in 2003 and becoming the first black woman to hold that office in California, went largely unnoticed by the Indian-American community.

Some argue that the community was not cognizant of biracial Harris's Indian roots since she was totally immersed in her black identity. Others grudgingly acknowledged that even though aware of her mother's Chennai origins, they eschewed seeking her out, perhaps influenced by the community's subliminal, or sometimes even overt, racism toward the African-American community—the kind of reverse racial stereotyping of a minority by another minority that was powerfully showcased in Mira Nair's 1991 movie *Mississippi Masala*, starring Sarita Choudhury and Denzel Washington.

Then there were others who contended that Harris had not publicly and vociferously acknowledged her Indian roots or "Indianness" and, as a consequence, the community could not be faulted for their reticence to reach out to her.

That Harris non-apologetically and proudly wore her black identity on her sleeve was no secret, as she would later write about in her 2018 memoir, *The Truths We Hold: An American Journey*, of how her Tamilian mother Shyamala Gopalan Harris—who came to the US at the age of 19 to attend UC Berkeley, and a few years later married fellow student Donald Harris, an African-American from Jamaica—raised her and her sister Maya Lakshmi as black girls.

Harris, who lost her mother in February 2009, ironically to cancer, in her memoir reminisced, "Though I miss her every day, I carry her with me wherever I go. I think of the battles she fought, the values she taught me.... There is no title or honor on earth I'll treasure more than to say I am Shyamala Gopalan Harris's daughter."

She writes, "My mother understood very well that she was raising two black daughters. She knew that her adopted homeland would see me and Maya as black girls, and she was determined to make sure we would grow into confident, proud black women."

But in her book, she did not deny her Indian heritage—far from it. In fact, she spoke fondly and with nostalgia of her Indian roots and her extended Indian family.

Harris wrote of how "my mother, grandparents, aunts, and uncle instilled us with pride in our South Asian roots. Our classical Indian names harked back to our heritage, and we were raised with a strong awareness and appreciation for Indian culture. All of my mother's words of affection or frustration came out in her mother tongue, which seems fitting to me, since the purity of those emotions is what I associate with my mother most of all."

But even though Harris's parents—her mother was then a breast cancer researcher and her father an economics professor—first separated and then divorced when she was just seven, her mother continued to raise her and her sister in a largely African-American middle-class neighborhood in Berkeley. So much so that when it was time for her to attend college, Harris, now a proud, strong black woman, journeyed all across the country to read for her undergraduate degree at the historical and prestigious black college, Howard University in Washington, DC, majoring in political science and economics and joining the famed Alpha Kappa Alpha sorority.

She has said she specifically chose Howard because her hero, the trailblazing lawyer and Supreme Court Justice Thurgood Marshall—the first black person to be appointed to the nation's highest court—was an alumnus there.

After graduating from Howard in 1986, she returned to the West Coast to the University of California's Hastings College of Law and, armed with a law degree in 1989, successfully passing the bar the following year, joined the Alameda County prosecutor's office as an assistant district attorney, focusing on sex crimes, which was the launching pad of her political ascent.

Harris won her first race in 2003, when she blazed her way through to be elected San Francisco's district attorney, defeating her former boss and two-term incumbent Terence Hallinan. In 2010, she was elected as California's attorney general in yet another upset win against a popular white Republican, Steve Cooley, who served as Los Angeles district attorney, and in another first, became the first black woman to hold this position.

And then in 2016, when California's Senator Barbara Boxer decided to retire, Harris threw her hat into the ring, and was elected in a landslide, routing 10-term US Representative Loretta Sanchez and became only the second black woman and first South Asian-American to be elected to the US Senate.

In 2010, a year after my interview, she was elected attorney general, I found that outreach to Harris by Indian-American political activists and fundraisers had begun. It had its small beginnings, and in 2013 in her first major public interaction with the Indian-American community, she attended the first Indiaspora Ball in Washington, DC, in honor of President Obama's reelection, where she engaged in animated conversation with the who's who of Indian-American community leaders, political and community activists, spanning three generations.

This was a time when Silicon Valley entrepreneur, angel investor, and philanthropist MR Rangaswami, who had founded Indiaspora in 2012, along with the likes of longtime Democratic Party activist Shekar Narasimhan, the founding chairman of the AAPI (Asian American and Pacific Islander) Victory Fund—the first and only Asian-American super PAC—and Deepak Raj, a New Jersey entrepreneur and philanthropist and chairman of Pratham USA—who would later go on to establish Indian-American Impact Fund—had emerged as the new breed of progressive Indian-American community leaders replacing the old guard of entrenched community leaders.

By co-opting the Generation Xers and millennials, they began making a concerted and structured effort, using the highly successful Jewish template, on supporting Indian-American candidates at all levels, be it national, state, county, and local, with the objective of moving the community from the parochial niche they found themselves in to the mainstream of politics.

This involvement got into top gear when Harris successfully ran for the US Senate in 2016, becoming the first Indian-American elected to the Senate, and on the House side fellow progressives Pramila Jayapal from Washington—the first Indian-American woman to be elected to the US House of Representatives—Ro Khanna from California, Raja Krishnamoorthi from Illinois, were also elected for the first time, joining Ami Bera from California, who was reelected for his third term.

But it was in 2018, when Harris was mulling a presidential run that the Indian-American Democrats and the community totally embraced her as one of their own and began hosting events and fundraisers on her behalf with other longtime Democratic activists and fundraisers like Ramesh Kapur of Boston, Dr RD Prabhu of Las Vegas, and Harris's close friends over several years, Silicon Valley entrepreneur and women's activist Shelly Kapoor Collins, founding partner of The Shatter Fund, and renowned civil rights lawyer Subodh Chandra of Cleveland, helping to rake in several million dollars to beef up her campaign coffers.

Harris, for her part, reciprocated with her own all-in embrace of the Indian-American community and her Indian identity, keynoting two conferences organized by the IMPACT Fund, including a "Women Who Impact" forum, and also was the headliner at two events organized by Pratham in the Bay Area in California and also a Pratham tri-state event held in New York.

At the all-day inaugural Indian-American Impact Project Summit 2018, held on June 7 at the National Education Association auditorium in Washington, DC, possibly the largest gathering in recent years of Indian-American congressional and state assembly aspirants, congressional incumbents, community leaders, political activists and donors, Harris along with her fellow Democratic US Senator Cory Booker of New Jersey, who was then a potential presidential aspirant for the Democratic nomination in 2020, provided the star power.

The summit attracted over 200 participants, largely Indian-American Generation Xers and millennials, and Raj Goyle, co-founder of IMPACT and former member of the Kansas House of Representatives, said, "This historic summit is proof that the Indian-American community has truly arrived on the political scene.

"Together, we can shape a future in which talented and patriotic Indian-Americans are fully represented at every level of government, from City Hall to the White House," he predicted.

His co-founder, Deepak Raj, acknowledged the gathering mission—"to get more Indian-Americans elected to all levels of public office"—and noted that the younger generation of Indian-Americans are rising to the challenge "and willing to go beyond the traditional barriers" to accomplish that task. "You will make it better for my children, our children, our grandchildren."

He said the stated goal was to have at least 15 to 20 Indian-Americans in Congress "and our community should be represented in many, many places—city council, state houses, Supreme Court, state governor's mansions, and who knows, thinking big, one day in the White House."

Harris, who delivered the closing keynote, in urging the Indian-American hopefuls to push past the naysayers, and declaring the community is having its "moment in time", recalled that well before she became the first Indian-American senator to serve on Capitol Hill, when she made her first foray on any ballot, many had discouraged the challenge she made in 2003 to unseat incumbent San Francisco District Attorney Hallinan.

"I was told like many of you may have been told or will be told, 'Maybe, it's not a good time, maybe they are not ready for you, it will be a lot of hard work.' I didn't listen. And, part of why I am here today, is to say, don't you listen."

Harris also said her bid to replace the retiring Senator Boxer was met with the same skepticism. "And, of course, again, I didn't listen, I didn't listen. What we did, we built a coalition of people who seemingly have nothing in common, but had everything in common. And, we brought people together, understanding that we've had experiences that have taught us from the early stages of our lives, that the vast majority of us, no matter where we were born, no matter what god we worship, no matter what languages are spoken at home, the vast majority of us, have so much more in common."

She also urged a collective fight against those who are busy "sowing hate and division among us".

Harris compared the political environment under President Donald Trump to the era that inspired her own parents' political activism in the 1960s as students at UC Berkeley, and also noted that her grandfather was "one of the original freedom fighters" for India's independence.

"This moment of time is a moment in time to that moment of time when my parents were active in the civil rights movement," Harris said. The moment, she said, requires the community to be part of the fight for American ideals.

Harris was back once again on October 2, to keynote another Indian-American Impact Fund conference to showcase Indian-American women power and sisterhood solidarity and several hundred Generation Xers and millennials congregated to celebrate Indian-American women leaders, who were front and center in the resistance to the Trump administration's perceived xenophobia, misogyny, anti-immigrant fervor, and bigotry.

Harris called the celebration "an incredible gathering", and showered kudos on her congressional colleague in the House, Jayapal, calling her "a colleague and friend and now we've realized that we are related".

"I cannot applaud Pramila enough," she said, "because I see her front and center leading the charge when there is an issue—when there is an issue on immigration, around children being separated, what we need to do around families."

Three months later, on January 21, 2019—Martin Luther King Jr Day—was when the worst kept political secret since early 2018 was out in the open. To no one's surprise, Harris formally declared her intent to seek the presidency in 2020, and the elation she ignited among her closest Indian-American friends and supporters, longtime fundraisers, and progressive activists in the community, who were eagerly waiting for this day, was beyond thrilling.

Goyle and Raj said, "As the first viable Indian-American candidate for president of the United States, she is a trailblazer for our community and a champion for our values. We applaud her decision and look forward to supporting her enthusiastically in the days and months ahead."

Priya Dayananda, director, federal government affairs at KPMG LLP, and one of DC's top lobbyists, declared, "Kamala Harris is an excellent choice. Our community should help her in every way possible."

Narasimhan said Harris's decision to run had elicited "We have arrived" reactions "from the next-generation". However, "In the first generation, they are still asking 'is she really Indian?' even though she cannot be just that!" he said.

Narasimhan predicted, "I would say she has a chance of winning the Democratic nomination and therefore should be taken seriously. So, she will get Indian-American support—we do like winners! In a crowded primary, we could be the margin of difference."

Rangaswami said, "I never thought in my wildest dreams that we would have an Indian-American running for president of the United States, but this is now a reality!"

Just four months into her campaign, despite a slate of over a dozen candidates, including Biden, Indian-American Impact Fund was the first

Asian-American political organization to endorse Harris. "In such a critically important election, one that will shape policy and politics for generations to come, Indian-Americans can't afford to stay on the sidelines," it said.

And added, "In the coming months, we look forward to mobilizing our network of resources to ensure Senator Harris secures the Democratic nomination and is elected the next president of the United States of America."

But this is not to say, she didn't have detractors in the community, particularly among the Indian-American GOPers, avowed Trumpites, and a consort of other critics, who alleged that her "new-found Indianness" ostensibly was driven by political expediency and to exploit the "cash cow" that is the affluent Indian-American community.

Also, Sikh-American attorney Harmeet Dhillon, a California committee woman of the Republican National Committee and a staunch Trumpite and rabid critic of Harris over the years, attacked Harris, accusing her of being a charlatan, and that her wooing of the Indian-American community was largely to covet their contributions and not because of any sincere love for her Indian heritage.

Dhillon, who at the time served as the national co-chair of Lawyers for Trump and Women for Trump, and organized several fundraisers for the Trump reelection campaign—and once when Trump visited California for a rally and fundraiser, received him at the airport and rode with Trump in "The Beast", the bullet-proof custom-built massive Cadillac presidential limousine—in describing Harris as a far-left extremist progressive, would refer to the legal battle she fought with Harris against the alleged discrimination of a Sikh-American.

The case revolved around a former Indian commander in the Indian Navy, Trilochan Singh Oberoi, who alleged he was denied employment as a corrections officer in California because he refused to compromise on his religious obligations and shave his beard.

Although the case, which began during the tenure of former California Attorney General Jerry Brown, was ultimately resolved after a six-year protracted legal tug-of-war with Oberoi being allowed to adhere to his mandated religious obligation, Dhillon asserted that "her [Harris's] legacy as a prosecutor is a terrible one", because she had sided with the Department of Corrections, arguing that Oberoi couldn't be fitted for a gas mask unless he shaved and that no exception to the rule had been made since the policy came into effect in 2004.

When the exhortations of Dhillon and some segments of the Sikh-American community brought up this case after Harris declared her presidential run, and the Religion News Service (RNS) on July 2, 2019, ran a report titled "Sikh activists ask Kamala Harris for apology over beard ban for California prison guards", Kate Waters, a spokeswoman for the Harris campaign, explained to the RNS in an email that Harris's hands were tied. "Attorney general of California, Senator Harris was obligated to defend state clients including the Department of Corrections," Waters said.

The state settled the case in 2011, ten months into Harris's tenure as California attorney general and six years after Oberoi had originally applied for the job, paying Oberoi $295,000 in damages and giving him a managerial position in the Department of Corrections. And, in 2012, Brown, who was then governor, signed a bill to protect workers wearing mandated religious clothing or hairstyles.

Harris also had to reckon with some progressives and segments of the African-American community who took issue with her record as district attorney, alleging that she was responsible for incarcerating a disproportionate number of African-Americans and that she had also stringently used truancy laws in public schools that led to scores of single black women being punitively targeted.

This charge was seized upon by US Congresswoman Tulsi Gabbard of Hawaii, the first Hindu-American elected to the US House of Representatives—also a Democratic presidential aspirant—who used it to clobber Harris during one of the Democratic presidential debates, after Harris had surged in the polls in the aftermath of the first debate.

In a viral moment, Harris took on the front-runner Biden on race issues during the time he served in the US Senate, specifically for his opposition to federally-mandated busing to desegregate schools and his making nice with segregationist senators.

At that debate, Harris, in slamming Biden over his position on busing, made it personal, saying, "There was a little girl in California who was part of the second class to integrate her public schools. And she was bused to school every day."

"And that little girl was me," she added.

In the debate that followed, Gabbard, in a stinging critique, went after Harris for her prosecutorial record when she was the attorney general of California, and in the absence of an aggressive comeback by Harris, in the weeks that followed, her standing as a top-tier candidate and one of the leaders of the pack, began to plummet and consequently her fundraising took a strong hit.

In the months that followed, besides falling significantly in the polls, Harris also began laying off staff and trailing in the money race and at one point in one poll suffered the ignominy of having Gabbard—who earlier was not even a blip on the radar—almost pulling parallel to her with five percentage polls, even though that put them nowhere among the top five contenders.

This simmering feud between Harris and Gabbard—both of whom were beneficiaries of the largesse of different segments of the Indian-American community to their respective campaigns—completely spilled over during the fifth debate in Atlanta on November 13, 2019, when Harris ripped into Gabbard, all but calling her a wolf in sheep's clothing in the Democratic Party.

Harris, since she launched her campaign, had been strongly supported by the largely progressive wing among Indian-Americans in the Democratic Party as well as the moderates, while Gabbard's support, including significant funding, had come from the Hindu-American community among Indian-Americans, particularly from the right-wingers.

But, at the time they were feuding, sources said that with Harris's percentage numbers plummeting in the polls, and Gabbard not "having a snowball's chance in hell" of securing the Democratic nomination, both had suffered a significant decline in their fundraising and this was unlikely to change anytime soon.

On December 3, 2019, when Harris announced that she was throwing in the towel—a month before the Iowa caucuses—an account managed by Trump's campaign tweeted, "Breaking News: Kamala Harris has ended her campaign for president. Congratulations Tulsi!"

Her withdrawal was a downer to her ardent supporters, including Indian-Americans who had invested heavily in her campaign. It also raised concern that Harris's attack on Biden at the first debate may have also signaled the end of their envisaged "Dream Team", of Harris as Biden's running mate, since Biden was pulling ahead as the most likely Democratic candidate who could beat Trump.

Harris, three months after delaying her endorsement of Biden, with the Biden nomination seeming a no-brainer, endorsed Biden on March 8, 2020.

She said, "When I started my run for president, I said America needs a president who reflects the decency and dignity of the American people; a president who speaks the truth; and a president who fights for those whose voices are too often overlooked or ignored. I still believe that to this day. That is why I am proud to announce I am endorsing my friend, Vice President Joe Biden, for president of the United States."

Biden immediately thanked Harris for the endorsement, saying: "Kamala—You've spent your whole career fighting for folks who've been written off and left behind—and no small part of that alongside Beau (Biden's late son, and former attorney general of Delaware, who was a friend on Harris). From our family: thank you," the former vice president said in a retweet of her endorsement.

This reinforced the hope by Harris's supporters, that perhaps the "Dream Team" was back on, because earlier, when Biden asked by reporters if he would consider Harris as a vice-presidential pick, said, "Of course, I would," turning around to answer the question as he walked onto his campaign bus. "Look, Senator Harris has the capacity to be anything she wants to be. I mean it sincerely. I talked to her yesterday. She's solid, she can be president someday herself, she can be vice president, she could go on to be a Supreme Court justice, she could be attorney general. I mean she has enormous capability."

In August, a week before the Democratic Convention (August 17–20), Biden, who had vowed that his running mate would be a woman, and had been urged to appoint a woman of color by US Congressman from South Carolina, Rep Jim Clyburn, and winnowing a long list of candidates before settling on Harris—placed a video call to her and asked, "You ready to go to work," manifesting once again, a case of "the rest is history" in the life of Harris.

The *New York Times* reported on August 13, 2020, that "no candidate scored as highly as Senator Kamala Harris on the Biden campaign's core criteria for a running mate, including her strength as a debater and ability to help him win the White House."

And, onward to the White House it was, when four days after the general election on November 3, after the bulk of the mail-in ballot were in during a surreal year dominated by the Covid-19 pandemic, the Biden–Harris ticket had prevailed and relegated President Donald Trump to a one-term president. And a black-American/Indian-American woman of color had scaled to heights never before experienced in either history of the black-American or the Indian-American immigrant experience.

On January 20, when Harris—whom both African-American and Indian-Americans could stake a claim to—was sworn in by Sotomayor with her left hand placed on two Bibles—one, which belonged to her inspiration, Supreme Court Justice Marshall, and the other that belonged to family friend Regina Shelton, whom Harris called a "second mother", both of which were held by her Jewish-American husband Doug Emhoff, the country's first second gentleman—race, religion, ethnicity, or gender mattered little to attain the highest offices in the nation.

Consequently, that's what Harris brings to the table. As Yonat Shimron has written in the Religion News Service that "in a time of expanding religious pluralism, the country's younger generation, many of them children and grandchildren of immigrants, will recognize in Harris a kind of multifaith and spiritual belonging unfamiliar to the mostly-white Christian-majority of past decades."

With the black-American/Indian-American Kamala Harris connection and the Jewish-American second gentleman, and Biden being only the second Catholic after President John F Kennedy to be president, it may not matter in the future whether one is sworn in and takes an oath to the US Constitution on the Bible, Bhagavad Gita, Torah or Quran. And now Indian-Americans and African-Americans can look forward to celebrating Christmas, Diwali, Kwanzaa, Hanukkah, Eid, and Baisakhi with equal gusto and togetherness in a multifaith, pluralist America.

EXCERPTS FROM MY 2009 *INDIA ABROAD* INTERVIEW:

On her dual ethnicity: I'm very proud of my cultural heritage. I am very proud to know that in my success, I provide a role model for those who identify with me for reasons of culture or ethnicity or gender or profession or professional goals, or just because they see something that inspires them, whoever they are and whatever their walk of life or background.

On her inherited culture and heritage: My mother was very proud of her Indian heritage and taught us, me and my sister Maya, to share in the pride about our culture.... India is the largest democracy in the world—so that is part of my background, and without question has had a great deal of influence on what I do today and who I am.

On the roots of her civil rights: My grandfather and grandmother enjoyed the time they spent with people of all walks of life (at Berkeley) who were involved in the civil rights movement. I believe that one of the benefits of having traveled the world and having known different cultures is that you really understand and see very clearly that people, whoever they are, whatever language they speak, have so much more in common than they do differences.

On the importance of the ethnicity: We have to stop seeing issues and people through a plate-glass window as though we were one-dimensional. Instead, we have to see that most people exist through a prism and they are a sum of many factors.

On her association with Barack Obama: I supported him when he ran for the Senate from Illinois. And one of the first events he did after he was elected to the United States Senate was in support of me in San Francisco, when I was about to run for reelection as district attorney. So yes, we have a history of supporting one another.

On a number of Indian-Americans holding senior positions in the Obama administration: In the process of electing Barack Obama president of the United States, the South Asian community became very involved and empowered. It encouraged people to see that they can themselves be leaders, not only around community organizations and activism, but also that they can run for office.

Kamala Harris and the Great Indian-American Diaspora

SHASHI THAROOR

The night the news came of the victory of the Biden–Harris ticket in the US presidential elections, Vice President-elect Kamala Harris—standing in front of a crowd of cheering, applauding, roaring, and sometimes weeping supporters—spoke in terms worthy of a great historic occasion.

At a podium placed before an array of parked cars in which the audience had driven in to preserve social distancing norms, Harris, dressed symbolically in the white suit that evokes the women's suffragette movement (and that is becoming her trademark), declared emotionally that she was "thinking about her [mother] and about the generations of women—black women, Asian, white, Latina, Native American women—who, throughout our nation's history, have paved the way for this moment tonight".

The moment was fraught with meaning, and for the hundreds of happy, flag-waving supporters that night, it signaled a breakthrough many had scarcely believed possible. America's first woman vice president represents multiple minorities: she is the first person elected to nationwide office who can claim black, South Asian, and Caribbean descent (and a Jewish husband to boot). For the thousands of little black girls who made "My VP Looks Like Me" T-shirts go viral over the next few days, Harris represented an expansion of their horizons.

But there was one slightly false note to all the fulsome tributes that flowed that night. Celebrating the ascent of a woman—the first, she proudly said, but not the last—the new US vice president-elect paid tribute to her late mother, Shyamala Gopalan, who in 1959 "came here from India at the age of nineteen" and "believed so deeply in an America where a moment like this is possible". But, said Harris, "Maybe [her mother] didn't quite imagine this moment."

Why not? An admiring Indian could well ask. Such a moment may not have been easy to imagine in the US, where there has been only one female presidential candidate from a major political party and two vice-presidential ones ever—and all unsuccessful. But in South Asia, the glass ceiling was shattered long ago. Just a year after the teenage Shyamala Gopalan arrived in the US, Sirimavo Bandaranaike became the prime minister of Sri Lanka in 1960 upon the tragic assassination of her husband and then premier, Solomon.

Thus began a long list of Asian female heads of government. From Indira Gandhi in India to Benazir Bhutto in Pakistan and Khaleda Zia and Sheikh Hasina Wazed in Bangladesh, taking in two presidents—Chandrika Kumaratunga in Sri Lanka and Pratibha Patil in India—South Asia has had no shortage of female leaders. So while no one can deny Kamala Harris the unique distinction she has acquired of being the first female vice president of the world's oldest democracy and, more to the interest of Indians, the first of part-South Asian descent, the concept of elected women holding the highest offices of the land is hardly novel to the South Asian region from which her mother hailed.

The US didn't, but so many democracies around the world did, that the distinction was somehow robbed of impact worldwide. But what was indeed impactful, especially in India, was the astonishing realization that the daughter of a woman born in Chennai was now a "heartbeat away" from occupying the White House.

In analyzing this development, I propose to review, in the pages that follow, the global phenomenon of the Indian diaspora, its specific American manifestation, and the further departure that Kamala Harris's ascension represents from all standard typologies.

Only Country with Acronym for Expats

India is probably the only country in the world that has not only given official recognition to its expatriates but has even devised a formal acronym for them. NRI, or Non-Resident Indian, is a term that, over the last three decades, has found a firm place in the national vocabulary, though it is yet to be reflected in any dictionary. In my 1997 book *India: From Midnight to the Millennium*, I jokingly suggested that the real debate was whether NRI stood for "Not Really Indian" or "Never Relinquished India". The nearly 25 million people of Indian descent who live abroad fall, of course, into both categories. And in recent years, as the government has set about cultivating them through generous new policies, the establishment of a Ministry for Overseas Indian Affairs (MOIA), and annual Pravasi Bharatiya Divas (PBD, or Overseas Indians' Day) events in India, it's clear one can apply a third variant to the acronym—the "Now Required Indians".

I recall a PBD in Mumbai attended by the vice presidents of Suriname and Mauritius, both the former prime ministers of Fiji and Trinidad and Tobago, Malaysian politicians and Gulf-based entrepreneurs, tycoons from Hong Kong and titans from the United States, all united by the simple fact of shared heritage—the undeniable reality that even exiles cannot escape when they look into the mirror. They were united, too, in the words of the typically thoughtful and inspiring inaugural address by then Prime Minister Manmohan Singh on that occasion, by an "idea of Indianness". It is an idea that enshrines the diversity and pluralism both of our country and of its diaspora. In a land that is home to Indians of every conceivable caste and creed, the PBD celebrations continue each year to afford to Indians—including former Indians—of every conceivable caste and creed the welcome assurance that they were indeed "at home".

Non-Resident Indians have certainly come a long way since the days when Indian prime ministers sanctimoniously urged them to be loyal to the foreign countries in which they had settled. As late as 1974, an Indian foreign minister told the parliament that "overseas Indians" had chosen to live abroad and so were responsible for their own condition: the government of India had no obligation toward them. But since then, New Delhi has developed expectations of its NRIs, and a reciprocal sense of obligation, too, has followed. Today NRIs are seen as people on whom the motherland and its elected representatives have a legitimate claim. It is a claim willingly conceded by many NRIs; for every extremist or secessionist abroad (a category whose numbers are mercifully dwindling), there are a hundred who continue to demonstrate a remarkable degree of interest in, and commitment to, the land of their birth (or of their forebears).

The law that first defined NRIs did so in broad terms and the term NRIs applied to expatriate Indians irrespective of their current citizenship; today it is restricted to Indian citizens living abroad, whereas people whose emigration has acquired the permanence of foreign nationality are referred to as PIOs, or Persons of Indian Origin. "A Person of Indian Origin (PIO) means a foreign citizen (except a national of Pakistan, Afghanistan, Bangladesh, China, Iran, Bhutan, Sri Lanka and Nepal)," says the government, "who at any time held an Indian passport; or who or either of their parents/grandparents/great-grandparents was born and permanently resident in India as defined in Government of India Act, 1935 and other territories that became part of India thereafter, provided neither was at any time a citizen of any of the aforesaid countries (as referred above); or who is a spouse of a citizen of India or a PIO." New Delhi's anxiety to define the category as broadly as possible has led to some interesting terminological calisthenics. Not only can anyone with one Indian grandparent or even a great-grand parent declare himself a PIO and claim the benefits of that designation but the spouse of a citizen of India or a PIO shall also be deemed to be of "Indian origin" though he/she may be of non-Indian origin.

These criteria, though liberal by international standards, still omit some who are visibly of Indian origin. One obvious problem, of course, is that if the PIO definition were to be interpreted literally, practically every citizen of the former British Raj in India, as well as those of neighboring countries, could qualify as being of "Indian" descent, but politics requires their exclusion. The original NRI definition had also disqualified descendants of some of the earlier waves of Indian migration, mainly in the last century, to such far-flung outposts of the Empire as Malaya and Mauritius, Ghana and Guyana, Singapore and Suriname. In most cases, nationals of those countries, though manifestly of Indian origin, are descended from migrants of earlier generations, higher up the family tree than their grandparents. Since, in this era of shrinking planetary distances, many of those expatriate communities have, in recent years, renewed their links to their ancestral lands, their connection is now recognized in the term PIO. So NRIs and PIOs together constitute the Great Indian Diaspora.

Waves of Diasporic Movement from India

There have been four broad waves of diasporic movement from India. The first, in precolonial times, featured Indians leaving our shores as travelers, teachers, and traders; the second involved the enforced migration of Indian labor as indentured servants of the British Empire; the third, the tragic displacement of millions by the horrors of Partition; and the fourth, the contemporary phenomenon of skilled and educated Indians seeking opportunity and challenge in our globalized world. I would probably divide the fourth wave further into two distinct categories: one of highly educated Indians, often staying on after studies abroad in places like the US, and the other of more modestly-qualified but even harder-working migrants, from taxi drivers to shop assistants, who for the most part see their migration as temporary and who remit a larger proportion of their funds home to India than their higher-earning counterparts. But in today's world, both sets of "fourth wave" migrants remain closely connected to the *matrbhumi*: the ease of communications and travel makes it possible for expatriates to be engaged with the country they left behind in a way that was simply not available to the plantation worker in Mauritius or Guyana, a century ago. To tap into this sense of allegiance and loyalty through an organized public gathering was an inspired idea; hence the annual PBDs, supported by a "one-stop shop" in the form of a dedicated Ministry for Overseas Indian Affairs. Though the ministry was merged by the Narendra Modi government into the Ministry of External Affairs (MEA), one secretary of the ministry is still dedicated to the work of the overseas Indians, and a minister of state in MEA is usually tasked with giving overseas Indians the level of political attention their importance deserves.

The stories of this "fourth wave" vary. Many of the first Indian emigrants to Britain, for instance, went in search of an education and stayed on to work. Then, from the 1950s on, came less-educated members of the working class, attracted by the liberalization of British entry laws during the labor shortages of the postwar boom years. A third stream of Indians came in the 1970s via East Africa, from where many were expelled in the xenophobic fervor that swept some African states after their independence. All three groups, and their offspring, have acquired a reputation for hard work, business sense, and ethnic clannishness. Their success and, paradoxically, their failure to assimilate fully into the British society have made them ideal NRIs—still owing residual loyalty to their Indian past, and usually well-off enough to do something about it. This has appealed to all those in India who wish to court their support.

In North America, the "waves" took place in a different order. The first Indian immigrants to the US and Canada came as early as the 1890s, when shiploads of Sikhs settled on the Pacific coast and established thriving farming communities in British Columbia and California. Racist entry-legislation—prompted by such events as anti-Indian riots in the state of Washington in 1907—prevented them from adding to their numbers, however, and it was only a thin trickle of students who came to the US from India after the 1920s. (As late as 1935, signs on the doors of certain California establishments declared, "No jobs for Japs or Hindus".) The number of Indian students began to increase after Indian independence, and an increasing proportion of them stayed on, bringing high levels of academic attainment and valuable scientific and engineering skills to their new country. By the early 1970s, the small but influential Indian minority was estimated as having the highest per capita income of any ethnic group in the US—the median family income of the Indian-American, according to US census figures, exceeds the median income of white Americans by a wide margin. That is still the case in 2020.

Opening the Sluice Gates

It was the more liberal Immigration and Naturalization Act of 1965 that opened the sluice gates to the United States for Indians. But while the trickle of Indian professionals became a stream, in the more recent years it is illegal immigration that has swelled the flow into a torrent. Working-class Indians found their way into the US for the first time in the late 1970s and early 1980s, toiling on construction sites, taking over newspaper kiosks on street corners, operating rundown motels, cooking and serving in Indian restaurants, and driving taxicabs. Their success has been based on the strength of qualities regarded as "typically Indian"—hard work, discipline, self-sacrifice, and thrift. The way in which Indians have taken over unprofitable motels across the United States, and run newsstands in New York City or late-night groceries in London, is widely seen as reflective of these qualities. A pair of "amnesties" gave the illegals among them the legal status they needed to bring their families over, and today this "underclass" of Indian immigrants accounts for nearly half of the estimated 3,400,000 PIOs in the United States.

That figure may even be an undercount, omitting as it does many who are still illegal and those who trace their direct descent from another center of the Indian diaspora, such as the Caribbean. But allowing for the approximations that are inevitable in such an exercise, the Indian-American is now a familiar figure in US politics.

Indian-Americans are probably behind other Indian immigrants in making major financial contributions to their motherland. In the 1980s and 1990s, remittances home from NRIs—primarily the diligent Indian workers in the countries of the Arab/Persian Gulf—averaged the equivalent of some 40 percent of India's annual merchandise exports, or some 3 percent to 4 percent of gross national product (GNP), though both percentages have been dropping in recent years as India's economy has boomed. (In the state of Kerala, these remittances were responsible for generating a remarkable boom in the real estate and construction businesses, as money was poured in to new housing for NRIs and land values tripled in some areas.) In addition, NRI depositors in Indian banks have frequently bailed out the government in periods when it was strapped for hard currency. And yes, there are now the millions poured into cutting-edge, high-tech businesses in Bengaluru or Gurugram by investors from Silicon Valley. But we shouldn't get carried away—overseas Indians, especially Indian-Americans, still invest a lower proportion of their resources in India than overseas Chinese do in China. Encouraging them to do more—and giving them reasons to do more—is certainly a worthwhile task for the MEA's Department of Overseas Indian Affairs in New Delhi.

Meanwhile, no longer is there much cavil about a "brain drain". The argument that Indians who work abroad are doing a disservice to their country seems to me misplaced, especially in recent years as Indians abroad have given so much more back to their homeland than they could ever have contributed while staying there. The old fears of a "brain drain" seemed to me to have been supplanted by hopes of a "brain gain", as desi software designers and high-tech gurus from Silicon Valley have opened thriving firms in India, employing their countrymen and women, increasing the country's export revenues and pumping up the national gross domestic product (GDP). Indians going abroad after their studies have done a great deal to benefit the Indians who stayed at home. And with some second-generation PIOs coming to India to discover the land of their ancestors, and even work there, the less euphonious but more accurate term seems to be of "brain circulation".

So it seems otiose to ask: Why do NRIs matter to India?

The answer is simple: as a source of pride, as a source of support, and as a source of investments. It is entirely natural for Indians to take pride in the successes of their erstwhile compatriots abroad. I once remarked rather cruelly to an interviewer that the only country where Indians as a whole did not succeed was India. That is fortunately no longer the case, as signs of Indians' increasing prosperity are increasingly evident everywhere one travels in India, but Indians abroad have certainly given us all a great deal to be proud of. One recent statistic from the US shows that the Indian-American family's median income is over $100,000 a year, the same as Japanese-Americans, but nearly $20,000 higher than the figure for all American families. That kind of success is not merely at the elite end of the scale—in England today, Indian curry houses employ more people than the iron and steel, coal and shipbuilding industries combined. (Many are the ways, indeed, in which the Empire can strike back.)

So we can be proud of the impact Indians have made on foreign societies. But pride is not merely an intangible asset. When I was living in the US, I was struck by the extent to which the success of our NRIs had transformed the public perception of India in the US. A generation ago, when I first traveled to the US as a graduate student in 1975, India was widely seen as a land of snake charmers and begging bowls—poverty marginally leavened by exotica. Today, if there is a stereotypical view of India, it is that of a country of fast-talking high achievers who are wizards at math and who are capable of doing most Americans' jobs better, faster, and more cheaply in Bengaluru. Today "IIT" is a brand name as respected in certain American circles as "MIT" or "Caltech". If Indians are treated with more respect as a result, so is India, as the land that produces them. Let us not underestimate the importance of such global respect in our globalizing world.

Increasing Affluence and Influence

The presence of successful and influential NRIs in so many countries also becomes a source of direct support for India, as they influence not just popular attitudes but governmental policies, to the benefit of the mother country. A list of successful NRIs/PIOs would range from the likes of Dr Har Gobind Khorana, Nobel Prize winning geneticist, and Dr Subrahmanyan Chandrasekhar, Nobel Prize winning astrophysicist, to the Oscar-winning actor Ben Kingsley, the millionaire British industrialist Lord Swraj Paul, and the conductor Zubin Mehta, as well as self-help guru Deepak Chopra and Didar Singh Bains, the United States' biggest peach farmer. The novelist Salman Rushdie has a claim to the PIO designation (and sued successfully for the restitution of property his father had owned in India). Most of India's nationalist leaders, from Jawaharlal Nehru to the anti-Emergency opposition leader Jayaprakash Narayan, were NRIs at one time, though the term had not been invented while they lived abroad.

With increasing affluence and visibility, the Indian-American is also beginning to develop political clout, and that is where the story takes a contemporary turn. In Mauritius, Fiji, Guyana, and Trinidad and Tobago, Indians have long occupied the highest offices; but for Portugal and Ireland to have prime ministers of Indian descent is remarkable. In Britain, both the current chancellor of the exchequer and the home secretary are of Indian origin, and for some years the parliament has sported a few, both in the House of Commons and among the nominated nobility in the unelected House of Lords. In the US, there are now four Indian members of Congress, calling themselves a "Samosa Caucus" in the House of Representatives, and that number was five until Senator Kamala Harris won elevation. It is worth recalling, though, that two Americans of Indian descent, Dalip Singh Saund and Bobby Jindal, did serve three and two terms in the United States House of Representatives, respectively, in the past. But neither flaunted their Indian-American credentials—Saund kept his first names out of public view (he ran on the slogan "Elect Judge Saund")— and Jindal, who went on to be governor of Louisiana and an unsuccessful presidential candidate, is an interesting case study, which I will examine below.

Bobby Jindal's Story

The election of Bobby Jindal as governor of the US state of Louisiana was greeted exultantly by Indians and Indian-Americans around the world, and then his failed candidacy for the White House had us all agog. There's no question that this was an extraordinary accomplishment: a young Indian-American, just 36 years old, not merely winning an election but doing so on the first ballot by receiving more votes than his eleven rivals combined, and that too in a state not noticeably friendly to minorities. Bobby Jindal became the first Indian-American governor in US history (paving the way for Nikki Haley, born Nimrata Randhawa, in South Carolina a few years later), and the youngest chief executive of an American state. These are distinctions of which he can legitimately be proud, and it is not surprising that Indians too felt a vicarious sense of shared pride in his remarkable ascent.

But was our pride misplaced? Who really is Bobby Jindal and what does he really stand for?

There are, broadly speaking, two kinds of Indian migrants in America: though no sociologist, I'll call them the atavists and the assimilationists. The atavists hold on to their original identities as much as possible, especially outside the workplace; in speech, dress, food habits, cultural preferences, they are still much more Indian than American. The assimilationists, on the other hand, seek assiduously to merge into the American mainstream; they acquire a new accent along with their visa, and adopt the ways, clothes, diet, and recreational preferences of the Americans they see around them. (Of course there are the in-betweens, but we'll leave them aside for now.) Class has something to do with which of the two major categories an Indian immigrant falls into; so does age, since the newer generation of Indians, especially those born in America, inevitably tend to gravitate to the latter category.

Bobby Jindal is an assimilationist's dream. Born to relatively affluent professionals in Louisiana, he rejected his Indian name (Piyush) as a very young child, insisting that he be called Bobby, after a (white) character on the popular TV show *The Brady Bunch.* His desire to fit in to the majority white society he saw around him soon manifested itself in another act of rejection: Bobby spurned the Hinduism into which he was born and, as a teenager, converted to Roman Catholicism, the faith of most white Louisianans. There is, of course, nothing wrong with any of this, and it is a measure of his precocity that his parents did not balk at his wishes despite his extreme youth. The boy was clearly gifted, and he soon had a Rhodes scholarship to prove it. But he was also ambivalent about his identity: he wanted to be seen as a Louisianan, but his mirror told him he was also an Indian. The two of us jointly won something called an "Excelsior Award" once from the Network of Indian Professionals in the US, and his acceptance speech on the occasion was striking—obligatory references to the Indian values of his parents, but a speech so American in tone and intonation that he mangled the Indian name of his own brother. There was no doubt which half of the hyphen this Indian-American leaned toward.

But there are many ways to be American, and it's interesting which one Bobby chose. Many Indians born in America have tended to sympathize with other people of color, identifying their lot with other immigrants, the poor, the underclass. Vanita Gupta, in Tulia, Texas, another largely white state, won her reputation as a crusading lawyer by taking up the case of undocumented workers exploited by a factory owner (her story was depicted by Hollywood, with Halle Berry playing the Indian heroine). Bhairavi Desai leads a taxi drivers' union; Preeta Bansal, who grew up as the only nonwhite child in her school in Nebraska, became New York's solicitor general and has served on the Commission for Religious Freedom, as well as in the Obama Justice Department. None of this for Bobby. Louisiana's most famous city, New Orleans, was a majority black town, at least until Hurricane Katrina destroyed so many black lives and homes, but there is no record of Bobby identifying himself with the needs or issues of his state's black people. Instead, he sought, in a state with fewer than 10,000 Indians, not to draw attention to his race by supporting racial causes.

Indeed he went well beyond trying to be nonracial (in a state that harbored notorious racists like the Ku Klux Klansman David Duke); he cultivated the most conservative elements of white Louisiana society. With his widely-advertised piety (he asked his Indian wife, Supriya, to convert as well, and the two are regular churchgoers), Bobby Jindal adopted positions on hot-button issues that place him on the most conservative fringe of the Republican Party. Most Indian-Americans are in favor of gun control, support a woman's right to choose abortion, advocate immigrants' rights, and oppose school prayer (for fear that it will marginalize non-Christians). On every one of these issues, Bobby Jindal is on the opposite side. He's not just conservative; on these questions, he is well to the right of his own party.

That hasn't stopped him, however, from seeking the support of Indian-Americans. Bobby Jindal has raised a small fortune from them, and both when he ran unsuccessfully for governor in 2003, and successfully in 2007 and 2011, an army of Indian-American volunteers from outside the state turned up to campaign for him. Many seemed unaware of his political views; it was enough for them that he was Indian. At his Indian-American fundraising events, Bobby is careful to downplay his extreme positions and play up his heritage, a heritage that plays little part in his appeal to the Louisiana electorate. Indian-Americans, by and large, accept this as the price of political success in white America: their attitude was—it's just good to have "someone like us" in such high office, whatever views he professes to get himself there. But Bobby has never supported a single Indian issue; he refused to join the India Caucus when he was a Congressman on Capitol Hill, and is conspicuously absent from any event with a visiting Indian leader. It is as if he wants to forget he is Indian and would like voters to forget it too.

The contrast with other elected Indian-Americans is instructive: not just the racially-enlightened "progressive" Democrats in the House of Representatives, but even a right-wing Republican like Nikki Haley. Haley, as governor of South Carolina, ordered the removal of the Confederate flag from government buildings as a symbol of racism and was unembarrassed to attend a gurdwara with her parents; she visited India, worshipped at the Golden Temple, and while not ostentatiously identifying herself with Indian causes, did not distance herself from Indians either.

So *The Times of India* emblazoned Jindal's triumph on its front page, and Indians beamed proudly at another Indian-American success story to go along with Kalpana Chawla and Sunita Williams, Har Gobind Khorana and Subrahmanyan Chandrasekhar, Kal Penn, and Jhumpa Lahiri. But none of these Indian-Americans expressed attitudes and beliefs so much at variance with the prevailing values of their community. Indians can, if they wish, be proud that a brown-skinned man with an Indian name has achieved what Bobby Jindal has. But let us not make the mistake of thinking that we should be proud of how he behaves, or what he stands for.

This is what brings us back to Kamala Harris and the uniqueness of her Indian-American story.

The Kamala Harris Story

The 2020 American presidential election was marked by the rising influence of the Indian-American community in the US—though barely 1 percent of the electorate. Indian-Americans are already the second largest immigrant group in the US, and among the fastest-growing (nearly 150 percent in the last decade). They also are more affluent and highly-educated than any other ethnic group, with a median income nearly double the national average (estimated at $100,000 in 2015). And they have been remarkably politically active, as voters, campaigners, donors, and candidates, having produced in the last two decades two state governors, a senator, six members of Congress—and now a vice president.

Both sides actively courted Indian-American voters, of whom a significant number reside in key "swing states" like Texas, Michigan, and Pennsylvania. Both Trump and Biden campaigns released television commercials in Indian languages on the leading ethnic networks broadcasting Indian fare in the US. The Hindu festival of Ganesh Chaturthi saw both campaigns wooing Indian-American voters with messages of greetings.

When Joe Biden picked the half-Indian, half-Jamaican California Senator Kamala Harris as his vice-presidential candidate, she openly embraced her roots, using a Tamil term to describe her Indian aunts in her acceptance speech at the Democratic National Convention. She spoke at length about her Indian ancestry, her visits to her grandfather and their conversations during seaside walks in Chennai. Well-known liberal Indian-American celebrities campaigned for the Biden–Harris ticket. A single fundraising event in September was reported to have raised a record-breaking $3.3 million from the Indian-American community for the Biden Victory Fund.

President Donald Trump was not far behind, responding to the Harris nomination with a campaign ad featuring Indian Prime Minister Narendra Modi, on whom he has often lavished praise. Trump shares rightist populist political leanings with Modi, a mutual suspicion of minorities and a barely-concealed Islamophobia. The two men have developed something of a "bromance", addressing large joint mass rallies, dubbed "Howdy Modi!" in Texas and "Namaste Trump" in Modi's home state of Gujarat. The Republicans created a group called Indian Voices for Trump, as well as four separate subgroups targeting the Indian-American vote bank, with three targeting Hindus, Sikhs, and Muslims separately.[1] Trump's handlers also ensured he presided over a rare naturalization ceremony at the White House, featuring—among others—a sari-draped Indian software engineer.

All of this prompted some observers to suggest that Indian-Americans, who are historically inclined to the Democratic Party, may shift their support to President Trump. There has certainly been a modest shift in the last eight years, when 84 percent of them voted for President Barack Obama in 2012. Indian-Americans may be the only group that has become more favorable to Trump during his term in office rather than less. But a YouGov poll still found 72 percent of Indian-American registered voters supporting

Vice President Biden. (The sari-clad engineer at the White House naturalization ceremony said she was voting for Biden too.) And when, in the second presidential debate, Trump described India's environment as "filthy", Biden quickly replied that he wouldn't insult a friend that way.

There is, however, a larger fault line emerging within the community. India's diaspora, though collectively influential, is deeply divided today across lines of ideology, religion, age, immigration history, and even caste. Modi may be seen as a polarizing figure by many Indians: he is passionately supported by many for his tough stances on Kashmir and Pakistan and his advocacy of an assertively majoritarian Hindutva ideology, the passage of a controversial Citizenship Amendment Act (CAA), and the construction of a Ram temple on the site of a destroyed mosque. But he is equally intensely opposed by other Indian-Americans of a more liberal and inclusive bent. Even while the former cheered every appearance in America by the Indian prime minister, the latter conducted protests against him outside his rallies, decrying his human rights record. While Modi's popularity among some Indian-American voters partly accounts for the Trump-ward shift in their voting inclinations, those Indian-Americans who reject Modi were also likely to have voted against Trump.

Both candidates had drawbacks with Indian-American voters. Trump's own harsh stand on immigration has affected the community; he has attacked Indians for taking American jobs and imposed severe restrictions on H-1B visas that have disproportionately hurt Indian tech professionals. At the same time, some Democratic politicians have been openly critical of Modi's Hindu nationalism, notably Indian-American Congresspersons Pramila Jayapal and Ro Khanna. Kamala Harris herself has echoed their concerns, notably on Kashmir.

The truth is that Kamala is the daughter of an "assimilationist" mother; but one who, unlike the vast majority of the Indian diaspora, chose not to assimilate into the dominant narrative of white America, but identified instead with the black community and the civil rights movement, and brought her daughters up to think of themselves principally as black-Americans. This is very unusual for the Indian-American diaspora, as the 1991 Mira Nair film *Mississippi Masala* showed. But it places Kamala Harris at a slight remove from making either the Jindal choice, of escaping from her desi identity, or the opposite, of embracing it too wholeheartedly. She is Indian-American and yet not wholly so, and for a potential US president, that is a good place to be.

India Won't Be Overlooked

With Biden's victory, it is clear India won't be overlooked, let alone forgotten, in an administration of which Harris is a senior member. But this cuts both ways. She is bound to be a strong voice for democracy and human rights generally, which could put her at odds with some of the Modi government's actions. When you care about a country, you won't be indifferent to it, and are more likely to take a stand on issues agitating the community.

That may not always be welcome—either to the Modi government or its more passionate supporters in the US, who seemed to have felt their salvation lay in President Trump's reelection. Trump had not always been ideal for India—his stands on trade and tariffs, immigrant and work visas, and environmental policies could hardly have been welcome in New Delhi—but he was uncritical of Modi's domestic politics and his Hindutva agenda.

The Indian-American community is more divided than ever before in its attitudes to the Indian government. Those Indian-Americans who realize that Kamala Harris will not automatically endorse everything the Indian government does were the ones who were least enthusiastic about her possible election.

The Dilemma of the Divided Self

To bring the themes which we have explored to a conclusion, the Indian diaspora thus represents a growing force worldwide and in the US, increasing in numbers and financial strength, beginning to flex their political muscle and widely seen as a national resource for the regeneration of their homeland. What is often overlooked in India, though, is that as individual human beings NRIs face a range of social problems implicit in the immigrant condition: alienation, anxiety about their identity, dilemmas about the values in which to bring up their children. Are NRIs/PIOs just what the term implies, Indians who happen not to reside in India and bear other passports, or are they Americans, Britons, Tanzanians of a different ethnicity than the majority of their new compatriots? Issues of discrimination in employment and housing, social and racial conflicts, differing levels of language skills and varying degrees of social acceptance complicate the response to this question. When Fijian or Malaysian Indians claim discrimination in their country, does India have any locus standi in the matter? And whatever passports they may currently hold, what are their true emotional loyalties when the interests of India and their new countries diverge? In Britain, a former Conservative Minister, Norman Tebbit, pointed out that Indian Britons at international cricket matches still supported the Indian team. (This was briefly undercut in June 1996 when England fielded, in their eleven for the first Test against India, no fewer than three players of Indian origin; but two of them soon lost their England places.) Salman Rushdie has written eloquently of the dilemma of the divided self, a dilemma all diaspora Indians, to a greater or lesser extent, live with every day. In an emotional sense, NRIs and PIOs are the prodigal sons and daughters of a motherland they have left but not forgotten, clinging to a sense of nationhood they cannot define but will not surrender.

But the positive side of the story is undeniable. Many would argue that, especially given the Indian government's open doors in the "liberalization" era, NRIs have the best of both worlds. As the late US-based physicist ECG Sudarshan put it, describing the unique situation of the NRI in relation to his home country and his country of adoption: "If you look at the world with two eyes, you see more. It is possible to live in two worlds."

The members of the Great Indian Diaspora are increasingly seizing every opportunity to exercise influence on India's behalf, contribute to India's development and profit from India's growth. Kamala Harris's victory has made it impossible for the world's largest democracy to be ignored by the leaders of the oldest.

Note

1. https://thediplomat.com/2020/09/indias-identity-politics-has-reached-its-diaspora-in-the-us/

Indian-Americans as "Ambassadors" of India

TP Sreenivasan

A book on Kamala Harris, the vice president of the United States, cannot be complete without the saga of the Indian diaspora in the United States. But that saga is of epic proportions, not only in size but also in depth and diversity. Harris's mother Shyamala Gopalan's epic struggle was very similar to many other Indian immigrants, who came to the US in a quest for knowledge. She had planned to return to India, but fell in love with the country and a fellow immigrant from another country, who shared her passion for science. Her trajectory became different from most other Indian immigrants as she married a black man from Jamaica and their daughters were born and brought up as black children at a time when she was herself attracted by the civil rights movement.

Harris's political life was determined by her black identity, but she was very much a part of the Indian-American success story. If the Indian immigrants had not been successful and prosperous, and if it had not been part of the building of America, Harris's life would have been different. But she did not have to be brown, and in a saree with a bindi, to be the inheritor of the great Indian civilization. Her color was a quirk of fortune and genetics as in the case of Barack Obama, who could have been born white and the history of the world would have been different. Cleopatra's nose is not the only part of the human anatomy that has influenced world history.

I am adding to this compendium a chapter on my experience of the activities of the Indian-American community I personally witnessed during the 10 years of my diplomatic life in the United States. I was in New York from 1980 to 1983 as a political counsellor in the permanent mission of India and as an ambassador/deputy permanent representative in the same mission from 1992 to 1995. Later I was ambassador/deputy chief of mission in the embassy of India in Washington from 1997 to 2000. I also traveled the length and breadth of the country during my stint in Washington. I have witnessed with my own eyes the growth of the community in size and stature and interacted with them socially and officially. I have a vast circle of friends in the US, including some who were my contemporaries in college back in India. Some of them became acknowledged leaders of the community and worked with me to enhance India–US relations. Two of them, the late Sunny Wycliffe and Parthasarathi Pillai, who won the Pravasi Bharatiya Samman, greeted me at the airport on my arrival and departure six times.

Change in Policy Toward Overseas Indians

Prime ministers of India and other leaders often tell Indian communities abroad that they are the real ambassadors of India since they are constantly in touch with the local population and India is judged by their faces and actions. Although this is largely true, some in the community begin to take it literally and claim recognition of their role in bilateral relations. I used to tell them that if they knew the salary of the ambassadors, they would not like to exchange places with us! Those who are dazzled by the diplomatic life express readiness to volunteer to be ambassadors. In the United States, ambassadorships are often given to those who make handsome contributions to the election campaign for the winning party and some have done well. In the case of the "honorary ambassadors" of India, only very few rise to the challenge of their status and look for briefings and opportunities for influencing public opinion in the host country. Among the Indian diaspora countries in which I have served (the US, Fiji, Kenya, and Austria), only in the United States have I seen a section of the community committed to the cause of India and willing to lobby for it by making investments to make themselves effective.

Many Indians do not quite see why they should be involved in India–US relations, though it is common sense to know that good relations between the two governments are important for the Indian immigrants to flourish. Many of them used to keep away from the embassy, except when they needed some of the services offered. Part of the reason for this was the overseas Indian policy spelled out by the first prime minister of India, Jawaharlal Nehru. He had said in the Indian parliament that India expected the Indian immigrants abroad to owe their loyalty to the countries of their adoption and that India would only remain alive to their welfare and cultural needs. It was his grandson, Prime Minister Rajiv Gandhi, who changed the policy in the eighties when he exhorted Indians abroad to participate in India's development through expertise, technology, and financing. The response was not overwhelming, but considerable.

Rajiv Gandhi's new policy was not one-sided. He pledged, unlike the previous prime ministers, that India would champion the cause of overseas Indians, regardless of the passports they held. India was, in the past, mere spectator when people of Indian origin had to flee, leaving their possessions behind, in the face of cruelty and discrimination. India simply welcomed those who returned and resettled them in designated spaces and helped them make a living. Ne Win's Burma was so harsh that it preferred to oust the Indians and become poor rather than prosper with their business acumen and hard work. Burma did not allow the fleeing Indians to carry anything other than the clothes they wore and no compensation was paid for the assets they left behind. The Indian embassy in Yangon still holds small pieces of gold, which were never claimed by the Indians who fled Burma (now Myanmar).

The first test of the new policy of Rajiv Gandhi was in 1989 when a military coup in the Fiji Islands disenfranchised the Indians who had made the country their home a hundred and fifty years ago. They were not driven out, but many of them wanted to leave if they could migrate to the neighboring countries and the US and Canada. As the Indian high commissioner to Fiji and other South Pacific island states, I offered them free visas to return to India, but there were no takers as India was too distant and too big for them. With no communications to consult Delhi, I tried to negotiate a better deal for the Indians with the governor-general, whom the army had not dismissed. In keeping with our policy so far of maintaining communal harmony, I did not take sides. I merely called for the restoration of democracy and communal harmony.

But when communications were restored, Rajiv Gandhi called me to Delhi to tell me that we should actively oppose the military regime and do everything possible to restore democracy by every means available. He himself initiated international consultations to bring in human rights bodies and also imposed trade sanctions against Fiji and got it expelled from the Commonwealth. After two years of hard struggle, Fiji expelled me and closed down the Indian embassy. But thanks to the efforts made at that time, democracy was reestablished and a truncated Fiji Indian community became part of the mainstream with equal rights.

The new policy meant that Indian communities everywhere received greater attention from the Indian embassies and several privileges were extended to the PIOs. What was until then a cultural interest in the Indian communities became a matter of priority from the political and economic angle. The reverberations of the change were heard in the countries with large Indian communities like the US and the interactions among Indian diplomats in different parts of the country intensified. The ambassador and the deputy chief of mission were put directly in charge of "Community Affairs", together with a senior officer who was assigned to look after them.

Ambivalence Toward Delhi

The support of the Indian community to the government of the day in Delhi was neither automatic nor institutionalized. Most Indians who had migrated to the US had come on their own and they did not consider themselves indebted to the government in any way. If anything, most of them had a grouse that they had to leave their motherland because the government had failed to give them jobs or other support to make a living. Even when they left, they were only allowed $8 to take with them, which was not even enough to hire a cab from JFK Airport in New York to the city.

When they came on holidays, they were harassed at the immigration and customs and even charged penal duties for the goods they carried to be gifted to the relatives. In other words, they owed their jobs and well-being more to the US than to India, even though they were educated and trained in India. Most of them maintained their cultural traditions externally but became white inside like the brown Oreo cookies. The second generation, caught between two generations, came to be known as the "American born confused desis" (ABCD), though they were not prejudiced against India.

When I came to Washington in 1997, having been ambassador to two Indian diaspora countries, Fiji and Kenya, I found that the Indian-American community could be grouped into (1) the top executives, businessmen, and politicians, who kept a distance from the embassy except during visits of Indian dignitaries; (2) the "patriots" who visited the embassy for national days, etc; (3) the leaders and members of community organizations who were constantly in touch with the embassy and helped the embassy organize events and kept in touch with senior politicians in India; and (4) the professionals, who were willing to help, if asked to do so. There was, of course, the vast majority, which thought of India only when they needed consular services. The challenge of the embassy was to put each section to take interest in India and to use their services to influence the administration, the senators, congressmen, media, and others.

The Indian community was in the habit of sporadically reacting to certain developments in India positively and negatively depending on the political inclinations of some Indian-Americans. There had been a virtual uprising in the Indian community when Emergency was declared in India by the Indira Gandhi government in 1975. They succumbed to the propaganda of the Western media that democracy was over in India and that the dictatorial regime will continue. Many demonstrations were held outside our diplomatic missions and there was serious concern about the future course of India. The efforts of the embassy to clarify matters did not carry conviction and the US government itself was hostile to India. The protests continued till the elections in 1977 and the change of government.

Another occasion when the Indian community was agitated against the government of India was in 1979–80 when Soviet troops occupied Afghanistan and India acquiesced in it because it stabilized the situation, though we were against foreign forces in any country. Once again, the Western world was up in arms against India and the Indian community joined in the outcry against India.

Even during my time in Washington, the Indian community, particularly Christians, got very agitated by reports from India that certain Christian priests and missionaries were being persecuted in certain parts of India. Since many Christians in the US are from Kerala, they also called me to complain. I tried to assure them that these were isolated incidents and the government of India would take care of the situation. Then we heard that certain Christian groups had begun writing to their senators and congressmen asking them to take up the matter with the Indian government. One day a fairly large group of Christians, mostly from Kerala, came to the embassy to protest. I went out and invited them to the embassy's conference room and gave them a hearing. I had no difficulty in convincing them that Christianity was not in danger in India, giving them the example of life in Kerala villages where Hindus and Christians lived side by side. Finally, they were fully satisfied and left the embassy after singing the Indian national anthem.

Change in Attitudes

Apart from these specific situations, the Indian community was generally dissatisfied with the way India was run and it was impatient about the lack of proper infrastructure in India, particularly communications. When ministers and others came from India to discuss better trade and economic relations, some Indian-Americans recounted their bad experiences in India, making the promotional activities counterproductive. Indian-Americans visiting India complained about the situation in India without taking into account the severe economic crisis. It was only after the economic liberalization and opening up of the economy that the Indian-Americans became friendly to the government of India. India–US relations also improved from the second term of President Bill Clinton.

Since the ambassadors to Washington were political appointees in the early years, most of them took an active interest in the community socially, but there is no evidence of the community having been prompted to organize themselves to lobby for Indian interests on the Hill or elsewhere. But the situation changed when the embassy hired a lobbyist at the instance of Prime Minister PV Narasimha Rao to stem the tide of anti-India resolutions and statements from the Senate and the Congress. Lobbying for foreign governments is quite legitimate on the Hill and many countries had hired expensive lobbyists to secure American assistance and other benefits. Kashmir and Khalistan activists were also hiring lobbyists, who prompted anti-Indian moves on the Hill. Our lobbyists pointed out how the Jewish community was active in promoting pro-Israeli activities and suggested that we should do the same with the Indian-Americans.

Systematic briefing of Indian-American leaders began by identifying Indian-American supporters of US senators and congressmen available in the public domain and we persuaded some of them to speak to their respective representatives to vote for India. The formation of the India caucuses in the Congress and the Senate was the concrete outcome of the cooperation of the community leaders with the embassy.

The biggest headache for the Indian embassy in Washington at that time was the annual Burton amendment, moved by Republican Congressman Dan Burton from Indiana, an inveterate critic of India, seeking a cut of 25 percent in the US developmental aid to India. Burton wanted to "punish" India for what he called its "unsatisfactory" human rights record, particularly in Kashmir, and treatment meted out to the minorities in the country. A majority of the members did not share his view, defending India's independent judiciary, free press, and elections. He also maintained a steady flow of correspondence with the president, the senators and the congressmen about human rights violations in India with the help of lobbyists provided by Pakistan. Over the years, the Burton amendment became a litmus test of India's popularity on the Hill and the effectiveness of Indian diplomacy. But, because of the efforts of the Indian-Americans, the support for the Burton amendment dwindled and reached rock bottom in 1997, the year I reached Washington.

In 1998, Burton decided to drop the amendment as he could line up only two lawmakers—Dana Rohrabacher (Republican) and Major R Owens (Democrat)—to speak in his favor. In sharp contrast, at least 21 congressmen, led by congressional caucus on India and Indian-Americans, Chairman Gary

Ackerman (Democrat) took the floor to successfully resist the anti-India proposal. They included House International Relations Committee Chairman Benjamin Gilman and its Asia and Near-East Panel Chairman Douglas K Bereuter (both Republican) and Frank Pallone (Democrat). Burton visited India subsequently to make amends as he needed Indian-American support to become the chair of the House Foreign Relations Committee.

The Burton amendment paled into insignificance when all hell broke loose on May 11, 1998 when India announced nuclear tests and declared itself a nuclear-weapon state. President Clinton came down on India "like a ton of bricks" and imposed comprehensive economic and personal sanctions against India in terms of the Glenn amendment. Since this was the first time that the Glenn amendment sanctions were imposed, the concerned authorities interpreted them so rigorously that it looked as though they would even affect the future of the Indian community in the US. Trade came to a standstill and many dual-use materials and equipment could not be purchased even in the market. Worst of all, there was no dialogue as the US took the position that there was nothing to be discussed. India simply had to indicate what kind of punishment it was willing to take for an act of betrayal.

The embassy decided to launch an information campaign to cover all sections of the American public and we fanned out to address whatever audiences we could get. It was at this point that the Indian community stood behind us like a rock, organizing various groups to listen to us. They themselves organized meetings and we simply had to provide the information. Even senators and congressmen began meeting us to know our views. Between the ambassador and myself, we covered most opinion makers with the support of the active and efficient young Taranjit Sandhu, who is now the Indian ambassador to the United States. Thanks to these efforts, the Clinton administration became defensive by the time talks began between Deputy Secretary of State Strobe Talbott and the Deputy Chairman of the Planning Commission Jaswant Singh. Even after Jaswant Singh became the minister of external affairs, he continued the conversations with Talbott for the sake of continuity rather than with the Secretary of State Madeleine Albright. He had a couple of meetings with Albright just to keep the protocol level of the contacts.

Community's Lobbying

I recall with gratitude, the work done by a group of young Indian professionals called Network of South Asian Professionals (NETSAP). One thing that struck me at that time was that the second- and third-generation Indians were more proud of the accomplishments of India than their parents were. Unlike their parents, who had some grievance with India on account of their old experiences of the government or the social system, they looked at India with clear eyes and appreciated the value of democracies there, and were generally willing to help India overcome its present difficulties. The nuclear tests had an electrifying effect on the young generation of Indian-Americans.

The Indian community exerted considerable pressure on their senators and congressmen to lift the sanctions against India. Senator Sam Brownback (Republican) came up with a number of amendments to the sanctions law, citing the losses sustained by the US economy, business, and education. Jaswant Singh never raised the question of sanctions as he was discussing larger issues of disarmament and non-proliferation. But the pressure from the Indian community outside reverberated in the meeting rooms around the world where the negotiators spent many hours.

Jaswant Singh's effort was to highlight the different threats to India and the need to meet them through appropriate armaments more to deter others than to attack. The long conversations he had with Talbott were supported by continuing lobbying by the Indian community leaders with the senators and the congressmen. The government in Delhi, its spokespersons, Jaswant Singh and Brajesh Mishra, the embassy in Washington, the Indian journalists stationed in the US and the unofficial Indian-American "ambassadors" worked in unison. By the end of 1999, a broad agreement was reached between the two governments, to the satisfaction of the rest of the international community, that India's nuclear capability did not pose a threat to the world. President Clinton visited India in early 2000 and Prime Minister Atal Bihari Vajpayee visited Washington at the end of the same year.

The banquet President Clinton hosted for Prime Minister Vajpayee at the White House was studded with the stars of the Indian community, some of them one had only heard of. I was on a table with filmmaker M Night

Shyamalan, director of the much-acclaimed *The Sixth Sense*, Deepak Chopra the popular new-age philosopher, Sabeer Bhatia, the founder of Hotmail and Kalpana Chawla, the astronaut. The CEOs of companies in the Silicon Valley were there in large numbers. As Clinton himself remarked at the banquet, "There are more than one million Indians here in America now. I think more than half of them are here tonight. And I might say, Prime Minister, the other half is disappointed that they are not here."

Community leaders from all over the US came to Washington and attended the reception the Indian community hosted for the prime minister. The Overseas Friends of the BJP had emerged as a leading group in the Indian community, much to the chagrin of the traditional leaders, but under instructions from Brajesh Mishra, we gave the responsibility for the reception to people like Dinesh Aggarwal and Bhishma Agnihotri, who was appointed "ambassador" for overseas Indians. He was originally posted to Washington, but since the US government would not recognize him as an ambassador, he was shifted to the permanent mission in New York, where a country could have several ambassadors. This practice was discontinued after the tenure of Agnihotri. The experiment of appointing an ambassador for overseas Indians was a total failure because he was not recognized by the US government and was not given any diplomatic privileges in Washington. After he joined the permanent mission of India in New York, he became a virtual roving ambassador to countries with a substantial Indian presence. For Agnihotri, it was a kind of reward for his loyalty to Vajpayee, whom Agnihotri had introduced as the "future prime minister of India" many years before he actually assumed the office of the prime minister.

Another accomplishment of the time was a dream come true of several Indian-Americans, who had worked on a project to install a Gandhi statue in front of the Indian embassy on Massachusetts Avenue on federal land. The US Congress had adopted a resolution in 1949 authorizing the India League of Americas to erect a memorial for Mahatma Gandhi in Washington. Forty years later, another Indian organization, Indian American Forum for Political Education (IAFPE), got another bill passed by the Congress in 1988. In 1997, Ambassador Naresh Chandra revived the proposal in the context of the fiftieth anniversary of Indian independence and got the statue unveiled by Clinton and Vajpayee together. Several Indians, who had worked for years on the statue proposal volunteered to donate money for the statue, but the government of India bore most of the expenditure. However, the money that the Indian community had collected was also utilized. A major contribution came in the form of a marble pedestal donated by an Indian-American, Sree Nair, an old friend of mine from Thiruvananthapuram.

"Cash Cows"

The Economist once called the Indian-Americans the "cash cows" of American politicians as they do make financial contributions to their favorite politicians. Unlike in India, the financial contributions made to politicians are published and there are limits to the amounts payable. But many mainstream politicians are attentive to Indian-Americans essentially because of the contributions they make. Some Indian-Americans contributed money in the names of their friends to enhance their contributions. A few months before I arrived in Washington, an Indian-American was caught making contributions in different names to politicians and it was suspected that he did so on behalf of the embassy. Though nothing was proved, Indian-Americans began distancing themselves from the embassy till the man accused was set free.

Since the Indian-Americans are prosperous, there is a wrong impression in India that money can be raised from them for developmental activities in India. In fact, a prominent Indian doctor suggested to Prime Minister Vajpayee that a bond should be established in which Indian-Americans could invest. We started calling him "Doctor Bond" as he repeated the suggestion at every opportunity. But, finally, when the bond was established with a very generous interest rate, but repayable only in rupees, Prime Minister Vajpayee was very disappointed that only less than 10 percent of the deposits came from the US. Nearly 90 percent of the deposits came from the Indians in the Gulf, who sent all their savings to India. The saying about Indian-Americans in India at that time was that they had their *tan* (body) in the US, *man* (mind) in India and *dhan* (wealth) in Swiss banks!

Another surprise was when India wanted to charge $1000 each for the PIO cards, which entitled American citizens of Indian origin to have the same facilities as NRIs with Indian nationality. In fact, when the chargeable fee had been discussed a few months earlier, Prime Minister Vajpayee had made an observation that the Indian-Americans would be willing to pay any amount for such a facility. When the card was introduced, it was considered too expensive and there were persistent representations to reduce the cost and the cards remained idle in the embassy till the cost was reduced.

The argument was that it was a heavy investment for a five-member family if each had to pay $1000. They also argued that taking visas for 20 years was cheaper than getting the PIO cards. The patriotism that the prime minister expected to see in this case was illusory. Indian-Americans do considerable humanitarian and philanthropic work in India, but they do not seem to be keen to support Indian government initiatives. They also do not trust that the government will return the deposits or spend their donations appropriately. When I returned to India, I met a number of American groups who came to India to help out with technology, but not financing. In other words, it is unrealistic to expect Indian-Americans to remit their savings to Indian banks or to make major investments in India.

Dual Citizenship

There were persistent demands from the Indian community for dual citizenship for a long time. Successive prime ministers had studies made of its implications and had come to the conclusion that constitutionally dual citizenship was not possible to be given to those who had assumed other nationalities. In fact, only very few "immigrant" countries permitted dual citizenship. With nearly 30 million Indians in many parts of the world with different passports, dual citizenship would have created immense problems. Recognizing this, the dual citizenship idea was abandoned and the PIO cards and overseas citizen of India (OCI) cards were issued to give foreign passport holders certain facilities in India, short of giving them voting rights.

When the constituent assembly had debated the provisions of citizenship, Dr BR Ambedkar was of the firm view that citizenship should go strictly by domicile. Later, Article 8 was incorporated which enabled the Indians living abroad to register themselves in the Indian embassies till they accepted citizenship. However, it must be mentioned that the overall policy of the government of India was to persuade the Indians overseas to take up the citizenship of the host countries. Unfortunately, many Indians preferred to "sit on the fence" or tried to have the best of both worlds.

Citizenship means loyalty to the country of citizenship. Being an Indian citizen means he should be loyal to India and uphold the provisions of the Indian Constitution. Dual citizenship means dual loyalty. And in times of strained bilateral relations between the two countries, the loyalty would be suspect. During World War II, when the United States went to war with Japan, there were 40,000 Japanese living in the United States, some had even taken US citizenship. The US government suspected their loyalty and detained many of them. During the Sino-Indian conflict in 1962, the minuscule Chinese community living in eastern India was subjected to persecution. Their loyalty to India was suspect and many were detained under the Preventive Detention Act. Realizing these complications, Indian-Americans seem to have given up the dual citizenship demand, but it may arise again. However, it has been established that it is neither possible nor desirable for India to give dual citizenship to any Indian who has acquired citizenship of another country.

Support for Nuclear Deal

When I left the US in early 2001, it appeared that India–US relations had reached a plateau and that there were no major issues to be resolved. On the nuclear issue, there was greater confidence between India and the US, but it would be impossible to formalize it in a treaty because of the legal problems. I thought that since India had not signed the Nuclear Nonproliferation Treaty (NPT) and the Comprehensive Test Ban Treaty (CTBT), no US government would be able to give legal recognition to India's nuclear capability. But President George Bush and Prime Minister Manmohan Singh reached an agreement on a nuclear deal in 2005, which was very innovative and mutually beneficial. The agreement was to bring India into the nuclear mainstream without signing the NPT. There were serious objections to this move both in India and the US; in India, because of the fear that India would enter a tight embrace with the US, and in the US because of the apprehension that the nuclear regime based on the NPT would be endangered and many more countries would aspire to become unauthorized nuclear-weapon states.

The active engagement of the Indian community was crucial in the next three years when the actual details of the agreement were being hammered out. The Senate and the Congress had a significant role to play in exempting a non-NPT country from the rigid export controls of the US and the guidelines of the Nuclear Suppliers Group and just as there was bipartisan support for the deal, there were also bipartisan objections. All the reports I saw in India and the US press credited the Indian-American community for influencing the American legislators across the board.

But an interesting observation was made by a young researcher at that time at the Brookings Institution, Dhruva Jaishankar, in the book, *Indo-US Nuclear Deal* edited by PR Chari that "the US legislators, who received significant backing from Indian-Americans were not necessarily among the chief proponents of the deal. Hillary Clinton, for example, was tepid in her support, despite being co-chair of the Senate India Caucus and a well-known recipient of support from Indian-Americans. Similarly, legislators from states with sizeable and influential Indian-American communities did not necessarily support the legislation. Most notably, Senators Barbara Boxer of California and Edward Kennedy of Massachusetts voted against the Hyde Act."

A counter to this could be that, had it not been for the lobbying by the community, more legislators would have opposed the deal. It is a fact that the community systematically worked for three years to make the deal possible.

At one point in the negotiations, some leaders of the community felt that India was dragging its feet on the deal because of pressures within India and they took a delegation to Delhi to impress upon the Manmohan Singh government to persist with the agreement. Ironically, though the fundamentals of the deal were ironed out by Jaswant Singh, and he would have signed the deal if it had fructified during the NDA regime, the BJP did not support the deal and in a way nullified it to a certain extent by promoting the Nuclear Liability Act in the Indian parliament. The leftist parties withdrew support to the government on this issue.

US corporate interests, in which the Indian-Americans had a voice, were certainly a major driving force in ensuring wide support for the deal. Among other initiatives, the US–India Business Council organized a group of corporate and community supporters of the agreement, which they called "The Coalition of Partnership with India", to coordinate lobbying efforts.

Community Polarization

After the advent of the Modi government in India, the Indian community got involved more and more in India–US relations. The rockstar reception that Narendra Modi received at Madison Square Garden in New York in September 2014 impressed even President Obama about the popularity Modi enjoyed in the US. Though the audience was essentially Indians, they had also brought along their American friends, making the gatherings multiracial. The "Howdy Modi" event in Houston was the first occasion of its kind when a US president himself attended a reception given by a community for its foreign leader. The support extended by Modi for the continuation of Trump as president moved a number of Indians from their Democratic moorings to the Republican Party. If the coronavirus had not come, and Trump had handled it wisely, the Indian-American support to Trump could have been decisive.

In the 2020 elections, the Indian-American votes got divided when Kamala Harris was nominated as Joe Biden's running mate on the Democratic ticket. The emotional and financial support the community gave her was phenomenal as they saw in her rise the fulfillment of the American dream of the Indian immigrants. The celebration of her victory spread far and wide in India, particularly the beaches of Chennai. Many Indians could relate to the brave journey of the young and ambitious Shyamala Gopalan, who embraced America and brought up her two daughters in adverse circumstances and more than fulfilled the wildest dreams of the Indian-American community, which had imagined their children to be the best doctors in the United States. The story goes that an Indian immigrant was witnessing the oath-taking ceremony of her son as a US president and when someone complimented her on her son's phenomenal success, she said with pride, "Oh yes, but his brother is the best cardiologist in our town!" Now many Indian-American mothers will be dreaming of themselves as the occupants of "Kamala Vilas", which was once the White House!

In spite of the euphoria over Harris's election, there is persisting suspicion that the Democratic government of Joe Biden will be critical of some internal policies of the Modi government. Democrats argue that India should live up to the democratic principles of the Indian Constitution and accept the advice of friends. But the overall expectation is that on hardcore issues of security and development, India and the US would work together in the next four years, with Biden and Harris at the helm of affairs in the US.

The role of the Indian-American "ambassadors" will only increase as the Biden administration begins to grapple with its humongous task of repairing and rebuilding the place of the US in the global dispensation. The changes he makes in this process may have some impact on India's own interests. For instance, he is not expected to take an open confrontationist position toward China as Donald Trump did. At the same time, they will remain competitive in business and global affairs. If China continues to be aggressive against India, it will become necessary for the Indian community to remain alert to the developments. Moreover, Indian business interests should also be protected as the economic relations between China and the US develop rapidly.

The India caucuses in the House of Representatives and the Senate need to be briefed and persuaded to promote India–US relations. Since these caucuses were built by the Indian community, the Indian leaders can play a very effective role by remaining in touch with the respective senators and congressmen. The guidance and support from the embassy will be crucial.

The US is in a critical stage and the general downturn in the economy will affect all sections of the people of the nation. The Indian community will have its share of problems till the US recovers. But it will be important for both countries if the Indian community remains active in promoting bilateral relations.

A Community Zooms into Political Spotlight

Maina Chawla Singh

In August 2020, the nomination of Kamala Harris as Joe Biden's running mate for vice president created a media stir which brought the Indian-American diaspora into prominent focus, adding a political pizazz to their already established successes in science, business, and academia. It injected a huge momentum among Indian-Americans across generations to organize themselves politically, campaign actively, and do what it takes to be seen and to be heard—as a political voice. So how can we map the story of this Indian diaspora community? Where should the saga begin? Should it begin with the stories of colonialism and the Indian indentured labor brought to America from the seventeenth century? Or the early hardworking Sikh farming communities of the late-nineteenth century who settled in Yuba City, California, and later worked on railroad construction?[1] Or should it be 1956, the landmark election of the pioneering Dalip Singh Saund as the first ethnic (Asian) Indian member of the US Congress? Or should it be 1965 when the passage of the landmark Immigration and Naturalization Act ended discriminatory immigration quotas skewed in favor of European immigration and opened the floodgates for highly-educated Indian engineers, physicians, and academics to arrive in the United States, in search of the "American Dream"?

Each of these is a historical milestone. However, for many reasons, the presidential elections of 2020 offered an opportune vantage point to examine how Indian-Americans have evolved as an immigrant community and acquired a prominent political voice. For one thing, the 2020 election campaign revealed that this over four-million strong diaspora community was wooed actively by both Republicans and Democrats working at local and national levels. In turn, Indian-Americans also stepped up as fundraisers, campaigners, and electoral candidates. Finally, at a moment when the US has elected as vice president a biracial woman born of immigrants from Jamaica and India, who has widely vocalized her appreciation of her Indian heritage and garnered support from many Indian-Americans, understanding the political consolidation of the Indian-American community becomes an important question.

We know that Kamala Devi Harris, in fact, did not grow up among the Indian-American community. Her mother Dr Shyamala Gopalan, emigrated several years before the 1965 Act, which is the moment in US history that most first-generation Indian immigrants identify with, because it facilitated large-scale immigration from India. Dr Gopalan's active participation in the civil rights movement is also not representative of community preferences, considering Indian immigrants have long displayed political apathy and shied away from activism. Yet Kamala Devi is an immigrant child, raised by an ambitious Indian scientist, and this aspect of her story resonates with a vast majority of Indian-Americans—the high-achiever parent-generation as well as their US-born immigrant children.

Today, although Indian-Americans constitute around 1 percent of the US population, their entrepreneurial success in Silicon Valley and wealth creation through professions in science, medicine, finance, venture capital, or the hotel business is well established. A 2015 survey revealed that 72 percent of Indian-Americans (below 25) had a bachelor's degree; 40 percent had a postgraduate, compared to the national average of 19 percent and 11 percent, respectively. Even within the successful cohort of Asian-Americans, Indians outshine the

Chinese, Filipino, Korean, and Japanese, because Indian-Americans lead by a significant margin in income levels and education. Seven in ten Indian-Americans who are 25 years or older have a college degree, compared with about half of Americans of Korean, Chinese, Filipino, and Japanese ancestry.[2]

But beyond these stories of start-ups and individual success, what about the diaspora community as a collective living within mainstream society? To map their story, it would be useful to track patterns of community behaviors and identify trends reflecting the broad self-perceptions of this community—ethnically, culturally, and politically. How do these self-perceptions drive social practices, religious choices, and philanthropic preferences? More importantly, how have these practices shaped the ways in which Indian-Americans are perceived within the wider multi-ethnic society in America? And, finally, what are the shifts taking place as the parent-generation of engineers, scientists, physicians, hoteliers, and business owners now faces an adult second-generation, who unlike their parents, were born as US citizens and have been conscious of their minority status since childhood? How is the community identity changing as many of these second-generation Indian-Americans are driven and passionate about US politics, much like Kamala Harris herself? These are key questions. Interrogating these issues has been the basis of my research on Indian-Americans.

I write this from a long-standing scholarly engagement with Indian diaspora communities. I have researched and lived in the US among the Indian-American diaspora for several years from 2009, interacting professionally and personally, across generational and ideological divides. As faculty at Georgetown and American universities, I taught courses on South Asia and Indian diaspora. My understandings of the second generation were textured by the Indian-American students who shared their experience and distinct perspectives of being immigrant children. They have navigated their ethnicities within mainstream American culture. Their narratives about "hybrid-identities" deepened my understandings of the immigrant experience. In Washington, DC, where I lived for several years, I reached out to second-generation professionals in public policy, civic engagement, or holding political appointments in the administration. Many of these professionals were speakers at my campus series on *The Changing Role of Indian Americans:*

New Trends and were later interviewed for this chapter. As the spouse of a senior Indian diplomat, I was fortunate to attend over 100 community events and 150 Indian embassy events across America. I had conversations with a wide range of diaspora men and women from different regions of India, now settled in parts of the US as diverse as Minnesota, Florida, Utah, California, and Indiana. Among them were physicians, professors, Silicon Valley entrepreneurs, small business owners, and community leaders from the first generation who were all Indian-born and naturalized Americans.

While the success stories of first-generation Indian-Americans in business, tech, or academia have been widely celebrated, the shifting trends toward active political participation among this diaspora has not received much scholarly attention. What is the nature of this political evolution? How does this mark a generational shift as the second generation shows heightened political engagement? What will be the future implications of this shift on community consolidation and how might this impact American politics? This chapter extrapolates on these questions by analyzing dominant trends, while remaining mindful of the heterogeneity among Indian-Americans. One must note that Indian-Americans are not a monolith—by religion, class, or linguistic affinities. Although a majority are Hindus, there are Muslims, Sikhs, and Christians in significant numbers. First-generation Indian-Americans grew up in India speaking different languages and following different religious traditions. Class variations are also significant and within this "model minority" as Indian-Americans are widely described, thousands are low-income. Additionally, in 2019, an estimated 630,000 Indians in the US were undocumented.[3]

The Foundational Years: Career, Culture, and Family

In October 1965, when President Lyndon B Johnson stood at the foot of the Statue of Liberty in New York signing the Hart–Celler Act into law, it ended preferences for white immigrants dating from the eighteenth century. The demographic consequences of this law were profound, both for America and for thousands of immigrants from India, opening the floodgates for thousands of highly-educated Indian engineers, physicians, and academics to migrate in search of their American Dream.[4] The early post-migration years for these Indian immigrants posed typical challenges of cultural adaptation and building economic security. In the foundational years, Indian immigrants to America tended to concentrate on navigating the cultural displacement—classic issues of nostalgia for the homeland and planning for more secure futures. Settling in professionally, socially and raising families swallowed up all their energies. However, from modest beginnings as researchers or entry-level engineers and scientists, this cohort moved steadily up the career ladders.

Some observable features about the community emerged early on regardless of whether they were living in Kansas or California, Boston, New York, or Miami. An ethic of hard work, family cohesion, and stability, emphasis on a faith-based home culture and education for the children were high priorities. During interviews, many of my second-generation respondents recounted scenarios of Indian families working across suburban Pennsylvania, Kansas, Ohio, or Minnesota living pretty isolated lives. These children from suburbs grew up in school districts often as being "the only brown kid". Parents strove to live in safe neighborhoods, as upper-class as they could afford. At home, they were diligent to instill cultural awareness of roots through food, language, and summer holidays visiting extended families in India. Although they were conscious of cultural isolation, the kids were getting increasingly "Americanized" at school, losing native Indian languages and ethnic roots. Thus, the parent-generation actively sought other Indian families to spend weekends together to expose their children to others who looked like themselves. As Tara, one of my students, described, "I grew up in Pennsylvania. We would drive sometimes 50 miles on the weekend for these potluck dinners with other Indian 'Uncles' and 'Aunties'. I think our parents really tried!" Many others echoed Tara's experience.

Religion, Culture, and Philanthropy

For all these informal groups, shared ethnicity and religion appeared to be important building blocks. These gatherings of potluck dinners to meet and celebrate Indian religious festivals like Diwali, Guru Nanak Jayanti, or Eid, metamorphosed over time into Indian associations with elected office-bearers and regular events. By the 1980s, New York, California, New Jersey, and Texas became clusters attracting a steady stream of new Indian immigrants. By the

1990s, there were enough individual successes among Indian immigrants to be noticed nationwide, not only as scientists in NASA, physicians in medical practice, the hotel–motel owners but also names like Vinod Khosla, founder Sun Microsystems, Vinod Dham, known for the Pentium micro-processing chip, and Romesh Wadhwani of Symphony Tech. The power of Indians in Silicon Valley was beginning to grow visibly. As Indians felt more self-assured professionally and economically, their cultural organizations which had by now mushroomed everywhere, including in states like Kansas, Utah, Minnesota, and Mississippi, became larger and more lavish in their cultural celebrations. Diwali was always top-ranking and celebrated with a splash, typically over a weekend around the actual festival which falls on a different date each year as per the lunar calendar. Indian organizations in different parts of the US still boast about how large and lavish their Diwali gala is. As the years went by, Indian organizations became more rooted in local districts and towns. They bought land to build temples, gurdwaras, and community centers which could house everything from religious prayers, Indian wedding ceremonies, to Indian dance classes, and teaching vernacular Indian languages, reflecting the desire of many parents to offer cultural exposure to their US-born children.

Although the earliest traditional mandir in the US is said to be the Shiva Murugan Temple in Concord, CA (1957), today Hindu temples and gurdwaras thrive in cities big and small. I was fascinated to visit the Sri Ganesha Hindu Temple in a place called South Jordan, Utah, which was built with community contributions in 1993. And, this is not the only Hindu temple in that vicinity—there are three others! While I knew that California with its concentration of Sikh communities has over thirty gurdwaras, it was insightful to visit a gurdwara in Boulder, Colorado, and Bloomington, Minnesota, where I least expected to!

Although professional networks like PANIIT (alumni of Indian Institutes of Technology) and AAPI (Association of American Physicians of Indian Origin) were active associations, they were primarily focused on networking for career advancement or related policy-making. Over the years, they have held conferences, galas, and fundraising events, much in the patterns of American models of organizational activity. Leadership positions in these organizations are highly coveted for the visibility they bring. However, despite a wealthy membership, in terms of causes, these Indian organizations were inward-looking—either focusing on diaspora community betterment or supporting charities in India. As Ramesh Patel, a hotelier, said, "Politics was too far from us. And, too messy. We were small numbers. Who would care about us as voters?" And Neelam Rao, a physician said, "Even after I got my US citizenship, I didn't feel inspired to vote."

Thus, through the 1980s and 1990s, even as Indian-Americans spread across the US working at its universities, hospitals, laboratories, or even working in grocery stores or driving cabs, their American Dream was about hard work, not hard politics, and rarely about mobilizing to challenge policy or "fix" issues that shaped their lives. In fact, in 1990, when US-born Kumar Barve (whose grandfather came from Indore in Central India), ran for elections to the House of Delegates in Maryland, he had no peers and no role models. Few in the Indian-American community contributed money or time to his campaign. Barve described his experience when I interviewed him. "Most believed it was really idiotic…how would a man with a name like Kumar Barve get elected?" chuckled Barve.[5] Barve became the first Asian-American of Indian origin to be elected to a state legislature in the US. He served as majority leader of the House of Delegates in Maryland (2002–2015) and is viewed by many Indian politicos as the doyen of Indian-Americans in politics.

In terms of community consolidation, trends during the 1990s did not show dramatic change. They continued to focus on cultural and social aspects. Although Indian organizations increased in numbers, many were, in fact, splintering along narrow, regional, linguistic, or caste lines. Thus, hundreds of registered Indian-American organizations were serving limited memberships, with little strategy about leveraging power in local governance. The membership consisted of the first-generation who had strong ties with remaining family in India. They cared for charities in India, and they cared about US–India relations. Although they were eager to embrace American citizenship, there was little vision for collective mobilization. To be fair, some professional organizations were somewhat exceptional in attempting to create pockets of influence by the 1990s. One of them was AAPI, which lobbied for lifting of restrictions on foreign-trained doctors working in the US. Fundraising for political purposes was also set in motion by organizations like the Indian American Friendship Council (founded in 1990) which claimed to be "the leading Indian-American group promoting relations between India and the United States".[6]

Although the majority of the first generation stayed away from political engagement, there are some notable individuals who were pushing for a change in Washington, DC. Their vision was for Indian-Americans to consolidate and make a mark. Gopal Raju was one such individual. He founded *India Abroad* (1970), the weekly newspaper which flourished as a prominent ethnic media publication and an influential voice. It was the staple source of news for Indians to hear community goings-on from across America. Indian immigrant families were regular subscribers, and the children who grew up to join politics often remarked about how parents who may have disapproved of their career choices were excited and appeased if they were featured in *India Abroad.* Although Gopal Raju passed away in 2008, *India Abroad* remained a widely read chronicler of Indian diaspora activities under its prominent executive-editor Aziz Haniffa. Gopal Raju also established other nonprofit philanthropic organizations outside of his main business in publishing and media. In the 1970s, he founded the Indian American Foundation (IAF), which raised millions of dollars to fund medical, educational, development, and disaster relief projects in India. In 1993, he set up the Indian American Center for Political Awareness (IACPA) and also ran the India Abroad Fellowship Program at Columbia University.

The IACPA was a visionary idea designed to place Indian-American college students in summer internships in Washington, DC, within the offices of members of the US Congress and US Senate. The IACPA idea was germane to the founding of The Washington Leadership Program (WLP), a thriving initiative which brings young Indian-American college students for a summer internship program and places them on Capitol Hill to get familiar with the political process. Over the years, I met and interviewed several WLP fellows some of whom in fact did join active politics. Jay Goyal (Democrat) was one, who was elected as member of the Ohio House of Representatives for three terms. The other was Niraj Antani (Republican) who was elected to Ohio House of Representatives in 2014.

Generational Shifts: New Models of Political Engagement

In general, Indian-Americans as a community stayed away from investing in political causes and seriously discouraged children from engaging in political activity. However, from 2000 a demographic shift began creeping in. Asian Indian population in the US grew from almost 1,678,765 in 2000 (0.6 percent of US population) to 2,843,391 in 2010 (0.9 percent of US population), a growth rate of 69.37 percent. Indians became one of the fastest-growing ethnic groups in the US.[7] Something else was also happening. The children raised by the parent-generation of engineers, physicians, academics, and businessmen were now in the adult world. Their growing-up experiences were widely divergent from what their parents recounted of their childhoods in Hyderabad, Madras, Chandigarh, or Ahmedabad. Unlike their parents, the Indian-American children were well aware of being minorities from an early age. They were born in towns across the US and had navigated school lives beginning with their Indian names being mispronounced or hearing jibes about Indian curry smells, or Indian deities, and such things. They knew from childhood what it was to be a cultural and racial "other". That was the reality they knew whether they grew up in Dayton, Ohio; Houston, Texas; Seattle, Washington; or Edison, New Jersey. Importantly, however, unlike their parents, they also studied American history and understood that discrimination and racism in the US were structural. They had been taught the US Constitution and knew how it affected their rights. They were born American but had lived complex hyphenated identities. This textured their perspectives, priorities, and life choices. For these high-achieving desis (colloquial for the Indian diaspora community), universities became the spaces to resolve struggles with identity—ethnic, sexual, and also political. Unlike their parents, these desi youth had childhood histories of being immigrant children, not adults who had come to grad school or into jobs. America and its politics mattered to them. They knew that policies mattered. They were responsive to conversations about social justice, racism, and healthcare benefits. When they saw local campaigns, they signed up to support causes.

From school projects on experiential learning, many signed up as volunteers helping socially disadvantaged communities.

"I always wanted to be a neuroscientist," says Neil Makhija who grew up in Pennsylvania, "but I started to realize that what I wanted to see change was how public policy could enable innovation. I felt like I could do more, not on a lab bench, but through the law." After practicing law for a few years, he ran for electoral office. In 2020 Makhija was appointed executive director of the IMPACT Fund, a dynamic organization founded in 2016, which has played a key role to train, endorse, and support Indian-American Democratic candidates to win elections in 2020.[8]

In short, the US-born generation was conversant and held views on the prevailing politics in America—unlike the majority of the parent-generation, for whom their individual professional success and wealth generation were pretty much the guarantees considered worth investing in. Not surprisingly, parents expected their US-born children to excel in academics, get accepted to premier universities and eventually to replicate parental success and become engineers, physicians, techies, stretching somewhat to include finance and law. Many of my Indian-American students chuckled about how careers in media, public policy, politics, music, or art were heavily discouraged as risky options for the future. Family dinner-table conversations were clear about these priorities as the children were mulling career choices through high school. These prescriptions, however, were not swallowed uncritically by the children. In fact, from the first crop of Indian-Americans who ran for electoral office in the 2010s, many had professional degrees in science, medicine, engineering, or law and had begun as professionals in their respective fields before entering the political arena.

The Obama Factor: "Yes We Can"

As the first decade of the twenty-first century was ending, the emergence of Barack Obama fired the imagination of thousands of Americans, especially nonwhite young men and women. US-born Indian-Americans were among them, and Obama's White House saw a string of appointments from the Indian-American community, generating waves of excitement and media headlines. Around Obama's own inauguration as president, some key Indian-

American appointees were announced, which created quite a buzz among the community as well as in media "back home". Sonal Shah, an economist who grew up in Houston, Texas, was one of the early Obama appointees, first to his transition team and later as the director, Office of Social Innovation and Civic Participation in the White House (April 2009–August 2011). Her appointment in 2008 was reported as "Gujarat village euphoric as daughter joins Obama team".[9]

In 2009, Preeta Bansal, a lawyer who grew up in Kansas was appointed as the general counsel and senior policy advisor in the Office of Management and Budget. Similarly, in 2010, headlines announced about Farah Pandit, "Obama names Indian-American Muslim as Special Envoy to the Islamic World".[10] Farah Pandit's parents were immigrants from Kashmir. In January 2009, Neal Kumar Katyal, professor at Georgetown University Law School, was appointed principal deputy solicitor general, becoming at the time, the highest-ranking Indian-American in the US Department of Justice. The same year, executive Aneesh Chopra, with degrees in public health and public policy, was appointed chief technology officer of the United States, a position newly created by Barack Obama's administration. In 2010, Rajiv Shah, appointed as head of USAID, became the highest-ranking person of Indian origin in any presidential administration. In 2013, *The Hindu* reported, "Chandigarh-born Srinivasan was appointed to the US Court of Appeals for the District of Columbia Circuit in May 2013". Sri Srinivasan became the chief United States circuit judge of the United States Court of Appeals for the District of Columbia. In 2014, Dr Vivek Murthy, a physician, was appointed surgeon general of the United States. This spate of appointments brought young Indian-American faces into high visibility. By this time, Indian media was reporting "Over 50 Indians in Barack Obama's White House Team".[11]

During the early Obama years, I had the opportunity to interact with all of the above individuals and found them to be remarkable professionals. Needless to say, all these appointees were Democrats. It was interesting to discover that although many of them had held reasonably important professional positions even before they joined the Obama administration, the Indian community in general did not know these immigrant children except in the communities where they had been raised. On the other hand,

Bobby Jindal, governor of Louisiana, and Nikki Haley, governor of South Carolina, appointed in 2008 and 2011, respectively, were widely known as the two Indians in high office. Some community organizations lauded Haley and Jindal as symbols of Indian-American success in public office. But among a majority of community members, they triggered negative responses. Young Indian-Americans in particular were highly critical of the fact that both Bobby and Nikki had dropped their Indian names (Piyush and Nimrata, respectively). They rarely spoke about their Indian heritage, and both had converted to Christianity. Identity was important to second-generation immigrant children because it had been their issue from an early age. They are American but do not support erasures to their ethnic selves.

Despite these high-ranking appointments in the administration, Indian-Americans had achieved only marginal representation in the political space. The power of some Indian commercial lobbies, like India Interest Group Lobby, had increased in Washington, DC. Meanwhile, the India Caucus emerged in the Senate (2004)—the first country-focused caucus for both houses of Congress. Around that time, the Indian diaspora began attracting media attention when scattered groups of wealthy first-generation Indian-Americans successfully mobilized from 2005–2006 to assert support of the India–US Civil Nuclear Agreement (the Henry J Hyde US–India Peaceful Atomic Energy Cooperation Act passed in 2008). Watching this, some analysts spoke of the emergence of an "India Lobby". Unfortunately, this initiative, which was driven by first-generation wealthy individuals (almost entirely men), showed no continuity in sustaining its momentum.

By now on the West Coast and in New York, America's financial capital, Indians were gaining nationwide recognition in tech and business. Indra Nooyi was named CEO of PepsiCo in 2006, Shantanu Narayen was appointed CEO at Adobe in 2007, Ajay Banga became CEO and president of Mastercard in 2010, Satya Nadella became head of Microsoft in 2014, and Sundar Pichai was appointed CEO of Google in 2015. We may note that all of these professionals were educated and raised in India in the 1980s or later. Therefore, their experience does not quite fit the broader contours of the Indian-American diasporic experience. They did however constitute a parallel thread of the Indian success story, adding much to its visibility.

Indian-Americans and Electoral Politics

Meanwhile, in the electoral space, Indian-Americans were entering state legislatures. By 2006, Indians got representation in six state legislatures (New Jersey, Maryland, Iowa, Minnesota, Kansas, and Ohio). Among them were Satveer Chaudhary (Minnesota), Swati Dandekar (Iowa), and two young men, Raj Goyle, an attorney who grew up in Kansas, and Jay Goyal, an industrial engineer from Ohio, who was just 27 at the time. Goyal became the youngest lawmaker in Ohio's State House and served three terms from 2007 to 2013. Aruna Miller, an engineer, became delegate to Maryland State Assembly in 2010 and got reelected in 2014.

During these years, there was significant shift in focus among young Indian-Americans who signed up to campaign. There was also a concerted push in some circles to aggressively invest in building up Indian-American candidates to enter politics. The Indian-American Leadership Initiative (IALI) which was founded in 2000, became active in endorsing and fundraising. I wish to note some exceptional first-generation Indian-Americans who were fired up about the community making a mark in US politics. In 2009, I met two prominent DC-based influential Indian-Americans from the first generation—Shekar Narasimhan and Dr Mahinder Tak. During the run-up to Obama's election, Narasimhan and Dr Tak were appointed co-chairs of the Democratic National Committee's Indo-American Council. Narasimhan is a highly successful tech entrepreneur, and Dr Tak is an oncology-radiologist who also served in the US military. She also owns the largest collection of contemporary Indian art in the US and serves on the board of several art foundations. Although many wealthy Indians had been donating to individual campaigns of mainstream American candidates, the active political engagement of Narasimhan and Tak sets them apart from their cohort. Their influence in DC circles has been noteworthy as they have long been political donors and have hosted high-profile fundraisers for Obama and Clinton campaigns. Most important has been their support for the next-gen of Indian-American political aspirants. They have generously leveraged their networks to support and fundraise the early-stage electoral campaigns for several Indian-Americans who later became well-known members of Congress including Ro

Khanna, Ami Bera, Pramila Jayapal, and several others. As influencers who are generous with their time and money, both Narasimhan and Tak are widely known to young Democrats who may be running from different districts across America. Such individual initiatives paved the way for more organized initiatives like the IMPACT Fund.[12]

In 2010, there was another push forward in the political arena, this time at the national level. A record number of six Indian-Americans ran for US Congress in the mid-term elections of 2010. By then, IALI PAC had a presence and was able to endorse and offer campaign funding to candidates. Among them were Ami Bera (California), Raj Goyle (Kansas), Ravi Sangisetty (Louisiana), Reshma Saujani (New York), and Dr Manan Trivedi (Pennsylvania). Kamala Harris was also supported by IALI for attorney general (California). Of these, only Dr Ami Bera and Kamala Harris were successful. In January 2013, Tulsi Gabbard, a Hindu-American woman and a war veteran from Hawaii, and Dr Ami Bera, a physician from California, were sworn in. Tulsi Gabbard, although not of Indian origin, appealed to a lot of Indian-Americans as she projected her Hindu identity upfront, taking her oath in Congress on the Hindu holy book Bhagavad Gita, a gesture which garnered much attention.

By now, the Indian community began to display unprecedented political energy especially in the socio-political circles of Washington, DC. I wish to cite a Washington, DC, tradition—the Presidential Balls that are held as parallel celebrations to the Presidential Inauguration. They are fancy, formal, prestigious, and expensive affairs organized by interest groups or communities. There had never been an Indian one. In January 2013, the first ever Indian-American Presidential Ball was held. The initiative was spearheaded by a dynamic organization called Indiaspora, which was founded by Silicon Valley software entrepreneur MR Rangaswami, and had been launched in 2012. I recall walking into this spectacular event at the plush Mandarin Oriental Hotel, Washington, DC. Most men and women had opted to dress in "formal traditional Indian". Resplendent Indian dresses and sarees were swishing past black suits, tuxedos, and even sherwanis. Color was everywhere. The scene was a marked contrast to the many Washington, DC-style events I had attended, typically the "dress-in-black" events. The entertainment had to compete with the chatter and the din of a packed hall. Chef Maneet Chauhan's cuisine, the dance troupes, and the band called *Red Baraat* all reflected this celebration of Indian-American identity. Indian-Americans from across America and across generations were there. Silicon Valley danced alongside Washington interns and staffers. Tulsi Gabbard, Ami Bera, and Kamala Harris were all there.

This Ball was a statement in national circles inserting a certain presence of the Indian diaspora. The Indian-American buzzer had been switched on. In 2016, a record number of five Indian-Americans were elected to US Congress. All of them Democrats. Kamala Harris was one of them, and the first to be elected to the Senate. Pramila Jayapal won from Seattle, the first Indian-American woman to accomplish this feat in the House of Representatives. Raja Krishnamoorthi from Chicago, Ro Khanna and Ami Bera from California, completed the list.[13] Since 2016, the US Congress has had these five Indian-American members, the largest cohort so far. Together they have created their own Samosa Caucus, named after a beloved Indian savory snack, now widely popularized by Indian diasporas in sundry regions of the world.

With rising aspirations to wield influence, Indian-Americans have often looked at the Jewish-American community with both admiration and envy for the influence they have captured in the worlds of finance, business, media, and politics. The ability of the Jewish diaspora to lobby with Congressional candidates and garner support for Israel is often cited by Indian-Americans, especially of the first generation, as something to strive for. When I arrived in DC in 2009, I had just published my book on the Indian-Jewish diaspora in Israel. *Being Indian, Being Israeli* (2009) was based on the fieldwork I had conducted in Israel among Indian-Jewish communities. The subject evoked much curiosity among American Jews who knew little about India's Jewish heritage. During the fifty odd book talks I presented at campuses and Jewish community events across America, I had the opportunity to meet hundreds of American diaspora Jews and observe Jewish community organizations. Many of these talks were co-hosted by Jewish community centers or local chapters of the American-Jewish Committee who had also partnered with local Indian organizations. I therefore got a chance to observe that the interactions between Indian and Jewish-American communities are warm and cordial. However, from observations gathered through these interactions in New York, Miami, Cleveland, Baltimore, and Los Angeles, where Jewish communities are most impactful, it became obvious that although the two diaspora communities display some shared values of family cohesion, education, and so forth, the Jewish model is not a perfect fit for Indians. Indian-Americans would find it hard to identify with the "existential threat" that many Jews identify with, nor can motherland India be perceived as "endangered" as is Israel.

Harris's Story a Milestone, not a Destination

It is true that Kamala Harris's election, in one stroke, has brought the Indian-American diaspora into the spotlight of national-level politics in the US. It is also true that Harris's public pronouncements claiming her Indian heritage with pride and her glowing praise for the values instilled by her Indian mother have resonated with large sections of the Indian-born generation who see Harris's family story of migration echoing their own. For the US-born children, Harris's journey is that of an immigrant child who has negotiated issues of cultural "otherness" and stands today as the confident high-achiever immigrant American, who has not disavowed her ethnic or racial identity. Of course, Harris does have her detractors—the Trump supporters or those who have issues about Harris's biracial identity. In general, however, Harris's outreach to Indian-Americans is a win-win for her and the Indian community, bringing to her a constituency of educated and well-off voters.

But Kamala Harris did not grow up among the Indian-American community, nor have they known her before she ran for office. So, how much will her election contribute to the community's cache? I believe Harris will be an inspiration for younger Democrat-leaning leadership in the community and will spur them on to aim even higher. This will strengthen political momentum in which Indian-Americans have lagged behind. The story of Kamala Devi can be claimed by anyone who may have a name like Sree, Rahul, Shilpa, Gautam, or Priyanka, as a story of aspirational fulfillment. But this momentum does not *hinge* on the success of Kamala Harris or more Indian-American appointees by the Biden administration. The trends in 2020 have revealed high levels of political ambition among Indian-Americans. Electoral candidates and advocacy groups have managed to galvanize the community despite the constraints of a Covid year of lockdowns. Over 50–70 Indian-American candidates ran for electoral office across America in 2020. Pandemic-related restrictions had affected the ability to knock on doors to campaign, but social media outreach through a barrage of online panels, videos, discussions, and interviews effectively connected the candidates to their constituents, in their homes.

This energy to have a voice in politics will only deepen in the years to come, especially among the US-born generation of desi politicos. Harris's story is only a milestone in that journey, not a destination.

Notes

1. "Punjabi Sikh-Mexican American Community: Fading Into History". *The Washington Post,* Aug 13, 2012 https://www.washingtonpost.com/national/on-faith/punjabi-sikh-mexican-american-community-fading-into-history/2012/08/13/cc6b7b98-e26b-11e1-98e7-89d659f9c106_story.html
2. Report: PEW Research Center (2012) https://www.pewsocialtrends.org/2012/06/19/the-rise-of-asian-americans/
3. *The Mint*, June 18, 2019. https://www.livemint.com/news/world/number-of-undocumented-indians-in-us-has-increased-sharply-report-1560853753639.html
4. The Nationality Act 1965 https://en.wikipedia.org/wiki/Immigration_and_Nationality_Act_of_1965
5. Interview, Kumar Barve. January 10, 2010
6. Indian American Friendship Council . https://iafc.us/home.php
7. Report : PEW Research Center. "Key facts about Asian Americans, a diverse and growing population" September 8, 2017. https://www.pewresearch.org/fact-tank/2017/09/08/key-facts-about-asian-americans/
8. See IMPACT FUND https://www.iaimpact.org/updates/indian-americans-in-politics-policy-and-government-create-leadership-pipeline
9. https://www.indiatoday.in/latest-headlines/story/gujarat-village-euphoric-as-daughter-joins-obama-team-33343-2008-11-13
10. http://timesofindia.indiatimes.com/articleshow/5577147.cms?utm_source=contentofinterest&utm_medium=text&utm_campaign=cppst
11. https://www.deccanchronicle.com/131230/news-world/article/over-50-indians-barack-obamas-white-house-team
12. I attended the launch-event of the IMPACT Fund held on the sidelines of the Democratic Convention in Philadelphia in 2016. Among the guests was Cory Booker , Democratic Senator from New Jersey who is a popular candidate among

Indian-American voters in New Jersey. IMPACT is co-founded by entrepreneurs Deepak Raj and Raj Goyle.

13. https://www.firstpost.com/world/us-election-2016-record-5-indian-americans-including-kamala-harris-set-to-be-elected-to-us-congress-3096710.html

From Struggling Immigrants to Political Influencers: How a Community Came of Age

Tarun Basu

Introduction: The "Macaca Moment"

It is called the "Macaca moment" in American politics. On August 11, 2006, a Republican senator, who was also a presidential hopeful, racially slurred a young Indian-American, SR Sidharth, at a campaign rally in South Virginia, not far from Washington, DC. Spotting him with a video camera, which he was using as a volunteer tracker, Senator George Allen called him out as a "macaca"—a derogatory term used by colonialists in Africa—and leered, "Let's give a welcome to macaca here. Welcome to America."

That gaffe exploded in the political world and made international news. Senator Allen apologized, but in a rapidly-changing multicultural America, it cost him his reelection.

"I remember that day—August 11, 2006—because it was when a politician used his power to demean a member of my family, a *son* of our community, born and brought up in the United States," recalled Shekar Narasimhan, chairman of the AAPI (Asian American and Pacific Islanders) Victory Fund, an impactful organization that supports political empowerment of Asian-American communities. The young Indian-American who was publicly vilified was his son, now a successful finance professional.

The incident, in a way, led to a "sense of awakening" in the Indian community that they not only needed to organize themselves but also be political influencers if they were to live with dignity in their adopted country.

In a serendipitous turn of fortune, exactly 14 years later to the day, on August 11, 2020, Joe Biden named Kamala Harris as his vice-presidential candidate.

"This was a very different kind of leader who used his power to lift up a member of our 'desi' family, a *daughter* of our community," says Narasimhan who calls Biden "my friend" and was officially listed as one of the major mobilizers and donors to the Biden campaign.

"Kamala Harris is the manifestation of our American dream," Narasimhan added.

Indian-Americans for Biden

President Biden has been long known to have a lot of friends in the Indian-American community. As two-time chairman of the powerful Senate Foreign Relations Committee, Biden who describes himself as a "liberal internationalist" was always keen to get educated about India, and had a large Indian-American support base that backed him with generous campaign funds.

He was among the clutch of lawmakers who supported the landmark US–India nuclear deal, even stepping up to the plate at the last minute to kill a legislative amendment in November 2006 that sought to link the passage of the nuclear deal with India suspending military deals with Iran —a condition New Delhi would never have accepted.

One of his close friends is Swadesh Chatterjee, an immigrant from Kolkata in the late seventies and a prominent entrepreneur in North Carolina, who used his long association with Biden as a community activist to get him involved in issues that mattered to India. Chatterjee recalls telling Biden at a business event at the St Regis Hotel in Washington, DC, as far back in the mid-nineties, that it was time to get something concrete done for India, beyond photo-ops that Indian-Americans were known to crave for.

To this, Biden quipped: "So you guys don't want any photos with me anymore?"

Convergence of History

In 2006, two historical stories converged: One involved strategic deepening of the US–India relationship; the other was a consolidation of organizational capacity within the burgeoning Indian community and its growing political clout.

Without the latter, it is unlikely that the bold US–India nuclear agreement would have made it over the requisite congressional hurdles in 2006 (more about this later).

The Indian-American community was becoming a formidable new asset in strengthening India's relationship with the world's only superpower and it was mutating—in the words of Stephen Walt, professor of international affairs at Harvard Kennedy School—into a "potent political weapon" in a public diplomacy strategy aimed at favorably influencing US policy toward India.

It was said that successful ethnic lobbies were those with an "elevated" socioeconomic profile like high education levels, good communicating skills, deep pockets with generous contributions to campaign funds, and Indian-Americans ticked on all these boxes as they grew in size, stature, and influence, becoming in effect the newest kid on the block.

Cut to 2020, and the election of at least 25 Indian-American congressmen/women and state representatives, the record fundraising by Indian-American associations, and one can at once realize how far the community had indeed traveled in its quest for political empowerment that has involved unprecedented mobilization and organization by a few pioneers and dedicated community activists.

"In the early eighties, there were two city council members from the Indian-American community in small towns. From those days we have traveled a long way to win many positions in several states, including the vice presidency of the US," says Dr Thomas Abraham, founder-president and chairman of the Global Organization of People of Indian Origin (GOPIO).

Storied History

If a social anthropologist sits down to chart the storied history of the Indian community in America—which has grown to over four million (US Census) to come into its own and be counted—he will no doubt mark in it a few milestones. These would be—1913: the Gadar movement initiated in San Francisco; 1923: US Supreme Court turns down the application of Bhagat Singh Thind, a US Army veteran, for citizenship; 1946: President Harry Truman signed the Luce–Celler Act permitting limited immigration from India (and the Philippines); 1956: the election of Dalip Singh "Judge" Saund to the US Congress broke multiple barriers as he was the first Asian-American and first Indian-American to be elected; 1965: US Congress passed the Immigration and Naturalization Act that opened the door to large-scale immigration from India; 1967: the formation of Association of Indians in America (AIA), acknowledged as the oldest Indian association in America; 1980: AIA got Indian-Americans their first political recognition by getting "Asian-Indians" listed as a separate category in the US Census; 1980: the National Federation of Indian American Associations (NFIA) was formed in New York at the First National Convention of Asian Indians in North America.

In one of the first such recorded references, at an event held at the Mike Mansfield Room of the US Capitol in April 1985 to honor Senator Bob Dole, then Senate majority leader who was to later become a Republican Party nominee in the 1996 presidential election, Indian-American community leaders made an impassioned plea for political recognition of their growing tribe.

"We as a community which is highly intelligent, highly educated and extremely hard-working are still not part of the decision-making process. The message is clear: We must be part of the process which makes decisions that affect us and our children," pleaded Dr Khatri on behalf of the National Association of Americans of Asian Indian Descent (NAAAID) which he claimed "is the only organization of US Citizens of Asian-Indian origin that faithfully represents the ethnic community and serves its members all across the country and all walks of life."

The NAAAID was led by its founder and honorary chairman, Dr Jan Pillai, a professor of law at Temple University who in 1986 went on to become an acting director of Federal Energy Regulatory Commission—"the first major appointment for the Asian-Indian community to the senior levels of the federal government".

American politicians seemed to have recognized not just the talent but the fundraising capacities of Indians early on. And a "rich Indian" mentioned in records as a big fundraiser for Senator Dole then was physician Zach Zachariah, who was among the early professional immigrants from India in the seventies. Zachariah is quoted by the *Los Angeles Times* of July 28, 1995 as saying, "It's much easier [raising money] for Dole than it was with [George HW] Bush [reelection] in 1992.... I don't give up easily. I keep after them until they're willing to give me $1,000 to get me off the phone."

Zachariah was reputed to have raised $750,000 for the Bush Sr campaign and evidence of this can be found in a letter written by Phil Gramm of the National Republican Senatorial Committee to Dole, seeking his presence in an Indian-American Issues Conference saying, "Indian-Americans have made tremendous economic and social contributions to this country. As a group, they are also one of the most organized and effective growing political coalitions today".

The letter went on to say that Dr Zachariah, who had provided "tremendous support for President Bush [Sr]", and Krishna Srinivasa, both respected leaders in the Indian-American community, wanted Dole to address the group "on issues relating to immigration and Indo-United States relations".

The thrust of early community involvement, as per available records, researched writings, and anecdotal recounting, go as far back as campaigning for India's independence in the early 1900s, with the start of the Gadar movement in San Francisco in 1913 and the India League in the 1940s. The early pioneers were quite involved in the campaign for India's independence, providing testimonies to the US Congress and seeking to influence American public opinion through the media, which was then not predisposed to immigration from South Asia.

Most illustrative of this attitude was the celebrated case of Bhagat Singh Thind, an academic who served in the US Army during World War I but was denied American citizenship by the US Supreme Court. In a judgment in 1923, the court upheld the racial exclusion of Indians and other Asians in implicitly protecting the country's white and Christian origins, reflecting as many would say the institutionalized xenophobia present at that time in American society.

Among the early pioneers was Jagjit Singh, better known as JJ Singh, president of the India League of America and founder and the first president of the India Chamber of Commerce of America. He was profiled in the *New York Post* as a rich Indian who had a clothing business on fashionable Fifth Avenue in Manhattan and was the archetype of a successful immigrant.

"He brought a slice of America into the India League" whose membership roster "included Detroit labor leaders, Sikh farmers in California, African-American activists in Harlem, Chinese immigrants, and a sprinkling of lawmakers." Urging Americans to support freedom for India, they compared Mahatma Gandhi to George Washington and printed the Declaration of Independence and its Indian counterpart, issued in 1930, side by side in pamphlets, dinner and event programs, and in the India League's newsletter. *The New Yorker* called him a "one-man lobby for Indian independence".

Singh helped Indian immigrants become legally American, pushing to undo the Supreme Court's 1923 decision that Indians could not become naturalized citizens. In July 1946, President Harry Truman approved the Luce–Celler Act, which allowed limited immigration from India (as well as the Philippines). Singh was invited to the White House to observe Truman sign it into law.

It was not, however, until the passage of the 1965 Immigration and Naturalization Act by Congress that the doors were opened to large-scale immigration of Indians, who soon began making their presence felt. This was a watershed moment not just for Indian-Americans but for all ethnic populations. The new Immigration Act abolished the national-origin quotas that had been in place, permitting the entry of many more immigrants into the "promise" of America.

The Act specified a preference for scientists and technological professionals. This gave Indians several advantages. Jawaharlal Nehru, India's first prime minister, had developed policies geared toward building world-class institutions of higher education like the Indian Institutes of Technology (IITs) and medical institutions. These policies resulted in an educated Indian population with a high proportion of technology and medical professionals who were permitted to emigrate for better prospects. Due to an inherited English-medium education from the British colonial rulers, many of these professionals spoke excellent English, giving them additional advantage over other ethnic groups that immigrated to the US from other parts of Asia.

The Indian population in the United States expanded rapidly. Between 1960 and 1980, it grew from under 9,000 to over 361,000. By 1990, the Indian population had reached 815,000 and by 2000 it approached 1.7 million (US Census). According to the 2010 United States Census, the Asian-Indian population in the United States grew from almost 1,678,765 in 2000 (0.6 percent of US population) to 2,843,391 in 2010 (0.9 percent of US population), a growth rate of 69.37 percent, one of the fastest-growing ethnic groups in the United States.

First Political Recognition

It was the Association of Indians in America (AIA), founded on August 20, 1967, that provided in the early years a unified voice to the people of "Asian-Indian" descent. It is acknowledged as the oldest association of Indians—and there have been many over the years—with chapters throughout the country. The AIA got Indian-Americans their first political recognition by getting "Asian-Indians" listed as a separate category in the US Census of 1980. The AIA also got Asian-Indians to be listed as a minority under the Asian-American and Pacific Islander category.

The AIA had three goals: to support the social welfare of Indians living in the United States and to ease their transition into the mainstream; to help members work for development in India; and to provide charitable, cultural, and educational means for Asian-Indians to participate in American community life.

However, the group failed to become a national entity, despite some individual aspirations of becoming more politically active. The early Indians who came were content to pursue their American dream, provide their children with good education, travel around the country, and bring some of their kin to the "promised land".

But politics was not their objective. They had come to America to lead a good life, not to dirty their hands with politics.

New Arrivals Changed Community Thinking

However, with the changes in immigration laws, the demography too changed and the majority of the community was soon the new arrivals of the 1970s, who were techies, doctors, and other professionals. These groups of new immigrants formed Indian associations in states and cities with a significant population of the community. Along with these, several language- and religion-based organizations were formed as arriving Indians sought social security. By the early 1970s, there were about 15 organizations in New York alone.

In a unifying effort to bring all these groups together, the Indian consulate in New York took the initiative to form a joint committee of Indian organizations. This slowly became an active body organizing major Indian national celebrations such as India's Independence Day, Republic Day, and Mahatma Gandhi's birthday. With more community groups enrolling in the joint committee, Indians sought to make their presence felt in the mainstream by participating in the American Bicentennial Celebrations in 1976 and American Independence Day and Parade of Nations on July 4, 1977.

The background of those who emigrated and their choice of state in which to settle—California, Texas, New Jersey—paved the way for Indian-American political mobilization, as this ethnic population slowly established itself as talented and successful immigrants in various areas—universities, hospitals, scientific and technological institutions, and businesses.

Federation of Indian Associations

With the success of the joint committee, there was a move toward formation of the Federation of Indian Associations (FIA) in New York City representing all Indian groups in the tri-state area of New York, New Jersey, and Connecticut. The FIA New York was launched in January 1978. From 1978 to 1981, it was fast growth for FIA with services such as medical counseling, employment counseling, emergency assistance, besides participation in various festivals and fairs.

The early 1978 saw the FIA campaign politically for the first time for a bill introduced by Senator Edward Kennedy (Democrat) to provide massive US aid for the rehabilitation of cyclone victims in Andhra Pradesh, a southern Indian state that sent a large proportion of Indian immigrants to the US. In 1979, FIA campaigned with other Asian groups to declare the first week of May as Asian-American week, which President Jimmy Carter signed into law. This has since then become the Asian-American Heritage Month in May.

First Convention of Indian-Americans

And the next logical step was to organize the first National Convention of Asian-Indians in North America. The convention took place at New York's Sheraton Center on Memorial Day weekend of 1980. Over 2,000 people attended the three-day convention with delegates from 24 states. The convention also served as a meeting place for the various alumni groups of Indian educational institutions, like the IITs and medical colleges.

Indians were finally realizing the potential of their growing numbers and uniting themselves to be a force for good.

The National Federation of Indian American Associations (NFIA) was formed at this convention. In the first half of the 1980s, the NFIA promoted the formation of FIAs in other cities—Chicago, Los Angeles, Cleveland, and Columbus. In 1988, San Francisco Bay Area formed FIA Northern California, while Washington, DC, area formed the FIA of the Capital Region in the mid-1990s. NFIA became a formidable force with over 200 member associations across the nation.

But political influence eluded them; some community leaders continued to feel it was best to stay away from mainstream politics.

Formation of Professional Organizations

In 1984, at its third biennial convention, NFIA organized the first conference of Indian physicians. It was a challenge to bring together the fragmented Indian medical groups, which had sprung up in different cities. The NFIA organized a White House briefing for the medical groups following which an open forum was held in the evening. The American Association of Physicians of Indian Origin (AAPI), which had just been formed in Michigan and had a chapter in Boston, expressed their wish to become a national-level professional body of Indian-origin doctors. The NFIA agreed and handed over the coordination to AAPI. AAPI is now the largest membership-oriented Indian professional organization.

In 1986, NFIA organized the first conference of Indian hotel and motel owners, another growing tribe, many of whom had fled persecution in East Africa. Haresh Panchal, owner of several hotels and motels in San Jose, California, coordinated this effort. After the conference, a national meeting was organized in Atlanta and the Asian American Hotel/Motel Operators Association (AAHOA) was formed at this meeting. It became an active organization representing thousands of Asian-Indian hotel/motel operators which has grown into another influential business lobby. Indian hotel and motel owners manage nearly half of the hotel/motel business across the US.

With NFIA's lead in consolidating Indian-Americans, another phenomenon followed, that is, provincial language-based groups started having their own conventions. The US Telugu group, known as Telugu Association of North America (TANA), was the first one to be formed in 1978. The Federation of Kerala Associations of North America (FOKANA) was formed after the NFIA general body meeting in Chicago in 1982, where eight Malayalis present at the NFIA meeting formed the organization. Similarly, other national language-based groups were formed, such as Kannada, Marathi, Bengali, Odia, Tamil, Assamese, and Rajasthani. In fact, these groups have larger attendance at their conventions—held mostly over the July 4 American Independence Day weekend—than the national Indian groups.

Thrust into the US Political Process

Community leaders now began feeling the need to be involved in the political process, develop a lobby for community causes, and influence policies and legislation in favor of the community and their native land. As Ashok Mago, who immigrated from New Delhi in 1974 and settled in Dallas, Texas, to become a leading community figure sought after by a succession of Indian ambassadors, noted: "Some of us realized that if we have to live here, raise our kids, give them a good education, we must take a more active interest in American public life, and know our politicians who run our lives."

Since the early 1980s, the community began supporting candidates in both the political parties and raising funds for political campaigns for local representatives, as many well-placed Indians began to feel that their interests were not being represented in the policies pursued by the state and federal governments.

For this reason, Indian-Americans began to mobilize.

The 1984 NFIA convention also saw the emergence of the Indian American Forum for Political Education (IAFPE), founded by Dr Joy Cherian in Washington, DC. Cherian was to later join the Reagan administration. The IAFPE is recognized for its work to enhance political awareness among the Indian-American community and encourage their civic engagement, the first such organization with an explicit aim to politically empower the community.

The NFIA and other community groups actively campaigned to preserve the family reunification clause in the early 1980s and were successful in their efforts. In 1987, when the Reagan administration decided to give massive military aid to Pakistan, including an airborne surveillance system such as the AWACS, NFIA campaigned with congressmen and senators to stop this aid. The US Congress, through the Pressler amendment, banned major military and economic aid to Pakistan unless it was able to justify and provide sufficient evidence that the funds were not being used for nuclear proliferation.

Early Mobilizing Efforts

Those were still early days in the community's activism, when visionaries like Dr Jan Pillai, Dr Joy Cherian, Thomas Abraham or Gopal Raju, the pioneering publisher of *India Abroad*, struggled to connect and unify the disparate, fragmented, but growing community, not just under an umbrella, but also to give them voice and heft so that they were taken seriously by their local or national lawmakers, their demands were addressed, and their rights and privileges protected.

Till then, all that a couple-of-million-strong Indian community seemed to be interested in, going by conversations and early writings, was to meet their congressman or senator on occasions like Diwali or Independence

Day, and have their photos taken with them and their families to place in their living rooms. The challenge for community mobilizers was to turn the photo-op seekers into political influencers strong and significant enough to be reckoned with.

And they realized that there were only a few ways to bind the community—through cultural clubs, Bollywood movies, or a community newspaper.

Abraham, a materials scientist who came from Kerala for postgraduate studies at Columbia University, became president of the India Club which became one of the richest student bodies among Indians in the US, and began using that money to promote young classical musicians and dancers from India. This gave Indian students a cultural identity that manifested in the organization of more Indian festivals and commemoration events.

Raju, who always thought big, had sought to leverage his multi-edition, professionally brought-out newspaper that he had founded in 1970 into a credible and influential voice for the community. He took pains—unlike other ethnic media of the time—to hire talented professional journalists in the US and in India, including retired hands from the *New York Times*, and the latest communication technology, to bring the latest news from India, and Indians across the world, in order to fill the news and information gap of the growing number of Indian professionals and students in America.

It was in the early nineties that Raju, at community gatherings where he popularized the professionally brought-out *India Abroad* paper as the "voice of the community", drew on the analogy of the Jewish community and said the India Abroad Center for Political Awareness (IACPA) which he had formed was aimed at "mobilizing the Indian community into a cohesive, influential group that would have clout and political leverage to impact on an issue". He said the IAPCA would seek to be the catalyst that helps to make the community more sophisticated and discerning in political activities such as fundraising and voting.

He said the IACPA's aims and objectives were, among other things, to have an infrastructure for collecting and sharing information about Indian-Americans throughout the country, their strengths, their weaknesses, and issues, including legislations that could affect their lives. Being a media owner, for him accurate information was the key to political empowerment.

A Community of Achievers

The organization of colorful and pageantry-filled Indian festivals and India Day parades built up a positive image for India as well as for the community across the country. Indian-American achievers such as the late astronaut Dr Kalpana Chawla, musician Ravi Shankar, Nobel Laureates Dr Har Gobind Khorana and the late Dr Subrahmanyan Chandrasekhar, Indian-American CEOs such as Indra Nooyi, Hotmail founder Sabeer Bhatia, Pulitzer Prize winning cancer specialist Siddhartha Mukherjee, the success stories of Indian entrepreneurs in Silicon Valley further burnished the community's image in public perception.

The growing number of students in American campuses, their admission to prestigious Ivy League institutions, their academic brilliance, particularly in STEM subjects that was not a favorite of the average American students, their English language proficiency, unlike other immigrant communities, and Indian students' dominance in the hugely popular National Spelling Bee gave the community a name and standing that few communities have been able to garner in such a short time.

In 1995, IACPA started the very innovative Washington Leadership Programme (WLP) to introduce Indian-American college students—who were going to step into a career path and were inclined to public life—to the political process in America through congressional internships. The idea was to enable them to get a first-hand look at how the political process worked, get the second-generation Indian-Americans hooked onto the American political process, and inspire them to pursue a career in public life.

Every year, a bunch of them were sent to India for orientation into Indian policymaking and thought processes, an exercise I was proud to be associated with, which gave me an insight into the thinking of the US-born "desis".

Solarz and Pallone: Early Community Supporters

One of the American politicians who realized the importance of the community and India was Congressman Stephen Solarz, the prime mover in setting up the India Caucus in Congress in 1994. He was also instrumental in setting up a South Asia Bureau in the State Department.

Solarz was probably the first politician to recognize the social capital (academics, doctors) and the economic capital (entrepreneurs, CEOs, philanthropists) of Indians. He cultivated the community, which also supported his campaign financially.

"He got other politicians to recognize the value of the community. Others began flocking to Indian-Americans after that," recalled Arul Louis, a veteran Indian-American journalist who has worked in both ethnic and mainstream American papers.

Solarz became an unofficial lobbyist for India even after he left Congress. "He studied issues relating to India–US relations and spoke and wrote about them with conviction, clarity and persuasiveness. He gave the impression that he was for India, right or wrong, but he had cogent arguments to substantiate his points in favor of India," wrote TP Sreenivasan, India's former deputy chief of mission at the embassy of India, Washington, DC.

Another staunch supporter, Frank Pallone (D-NJ) became the head of the House of Representative India Caucus, the largest country-specific caucus, making it exceedingly influential. It was formed after intense lobbying for the purpose of educating the Congress on issues concerning India. Indian-Americans were concerned at the way the government was portraying India as this was at a time the State Department was particularly critical of India's human rights policies in Kashmir.

A Senate "Friends of India" group was subsequently formed in April 2004. Senator John Cornyn (R-Tex) initiated the formation of the caucus—largely due to the initiatives of Texas businessman Mago who had taken Cornyn on a familiarization trip to India—and Senator Hillary Clinton (D-NY) became its co-chair. This caucus was the first and the only country-focused caucus in the Senate, making it a landmark for Indian-Americans.

And these caucuses have been since acting as pressure groups on critical issues of interest to India and Indian-Americans.

Growing Funding Clout

The growing fundraising capability of Indians—as they grew richer to have the highest median income among all immigrant communities—was a big factor in their rising political influence, with the economic and educational achievements of the immigrant group being described by a researcher as "perhaps a record in US social history".

President Bill Clinton, for example, was not much aware of the Indian community and let himself be pulled by pro-Pakistanis in the administration—Robin Raphael, for one, assistant secretary of state for South and Central Asian affairs he had appointed in 1995, who declared that the US did not recognize Kashmir's accession to India. But apparently once he got wise to the political funding capacity of the community, he became closer to India.

Clinton's breakthrough visit to India in March 2000, the first visit by a US president in 22 years, had no less than 150 Indian-Americans accompanying the presidential delegation in a clear sign that the community was being taken seriously by the administration as a bridge between the two countries.

During the Kargil conflict with Pakistan in 1999, the *Washington Post* reported how a new Indian-American activism "boosted India's fortunes". Indian-Americans flooded Congress offices with emails urging Pakistani forces to withdraw: "Ultimately, the lawmakers complied and a few days later, in a White House meeting, Mr Clinton cited Congressional pressure as one of the reasons in urging [Pakistan Prime Minister] Mr Nawaz Sharif to withdraw his forces."

Community Rallies around the Nuclear Deal

In the first decade of this century, the community rallied around—like never before—for the Indo-US civil nuclear agreement and lobbied intensely and successfully for its passage through the Congress which at one time seemed impossible. Their efforts were visible enough to elicit laudatory comments from the American business community, lobbyists, lawmakers, and even President George W Bush.

"The Indian-American community was vital to explaining this strategic bill to our fellow citizens. I appreciate so very much your carrying the message not only here at home, but in India. And I want you to know that your voice was very effective, and I welcome it," said the president.

Anecdotal accounts of President Bush's early interest in India, especially a man who had till then shown no great interest in foreign policy outside America's traditional strategic associations, was when he was being briefed prior to his oath-taking as the nation's forty-third president.

Ashley Tellis, one of the US architects of the nuclear deal and an Indian-American, has quoted Robert Blackwill—a Bush advisor who later became US ambassador to India—who paraphrased President Bush in the following manner on the subject of Indian-Americans: "Oh my God, here is a group of people so successful, so dedicated, so evocative of the American dream, then there are a billion of them somewhere in another part of the world; this is a country that we need to reach out to and have a new relationship with."

Some, apparently including Blackwill himself, have suggested that Bush's interest in India had originally been stirred by his encounters with successful Indian-Americans living in Texas, a state that has a large Indian-American community who are wealthy, educated, and skilled.

One of the Indian-Americans Bush had been in contact with in Texas was Durga Agrawal. Born in Lakhanpur, Jammu and Kashmir, Agrawal had earned a master's degree at the University of Houston. Along with a number of other Indian-Americans he helped build Texas's high-tech corridor, dubbed Silicon Canyon. Agrawal was also able to raise more than $100,000 for the Bush presidential campaign in his local Indian community.

In fact, Houston and Dallas, have been termed the "money-centers" of the Indian-American community and senators and congressmen are known to make a beeline for these two cities to raise funds.

President Bush had kept his focus on a core idea—that India is a thriving, pluralistic democracy, one of the good guys in international relations—and he was willing to sweep away nuclear non-proliferation dogmas to position India as one of US's closest partners, a move that was described as "one of the most significant developments in American foreign policy in the past decade." And to secure a domestic ratification of the nuclear deal with India, the Bush administration knew it would have to build a strong domestic coalition in favor of the agreement, and here is where the Indian-American community came in handy.

Former Indian Ambassador Ronen Sen described their role in getting the bill's passage through the Congress as the "biggest community mobilization of any community for a single item".

North Carolina businessman Swadesh Chatterjee, who was made the national president of the IAFPE for his organizational abilities and mobilizing skills, was approached by Ambassador Sen to help pass the bill through the Congress after President Bush's visit to India in 2006.

"It's like moving a mountain," Chatterjee said of the challenge ahead of them before the two met up at the Cosmos Club in Washington, DC, for what was to be the beginning of a fruitful embassy–community partnership. "We need to unite Indian-Americans and work together, but as you know, we are two million Indian-Americans and 10 million egos. We need to keep these egos in the deep freezer for a few years."

Unity Is Strength

It was then that a separate body was formed, at the behest of Ambassador Sen, called the US–India Friendship Council. Their goal was to convince lawmakers that ratification of this deal will pave the way for a strategic alliance between the US and India and unite the two democracies for a common goal, including a counterbalance to China's growing dominance and expansionism.

For once, all groups sunk their differences and came under this common platform. These included the US–India Political Action Committee (USINPAC) of Sanjay Puri, GOPIO of Thomas Abraham, AAPI, AAHOA; FIA—tri-state area, alumni of the Indian Institutes of Technology (PANIIT).

Also, in support was the US–India Business Council (USIBC), then led by the India-friendly Ron Somers, and the influential American Jewish Committee (AJC) that had been supportive of and worked often in tandem with Indian-Americans on certain issues.

DC *Chalo*

It was then that the old adage "Unity Is Strength" was manifest in the way the community organized itself to mount a massive grassroots campaign across the country to track congressmen and senators who were supportive of the bill and those who weren't.

Temples, gurdwaras, festive, and social occasions were used to sensitize and mobilize the community in an unprecedented way to bombard lawmakers with a letter stating why Indian-Americans had chosen to support the bill and why the bill's passage would be good not just for US–India relations but would increase trust and confidence between the Indian-American community and their legislative representatives.

Congressional offices were bombarded with these letters from Indian-Americans across the nation in a way that showed the symbiotic relationship between the community and their origin country. A total of 435 congressmen and 100 senators were recipients of the missive along with a flyer of a full-page advertisement all the Indian-American organizations jointly ran in the *Washington Post* and other national publications on the day of congressional hearings on the issue.

And the final push was what Chatterjee evocatively calls the "DC *Chalo*" (Let's go to Washington, DC) campaign where a bunch of Indian-American community leaders traveled by a bus, emblazoned with the banner "DC *Chalo*", making halts at congressional offices and meeting grounds, with one simple message—support the bill and in return the Indian-American will be a great asset for you, in fundraising, mobilization, and elections.

The Indian-American community had finally stood up and demanded to be counted. As Chatterjee says: "Handshakes with politicians and photos to hang on my walls were just not enough. The time was right to demand concrete action from our representatives in Washington."

Nancy Pelosi, House speaker, then House minority leader, was one of the skeptics who converted to their cause: "I did not realize how united you (Indian-Americans) are behind the issue."

Another convert was Senate Minority Leader Harry Reid, Democrat from Nevada. And his early influencer was none other than his Indian-American doctor, Dr RD Prabhu, who told him about the importance of the deal to the community and bilateral ties.

Reid, who had a statue of Mahatma Gandhi on his desk and had many Indian-American friends, remarked: "The two million Americans of Indian descent have enriched the nation in so many ways and helped build even stronger ties between our two countries."

It was Chatterjee who used his long association with Biden to get him involved in issues that mattered to India. Mago was also responsible for delivering on the Republican congressmen, including two senators from

Texas, after Ambassador Sen approached him to get more co-sponsors for the bill.

Just before Thanksgiving, the Senate voted overwhelmingly in favor of the bill that would enable President Bush to negotiate a civil nuclear agreement with India, a country that was an exception to the nonproliferation dogma that forbade nuclear trade with a country that did not sign the Nuclear Nonproliferation Treaty (NPT).

A Community's "Coming Out Party"

Nicholas Burns, undersecretary of state for political affairs in the Department of State, and the chief US negotiator with India, credited the win to the Indian-American lobby and said it was their "coming out party". And Norman A Wulf, special representative to the president on nuclear nonproliferation, conceded that the Indian-American community is probably the second most powerful lobby in US foreign policy after American Israel Public Affairs Committee.

It, however, took two more years of negotiating through the thicket of India's fractious politics and agreement on the fine print of this globally consequential deal for it to get the final assent of both legislatures and governments and the signing of the momentous US–India Civil Nuclear Agreement on October 8, 2008 at the White House.

And the community never gave up on it—pushing, prodding, cajoling, persuading top policymakers in both countries that the deal was in the interest of both countries and good for the survival of democracy.

As Chatterjee was to explain: "It is no coincidence that the era of deepest estrangement between India and United States was during the time when there were few Indian-Americans, and even fewer involved in public life.

Nor is it a coincidence that during the era of growing India–US cooperation, the community of Indian-American grew to some 3.18 million and became a united and powerful political force."

A Community in Generational Transition

Indian diplomats familiar with America say it's true that the community united as never before to clinch the 2008 nuclear deal, but once that happened and there was no singular or overarching issue on which to consolidate, the community once again became fragmented. There is no doubt that the community has arrived, but their mobilization will remain episodic, as they remain a divided lot—a microcosm of the larger society they are a distant chip of—and will never be able to match the power and influence of the American-Jewish community.

This is because the Jews think they face an existential threat and all their activities and lobbying are geared toward ensuring in staving off that possibility anytime in the future.

But Indian-Americans don't have that problem—or challenge before them—and although they have come a long way their hearts will beat less for India as the second-generation leaders, born and raised in America, will focus more on issues that matter to them rather than a country with which they relate only culturally and perhaps socially.

The interesting fact, as many community leaders say, is that all Indian-American politicians come to the community first to raise campaign funds. But then many forget them once they get elected, if not turn their backs on them. That is where, say many old-timers, the community groups need to put in sustained effort and ensure that the elected Indian-American politician, whether at the city, state, or federal level, retains links with his or her roots.

"It is good that more and more Indian-Americans are getting into politics, but how many of them are really supportive of Indian-American and Indo-US issues once they [are] elected?" asks Mago, the community activist from Texas.

In a way, the newest of community organizations, Indiaspora, founded in 2012 by tech investor MR Rangaswami, was envisaged as a bridge between the first and second generation of Indian-Americans. Rangaswami wanted the organization "to reflect the mindset of a community that has come of age" and build a community of leaders who would make an impact, not just in America, but globally.

So, for the first, time here was an organization that was not a volunteer group—like all previous community organizations—but one that had paid membership by dedicated professionals with a desire to "catalyze impactful initiatives" and "work to build stronger (Indian) communities at home and abroad".

Record Number of Indian-American Candidates

As the community is projected to grow to five million by 2021, with a large backlog of green card aspirants likely to become citizens with the passage of key immigration bills, and with second-generation Indian-Americans warming up to mainstream politics and contesting elections, the community is bound to make a big impact politically and socially in the coming years.

November 2020 had indeed been a month of celebration for the community that started with the election of Kamala Harris and ended with not only the election of so many Indian-Americans but also the appointment of a clutch of them to the new Biden–Harris administration. There is no denying that the community had indeed marked its arrival on the national political stage.

Indian-American election winners, from Nima Kulkarni to Jenifer Rajkumar, told of a growing political consciousness and conviction they needed to be at the decision-taking tables to not only be able to influence issues connected to the community but also have a role in larger governance.

Immigration attorney Nima Kulkarni, Democrat, who was elected to Kentucky house from the 40th District, said there are only a handful of Indians in the constituency, and yet she defeated a 22-year incumbent. Dr Shri Thanedar, 65, Democrat, a scientist-entrepreneur who in 2018 ran for Michigan governor, won his election to the Michigan house—the third Indian to do so—largely with the support of African-Americans and has plans to create "a new Black Wall Street in Detroit".

And Latha Mangipudi, a Democrat elected to the New Hampshire house for a fifth term, noted the help GOPIO and IMPACT gave her in her campaign, and has coined the term "Idli Caucus" to describe South Indian representatives even as Congressman Raja Krishnamoorthi had dubbed the Indian-American Congress delegation the "Samosa Caucus". Mangipudi promises to cook Mysore *masala dosa*s in her constituency.

Many upcoming second-generation politicians like Niraj Antani, who in 2014 became the youngest member of the Ohio state house, echoed Chatterjee's sentiments at a pre-election interaction.

"My parents worked hard to live the American dream. Everyone is able to realize the dream. We stand on your shoulders, to carry on the Indian values. There is a need for us to be at the decision-making table."

It is clear that the new generation of the Indian-American community and political leaders are more self-assured, see themselves more as American than Indian, are ready to identify with more South Asian issues when needed through organizations like South Asia Americans Leading Together (SAALT), in order to broaden their constituency, and are excited about the prospects opening up for them, especially in a more liberal-minded Biden–Harris administration.

Dr Gautam Mukunda of The Center for Public Leadership, Harvard Kennedy School, speaking at a pre-election event sort of summed it up: "People in US believe that Indian-Americans are capable of becoming leaders in the nation." Raj Goyle, Democratic politician in the Kansas House of Representatives from 2007–2011, echoed: "We are at an early stage. But there is lots to be excited about 2020 and beyond."

Notes

1. Dole Archives/University of Kansas
2. Building Bridges: The Role of Indian Americans in Indo-US Relations by Swadesh Chatterjee.
3. Foreign Policy Analysis, Jason Kirk/Virginia Military Institute.
4. US–India Nuclear Deal, Allison Marz Freedman, University of Pennsylvania.
5. Congressional Records
6. *The Atlantic*
7. immigrationtounitedstates.org
8. Global Organization of People of Indian Origin (GOPIO)
9. John Lancaster, John, *Washington Post*, 'Kashmir crisis was defused on brink of war'.
10. Hans Christian Kjolsethk/University of Oslo.

An Accidental Capitalist: How Indian-Americans Made Their Mark in Silicon Valley

MR Rangaswami

For the last four decades, I have had a front row seat to the Indian-American rise to power in Silicon Valley. What began as a trickle of programmers expanded to a juggernaut of a several hundred thousand people. From immigrants arriving for education and employment, they metamorphosed into builders of companies and communities. Almost one in twelve US start-up founders is now a member of the diaspora. About one in seven Silicon Valley start-ups has an Indian founder. Indeed, Indian-Americans have played a big role in Silicon Valley's tech sector success; in many cases, they engineered it.

My own Silicon Valley adventure began by accident. One piece of advice launched a career with events similar to those experienced by many other Indian-Americans. And while each immigrant's path was unique, all would agree on one thing: living through the rise and fall of the region's technology and business trends was a thrilling roller-coaster ride of big wins, heartbreaking losses, and exciting comebacks.

The 1980s: A Mythical Place

Many young Indians now dream of coming to "The Valley"—a place I didn't even know existed when I left Chennai for Ohio's Kent State University.

I didn't come to America with a grand plan. I was an Indian student in the 1970s who came to the US with a few dollars in his pocket and one modest goal: to get a master's degree. I planned to return to India with a master's in business administration (MBA) in hand, but I ended up getting a practical training visa and also a job offer.

I decided to take the position and stay in America. I moved to Houston to work as operations manager for a manufacturing company. Every day, although I was an executive, I donned a hard hat and steel-toed boots to help keep the factory running smoothly. After three years, I attended a certification program in software system best practices. My instructor enquired about my job during a break. When he gathered that I was good with software, he grabbed my arm, looked me in the eye, and said: "You have to go to Silicon Valley."

It was the best piece of advice I ever got.

I had begun to hear tales of this mythical "Silicon Valley" place. I knew it was a growing center of the technology business, but I was at a bit of a loss as to how I could fit in. There was no internet, LinkedIn or Facebook. So I went to the local library, sat down at the microfiche machine, and began searching old copies of the *San Jose Mercury News* and the *San Francisco Chronicle,* to read up on the companies in the area.

My research ended with a list of potential employers. I typed up cover letters, Xeroxed my résumé, and sent off a dozen inquiries through snail mail. Incredibly, one executive flew me out to California and gave me a job on the spot!

Start-up Life

I had accidentally joined my first start-up. My new job was a world away from my experience at the manufacturer in Texas. Here, we wore khakis, had working lunches in the conference room, and often shared a beer after work. As the in-house expert on manufacturing, I felt empowered to have an impact on our trajectory. I helped fine-tune the product and marketing of our software to US clients. Our revenue doubled during my first year—and my second!

And then we went bankrupt.

It was my first start-up—my first success, and my first failure. Little did I know there would be plenty more wins and losses in the years to come.

And that's the true story of Silicon Valley: 99 percent of start-ups fail. The media can't possibly cover all of the failures, so it focuses on the successes.

But back in 1986, I was shocked by the failure—and I was hooked. I never once thought of returning to Texas, or India. Deloitte snatched me up as a consultant. My software and operations management skills were in high demand; I spent the next couple of years parked there—advising clients, watching the industry, and waiting for my next move.

A Bit Like Home

In the 1980s, I still found it a bit surprising to see an Indian face in the hallway, parking lot, or supermarket near my apartment in The Valley. The US Census estimated 361,000 Indians were living in the entire country with only 5,200 calling Santa Clara county home.

Lots of young Indian men—and they *were* almost all men—met for lunch and a bit of informal networking at Pasand—a restaurant on the corner of Lawrence Expressway and El Camino Real serving authentic Indian meals to tech workers for miles around.

For my dose of India, I looked forward to packages from family with savory snacks like *muruku*s, *sev*, along with Bollywood movies on VHS. If you needed spices or groceries or other South Asian products, you headed to another Santa Clara spot, Bharat Bazar. The Birla family had been importing Indian specialties since the 1970s, and their offerings had grown along with The Valley's population of immigrants.

When it was time to impress an Indian visitor, we drove an hour up to San Francisco and booked a table at Gaylord Restaurant in the Embarcadero Center. It was the only upscale Indian food place in the entire Bay Area!

Little did I know this was going to be my beginning of the Indian saga in Silicon Valley.

"Time Share" Pioneers

By the time I settled in Silicon Valley, Indians were already making a name for themselves as skilled programmers for the rapidly-growing computer market. The IIT graduates often came to the US for graduate school during the 1960s and 1970s. Rather than returning to India with their degrees, they found engineering jobs at large hardware and software companies, during the "silicon" days of Silicon Valley's origins, and settled in California.

At that time, most enterprises—large companies of 1,000 or more employees—relied on mainframes for data processing. Mainframes were the first business computers and were famous for being massive in terms of physical size, computing power, and cost. Most enterprises could not afford to buy a mainframe, so they purchased computing time and storage from a giant technology company such as IBM.

The mainframe's timeshare business model was similar to that of today's vacation timeshare market: you buy a tiny fractional share of a holiday condominium to use when needed and avoid the maintenance and operational costs of the unit.

In the 1980s, the minicomputer started disrupting the mainframe and got into the enterprise computing market. Companies could now buy smaller, more affordable versions of a mainframe from makers like Hewlett Packard, Digital Equipment Corporation, and many others. This trend was just the opposite of the timeshare model—the client bought the minicomputer, programmed it, and maintained it on their own dime.

In 1982, Sun Microsystems pushed the business of computer power price point down another notch with the introduction of their powerful workstation computers. Co-founded by Vinod Khosla, Sun's success was one of the first signs that Indians were soaking up America's entrepreneurial spirit. Umang Gupta's launch of Gupta Software in 1984 was right behind.

The Big Leagues

A friend from a prior start-up, who was now working at another software company, approached me about joining his marketing team. The company was young but already public, with its business doubling every year. And even though I'd heard that line before, I was impressed with its products and comforted by its larger size.

I joined Oracle in 1988. The upstart database start-up was an early player in the next era of corporate technology called client/server computing. Employees used "clients"—often personal computers or terminals—to access application and database software stored on hardware "servers" over a private network. In the timeshare analogy, the client–server model is similar to owning your home and also owning a vacation condominium.

Oracle had outgrown its office space in Belmont, a bayside town at the northern end of the Silicon Valley area. Two employees had to share one cubicle, and more than a handful of them were Indians. And though there were few offices, founder Larry Ellison had one—and I was assigned a seat right outside his door.

Everyone could see that Ellison had what it took to succeed in business. He was a straight shooter and didn't suffer fools for an instant. Ellison was firmly at the helm, steering his ship toward what would eventually be a massive market share of the enterprise computing market, battling against tech titans like IBM and SAP in the process.

From my cubicle, I saw—and heard—Ellison at work. And though we exchanged greetings, he was every bit as intimidating as he is today. He was often in the business headlines for his business savvy and relentless focus.

So, you can imagine my shock when Ellison stopped at my desk.

"Come in later and present your business plan."

Never has an office seemed so small and a man seemed so large. But my presentation went off without a hitch. Ellison listened intently; then peppered me with pointed questions. I batted each one back with a solid answer. But Ellison kept a poker face the entire time. It wasn't until our next company meeting, where I heard him restate and articulate some of my ideas, that I knew I'd made a positive impression.

Like many Indian immigrants in The Valley, I'd begun to prove myself as an executive. I rose quickly through Oracle's ranks as it expanded its offerings. Though I'd started as a marketing manager, I finished my fourth year as VP of application marketing, introducing the company's new suite of interconnected business software products to companies around the world.

The 1990s: H1B, IPO, & Y2K

As the technology industry boomed, the Silicon Valley economy made headlines across the world. The move to a software-driven enterprise was driving revenue growth for all vendors, including makers of chips, servers, applications, and networking products from The Valley's Cisco.

At the same time, Cupertino's Apple and HP, IBM, Microsoft, and other players had spent the past decade powering the personal computing wave to new heights—a trend that experts believed would sink the legacy mainframe and minicomputer systems.

President George HW Bush signed the H1B visa into law in 1990. The legislation created a path for skilled workers to get a job in the US, obtain a "green card" for permanent residency, and become eligible for citizenship after four-and-a-half years.

Fluent in English, backed by excellent technical training, Indians were well-positioned to take advantage of the new visa policy to come to Silicon Valley. Technology companies needed more brain power than local hires could deliver, and they began to hire engineering experts from India and other nations to meet their development demands. It turned out this was the beginning of a symbiotic relationship.

A True Partner

I was fortunate to have a partner along for all my career moves. I'd met a cellist during my time in Houston and we agreed to make the move to Silicon Valley together. In 1992, Krisanthy and I exchanged vows at the pioneering vegetarian restaurant, Greens, overlooking the San Francisco Bay and Golden Gate Bridge.

Even though the Indian-American population had grown from 361,000 to 861,000 between the 1980 and 1990 censuses, Kris and I were still one of the few interracial couples in the Silicon Valley. But everyone could see we made a great team. And I could never have achieved my professional success without her personal support.

A Rich Community

Three technology businessmen—angel investor Kanwal Rekhi and semiconductor company founders Suhas Patil and Prabhu Goel—saw the need for a professional community to unite and foster success among Indian tech workers. They founded The Indus Entrepreneurs (TiE), which grew to be an influential organization. The network connected Silicon Valley Indians and gave them the tools to create their own start-ups, including mentors, funding, and partners. TiE enabled executives from big vendors like Sun, Cisco, Apple, and Oracle to head out on their own and build new companies.

By this time, pioneers like Khosla had already amassed considerable wealth and were joining the burgeoning ranks of venture capitalists, scouring The Valley and beyond for the next Oracles, Ciscos, Microsofts, and Suns. As these proven Indian tech millionaires became part of Palo Alto's "Sand Hill Road" establishment of tech venture capital investors, it became apparent that Indians like me were an integral part of the start-up ecosystem.

Failure Redux

When Oracle hit $1 billion in revenue, I began to look around for my next "start-up". In 1992, I found another enterprise resource planning (ERP) software company and took it up.

Arriving as chief marketing officer (CMO) of a rising star felt fantastic. I got straight to work, and realized that my experience at both small and large software makers gave me a unique ability to market to business clients of all types.

With excitement—and more than a bit of déjà vú—I saw the company's revenue double during Year 1. In Year 2, it tripled!

Year 3?

We hit the wall.

Just like my first start-up, the company began to flail.

Superbowl for a CMO

I had never written a résumé in my life—and still haven't—but I knew I would soon be in need of a new job. In The Valley as in the wild, one death spurs the cycle of rebirth. As a company neared failure, word would spread through the ecosystem of investors, recruiters, and executives. A great office space might soon be vacant and an experienced management team might soon be looking for their next start-up. In the nick of time, I got a call: another ERP vendor needed a seasoned CMO. The company was in hyper-growth and planned to go public soon.

I joined Baan as CMO in 1995. The company was based in Menlo Park and Amsterdam. It had jumped in the ring to battle the leading ERP vendor, SAP. Just before I joined, Baan had snatched a massive Boeing contract out of the German giant's hands. The deal pushed our senior management team to prepare its initial public offering (IPO) of stock on a public exchange.

Baan's IPO was my "Superbowl" moment—and I felt like a pro athlete the whole time. How many executives get to experience an IPO? There were only 4,000 public companies at that time. I was now in the big league.

As a professional, the work experience was unlike anything I had done before. I was quickly brought in to consult with our bankers—the group that would underwrite the stock offering. Baan was so compelling that we ended up being represented by the two biggest players: Goldman Sachs and Morgan Stanley. Normally, a company would be lucky to have either one or the other manage their offering.

Roadshow for an IPO

All this was preparing for Baan's "roadshow". The executives and bankers set out to travel around the world and meet with prospective investors before the IPO. We covered 25,000 miles and three continents in three weeks, all via private jet or in the comfort of first-class. It was exhausting and incredible!

Was I in New York City to ring the opening bell on the day Baan started trading? Nope. That wasn't a big thing in 1995. I wasn't even in the office! I was so beat from the roadshow that I went to visit my sister in Salt Lake City. By the time she served us a fabulous homemade South Indian meal, Baan had finished its first day of trading valued at $1 billion!

Immigrant Power

Baan's trajectory exemplified the classic Silicon Valley immigrant success story of the 1990s. In ours, a Dutch entrepreneur, Scottish CFO, and Indian CMO teamed up to take a company public in New York City.

But pick any ethnicity—Chinese, Russian, Israeli, German, and South African—and I can name a tech start-up with founders of that background. And of course, not to mention all the homegrown and international entrepreneurs flowing out of US universities who basically studied, "Tech Startup 101". The sharpest minds from around the world were playing a starring role in the innovation ecosystem—and Silicon Valley was a perfect home for it.

In 2020, journalist Fareed Zakaria urged Americans to recognize the unique circumstances of all minorities, rather than lumping non-white people into a "people of color" box. He says this is especially true for members of the diaspora and other recent immigrants who moved to the US by choice, not to escape circumstances in their home countries. There are hundreds of thousands of Indian-Americans of varying faiths, motivations, and personal situations, which makes us just like the white immigrants who have moved here over the centuries.

Zakaria's comment made me reflect on where I fit into The Valley's puzzle. There's no question that I stayed in America because of my family. The job offer made my decision to relocate to Santa Clara an easy one. Clearly, once I landed in the tech sector, I was swept up in the industry's expansion. Even though I experienced failures, the successes kept me engaged, reinforcing the power of innovative thinking and potential for rebirth.

Maybe losing my father at ten pushed me to try harder, and be more willing to take risks. In addition, my mother's resilience and support during that crisis gave me confidence, and spurred me to take on challenges during my life journey.

Or was I addicted to the buzz of being surrounded by The Valley's brilliant minds—or the energy of so many eager young entrepreneurs? The excitement of technology's "next big thing" on the horizon—or maybe just watching the horizon turn into spectacular shades of orange after another blue-sky day in the Golden State? Whatever the reason, "home" was now California.

Birth of an Angel

After two failed start-ups, I'd finally hit the jackpot, but I had no plans to trade-in my used Mazda. I knew a lot of my success could be attributed to timing and luck. So as my wife and I looked to start a family, I knew I had to take a break from my intense, round-the-world software adventures. We decided to settle in San Francisco, an arm's length from the Silicon Valley but close enough to dive in whenever needed.

I partnered with a friend and together we hung out a shingle as Sand Hill Group. Rather than an office on venture capital's famed Sand Hill Road, we spent $20 on www.sandhill.com. Instantly, we became "angel investors", a new type of investor who provides entrepreneurs with their very first round of seed funding in order to get a business plan together and later attract backing from a larger, more established investment firm.

Every week we would meet with new founders to talk about their start-ups. Reviewing each business plan was a laborious process. Out of all the companies we reviewed, we only backed a tiny fraction. Friends have guessed that we invested money in about one out of every five companies we meet; I believe the ratio is more like 1 out of every 100.

To the 99 deals we didn't back financially, we gave other assistance, often connecting the founders to other investors, key hires, or mentors in their space. We also gave advice about marketing, business development, technology, and ideas on how to fit into the community of start-ups and entrepreneurs.

Our Silicon Valley savvy helped our partnership do a decent job of betting on future winners—and passing on eventual losers. Sand Hill Group gained enough credibility that before we knew it, a sketch of my face was printed on the front page of *The Wall Street Journal* and *Forbes* had named me in their Midas List of the world's best investors.

Indeed, by the mid-1990s, the Indian diaspora had completed a virtuous cycle in tech innovation: Indian immigrants were proving their mettle as employees at large companies, climbing the corporate ladder, founding their own successful start-ups, and then investing their wealth in the next generation of entrepreneurs.

In fact, one study estimates that Indian-Americans controlled 7 percent of tech companies founded in the Silicon Valley from 1980 to 1998—and that's when Indians only accounted for 1 percent of the US population.

Countdown to Y2K

Though the "Y2K problem" had been discussed for a decade, many American companies were still woefully unprepared in the mid-1990s. Chief information officers (CIOs) knew their aging mainframe backbones that ran on "ancient" languages like Cobol and Fortran would not accommodate the calendar turning from two-digit years to four-digit years in the new millennium. In other words, "00" would be misconstrued as 1900, instead of the year 2000. Massive code rewrites were needed to prevent cataclysmic failure on January 1, 2000.

Indian programmers came to the rescue. While many US engineers now wrote codes in Unix and C, Indians were far more likely to still be programming in the old mainframe languages.

American companies and consultancies hired thousands of these experts to re-engineer their systems—just in the nick of time.

Thus, the offshoring services industry began. A cadre of companies staffed up in India to provide the much-needed Y2K programming services. These firms like Tata Consultancy, Infosys, and Wipro formed the basis for today's massive tech sector in Bengaluru and beyond. In many cases, Americans had no choice but to offshore this coding—and in many cases, they were hooked. The Indian firms could provide high-quality, low-cost developers who proved they could get the job done.

At the same time, Silicon Valley consultancies and companies hired thousands of Y2K programmers and brought them to work domestically on H1B visas. Together with the new influx of students arriving to study at American universities, young professional Indians were flocking to find jobs in the tech sector. And these skilled immigrants were legally able to bring their families along as well, further swelling Silicon Valley's Indian population and strengthening its roots.

Indeed, the face of the Silicon Valley was increasingly an Indian one now.

The 2000s: From Dot-com to the Cloud

The rise of internet technology and the World Wide Web was extraordinary. Whether you were a CIO at a Fortune 500 company, a shopkeeper on Main Street, or a retiree watching TV, there was a dot-com start-up aiming to revolutionize your way of life—and everyone wanted to get in on the action.

Watching wide-eyed as Jeff Bezos, Pierre Omidyar, Jerry Yang, and Reed Hastings debuted their companies, Silicon Valley's venture capitalists threw fistfuls of money into the innovation engine in order to create the underlying technologies and new business models that would power the dot-com era.

Indian-Americans like me were right there with the best of them. By early 2001, five of the start-ups I'd backed had filed to go public. I couldn't believe my luck: five companies in the IPO pipeline! It seemed too good to be true!

And it was.

The "bubble" burst. All five companies withdrew their offerings. All closed their doors. And I lost my entire portfolio.

The Dark Side

It was fabulous to help create a "winner"—funding a bright entrepreneur, shepherding a start-up's growth, and ushering the company to acquisition or IPO! Those deals felt good.

But the winners were few and far between—even with our serious due diligence. I bet that for every one of our deals that won, we backed ten start-ups that didn't make it.

Most entrepreneurs know success is a long shot. But some get so caught up in the stories about winners that they even go to the extreme of mortgaging their future to fund their dreams.

One older entrepreneur had built up a considerable pension savings through the American IRA and 401k retirement plans during his career. He was so sure about his business idea that he pulled out all of his retirement savings to fund his start-up. Unfortunately, he lost it all. Another founder used the money he had saved for his kids' college education to develop a prototype. The company never took off.

It was during this decade that critics say the locus of Silicon Valley culture shifted from innovation to money. Where the earliest transplants to The Valley might have come for the intellectual challenges, the opportunities, or the excitement, new arrivals came for the money—not just enough to fund a comfortable suburban life but the promise of millions. It felt like the new California Gold Rush!

Indian immigrants were just as caught up in the twenty-first century Gold Rush as others. Too often, the conversation at gatherings would revolve around IPOs, stock options, net worth—and then calculations to try and figure out the net worth of the start-up founder who went public most recently.

Much ink was spilled about the flood of money that flowed into Silicon Valley communities and pushed real estate prices into the stratosphere. Sleepy bedroom communities in the Bay Area were transformed by the influx of the wealthy: no longer could teachers or nurses or shopkeepers afford to live here.

New Kids in Town

The start-up culture delivered a steady stream of eager entrepreneurs to our office. Until the mid-1990s, founders had typically studied, worked for at least one large company, and experienced one start-up before launching their own venture. By the turn of the twenty-first century, founders were often right out of university or had dropped out to start on their own.

Though I was typically on the receiving end of an entrepreneur's pitch for backing, my mission as an angel investor was to help start-ups get their first round of funding from an established venture capital firm. I had forged solid connections with many venture capitalists (VCs) as a CMO and an angel; so by the time my start-up and I sat down in an office to make a presentation, we usually knew what we were up against—a serious examination of the start-up's technology, team, and market. Sometimes we secured additional investment, sometimes we didn't, but rarely was it an unproductive experience.

But as the dot-com era greatly enlarged the size of their funds and their staffs, the major tech VC firms began to take a lot more meetings. We would typically have to meet with a junior partner before we could meet with a senior dealmaker. The junior partners were very often in possession of a fresh MBA and little real-world experience.

I'll never forget one such encounter. We had jumped through hoops to bring in our entire executive team for a meeting with a senior partner. Instead, a fresh-faced VC straight from Silicon Valley central casting entered the conference room. He announced he would be subbing for his superior, who had been called away.

The team was visibly disappointed, but our CEO pushed on, taking twenty minutes to skillfully present the new product's technological approach, target market, competitive differentiators, and revenue potential. When it was time for questions, the junior partner looked at the team, eyes narrowed.

"Is your solution a pain killer or a vitamin?"

The executive team looked at each other in disbelief. As I waited for someone to formulate an answer to the ridiculous "only in business school" question, the founder stood up. He slapped shut his laptop and went for the door. The rest of us followed and never looked back. Not long afterward, a competing VC firm backed the start-up and led it to a solid exit.

Rebirth Begins in the Cloud

The hangover from the collapse of the dot-com bubble was painful. For many investors and founders, it was their first "era", their first start-up, their first deal, their first failure. They didn't know how to operate in a non-frothy, non-hyper growth world.

But Silicon Valley veterans, like myself, knew the drill. The birth–growth–death–rebirth innovation cycle ran in a constant loop. And we knew that below the buzz of the consumer World Wide Web, an entire ecosystem of internet-based business systems had spawned.

Web services and cloud computing had already arrived to change the very nature of computing—again. In this era, the business model returned to the timeshare model of the mainframe era. Companies, students, and consumers could access all the software, computing power, and storage they needed in the "cloud"—the name for this invisible tech center enabled by internet connectivity. Users can connect to the cloud via a smartphone, laptop, or any other web-enabled device and pay for only what they used. In other words, the buyer has a key to the vacation home but only needs to pay for how many times he opens the door, stays the night, and uses the pool.

The model where companies buy software on a pay-as-you-go basis became known as software as a service (SaaS). Pioneers like Marc Benioff's Salesforce and Aneel Bhusri's Workday spent the next few years evangelizing the benefits and lower costs of SaaS computing and catching up to market leaders Oracle and SAP. Deals by Indian financiers funded many of the deals that would help pull Silicon Valley out of the dot-com doldrums and back into the spotlight. Indeed, Indian venture capitalists had achieved parity with their native-born counterparts in the world of tech finance.

A Voice for Software

With two young daughters at home, I had no time to wallow in sorrow over my dot-com fortune that "might have been". I had to rebuild my portfolio. We began placing bets on the next wave of start-ups. And while I had always kept one foot in the business I knew best—marketing enterprise software—my pivot back to the industry helped me to realize my actual gift: building personal networks.

While the media had spent the last few years focusing on the millions being poured into the latest zero-revenue web darling, business application makers were continuing to rake in billions, year after year. I realized that the Silicon Valley's enterprise software industry needed a strategic voice.

Over the next decade, Sand Hill Group created conferences, events, and online media to deliver thought leadership and practical insights specifically aimed at software leaders. We also partnered with Silicon Valley's top analysts to produce groundbreaking research on the impact of significant trends impacting the software industry, including web services, open source, and artificial intelligence (AI).

Turning "On" Offshore

Offshoring development was one hot-button strategy that we spent years analyzing. Working with Indian services companies during the Y2K crisis, Fortune 500 companies had begun to outsource engineering work to India to help conserve cash following the dot-com crash of 2001 and the financial recession of 2008.

But on the other hand, software start-ups were reticent to move development away from The Valley by outsourcing development of their crown jewel: intellectual capital. We worked with both offshoring providers and software vendors to conduct a market research study to identify win-win processes, pricing, and workflow.

I then took part in the second "roadshow" of my career: convincing Silicon Valley leaders that Indian developers were a viable means of developing core software products. Instead of flying private jets around the world talking to bankers, I was driving myself up and down Sand Hill Road, holding two-hour working sessions that preached the virtue of India's developers to the CEOs of The Valley's most promising start-ups backed by venture capital firms: Sequoia, Mayfield, Kleiner Perkins, and Redpoint.

When founders came in seeking funding, I urged the VCs to ask about their offshoring strategies before investing. If that start-up was not using the most cost-effective engineering to develop their products, its competitors probably were. Today, offshoring development in India has become an integral part of engineering strategies at Silicon Valley companies and others around the world.

Impactful Events

Sand Hill Group also became known as a producer of must-attend gatherings of software movers and shakers. We held our first elite gathering in 1998, just as the dot-com era was heating up. The Enterprise retreat was an invite-only gathering for the "who's who" of the software world.

Flipping through my Rolodex, I contacted hundreds of high-level Silicon Valley executives, venture capitalists, entrepreneurs, and professionals I'd kept in touch with over the years. Many joined us for Enterprise, spending a weekend at a local resort discussing the unique business challenges and opportunities of software makers. The event continued for a decade, was reborn in 2017, and revived again in 2020 just before the pandemic hit.

Where Deals are Done

More than a place to gather for insight and camaraderie, strategic events are where deals happen in the Silicon Valley. As host of these events, I regularly heard about how one company acquired another, one start-up secured a follow-on round, or one executive was poached by a competing company. The beginning of these new relationships often began during dinner or drinks, or—very often—a round of golf. The last scene proved challenging for me because even though I love sports, I never really got into golf.

Well, actually, I did play one hole—the seventh at Pebble Beach. We held the Enterprise conference there so I had to join the others and take a swing at it. It's a par-3 overlooking the Pacific, and you have to hit the ball down or it will end up in the ocean. My first try dented the cart 10 feet away! I decided to stick to hosting.

Profits to Nonprofits

My entry into the world of philanthropy could also be classified as accidental. While planning the first Enterprise conference, I began to recruit an advisory board of Silicon Valley A-list executives and investors to shape its development, like Oracle President Ray Lane and investor Roger McNamee. After months of work, I was shocked to hear that none of the advisors could make time in their calendar to attend. There were just too many similar gatherings for the tech elite.

That's when the idea hit me: Enterprise would be the only nonprofit gathering of software CEOs. All proceeds would go to the newly-formed SHG Foundation, which would grant the money to charities benefitting women and children.

My marketing mind had discovered a differentiator that mattered. Every single one of my advisors attended the first Enterprise conference. In the process, I became a philanthropist. And though I helped direct SHG Foundation donations to dozens of grantees over the years, the exposure to successful Silicon Valley executives was even more valuable.

One of SHG Foundation's early grantees was Room to Read. Its founder, John Wood, had left a great career at Microsoft to "change the world". After a long career with the software market leader, he founded the nonprofit to foster a love for books by building native-language libraries in developing countries.

We knew his personal story would resonate with current executives in the industry. A few years later, we again invited Wood to speak at the Software conference. More than 1,000 people heard his incredible presentation, even giving him a standing ovation. Impulsively, I took the mic, "Hey John, the SHG Foundation wants to give $10,000 to Room to Read—and I challenge everyone in this room to match my gift!" The audience cheered and many mobbed him with donations as he left the podium. In the end, Wood's hour at our conference translated to 10 percent of Room to Read's annual budget.

Word spread among The Valley's social entrepreneurs that recognition by the SHG Foundation could be exponentially lucrative. One organization we backed, BUILD, delivers entrepreneurial experience to underserved high schoolers. When we realized founder Suzanne McKechnie Klahr was pregnant, we offered to mail her a check instead of traveling to our event to present. But Suzanne flew out, took the podium in Las Vegas, wowed the crowd, and flew home with our grant and much more.

From "Enterprise" to "Software"

We parlayed our success with the Enterprise retreat into a larger gathering of industry business leaders. Software 2004 was held in San Francisco and then moved to the Santa Clara Convention Center for three years. By Software 2007, more than 2,000 people packed two days of innovative discussions.

Hosting the Software 2007 conference was a crowning moment of my career in software. I had assembled the industry's top leaders and welcomed each one to the stage, including Microsoft CEO Steve Ballmer, Oracle president Charles Phillips, SAP CEO Hasso Plattner, Motorola CEO Edward Zander, and Salesforce CEO Marc Benioff.

It was also a crossroads for the industry, a showcase and a showdown of incumbents and disruptors. Salesforce's software-as-a-service offering proceeded to amass a market cap equal to that of Oracle and SAP, combined. Motorola's position quickly faded too as it was laser-focused on its Razr flip phone, while just 15 minutes down the Lawrence Expressway, Apple was prepping for the debut of its iPhone just a month later—a blockbuster success that eventually killed the Razr.

Our success did not go unnoticed: CMP Technology, one of the nation's top tech event producers, had purchased the Software conference the prior year. And the deal's timing proved fortunate: The 2008 financial crisis put a damper on all tech events.

A Familiar Face

As the emcee at these large events, I quickly became one of the faces of enterprise software in Silicon Valley. I didn't realize that advocating for causes and connecting like-minded experts was unique. To me, building impactful networks through small and large meetings was exciting.

Surprisingly, I began to regularly receive invites to moderate panels and keynote events around Silicon Valley. I took my show on the road to India every year as well, becoming the host of the Nasscom Product Conclave (NPC) in India. In this capacity, I took successful Indian-American CEOs and executives to India, and they inspired and taught thousands of Indian tech founders what it took to succeed.

My years as an angel investor delivered benefits beyond financial returns: connections with thousands of talented Indians and Americans. I recently did the math: by having two meetings with one or two founders each week for two decades, I estimate that I've met one-on-one with 2,000 people. That's a lot of breakfasts, lunches, and dinners.

I've been able to maintain and grow many of these relationships over the years. Now I am better able to connect these ambitious tech professionals to an even richer network of strategic contacts. It's the same way that my mentors helped me during my career.

And the cycle is virtuous, to be sure. One of my early mentors recommended me to Larry Ellison for a job at Oracle. Then, during my time at Oracle, I helped an Indian entrepreneur become an Oracle partner. Years later, I again helped him with his new venture, Aspect Development, a company that was purchased in 2003 for $9.3 billion—one of the biggest software exits ever. Today, that entrepreneur, Romesh Wadhwani, is one of the most powerful Silicon Valley investors and philanthropists. He now serves as *my* mentor.

The 2010s: Titan Takeovers

The tale of Indian-Americans as builders, leaders, and financiers of Silicon Valley's technology sector had evolved into a bona fide "success story". You didn't have to look hard to find outside validation of their influence: *Forbes* magazine counts eight Indians on its 2020 list of the 400 richest people in America and 14 on its Midas List of the most powerful venture capitalists.

Over the past decade, I watched as, one by one, the world's most powerful technology titans announced an Indian would be their new CEO. These appointments were not merely the result of an executive search or a push for diversity; these new leaders had spent years engineering, marketing, growing, and managing the company they would now steer into the future.

Take Sundar Pichai. After years of leading Android, Chrome, and Maps products, Pichai became CEO of Mountain View's Google in 2015 and its parent company Alphabet Inc in 2019.

Other up-through-the-ranks CEOs include Satya Nadella, who assumed the helm of Microsoft in 2014, and Arvind Krishna, who took over as IBM CEO in 2020 after a 30-year career with Big Blue.

Indian-Americans lead other Valley titans too: Shantanu Narayen has been CEO of San Jose's Adobe since 2007. Padmasree Warrior has served as chief technology officer (CTO) at Cisco, Motorola, and NIO USA and remains a role model for the ranks of female Indian executives to come.

In The Valley's networking world, Jayshree Ullal is CEO of Arista Networks and Nikesh Arora has been CEO of Palo Alto Networks since 2018. George Kurian leads NetApp and Sanjay Mehrotra is CEO of Micron. The list goes on.

In fact, one researcher estimated that by 2012, Indian-Americans co-founded 16 percent of Silicon Valley start-ups. I'd say that portion is much higher today. Importantly, Indian-Americans have also risen to top technology positions in major companies around the US. As CIOs and CTOs, these Indian-Americans are the buyers of corporate technology, and represent the target customers for Silicon Valley's tech start-ups. In addition, these buyers also utilize India's offshoring services. There's no doubt that the diaspora's network of technology leaders now collaborates in a very productive way.

Time to Give Back

Service and giving back are core parts of the Indian ethos. Many tech millionaires have begun giving to impactful causes. Indian-Americans owe much of their success to higher education—and they have shown their gratitude by donating more than US$1 billion to US universities.

Early Google investor Ram Shriram donated $61 million to Stanford University's engineering department. Symphony Technology Group's Romesh Wadhwani, Aneel Bhusri, and other billionaires have signed Bill Gates's "Giving Pledge" to donate the majority of their wealth to philanthropies.

Cultural Highs

I'll never forget walking into Whole Foods in Cupertino and running into a *dosa* counter. Now a mainstream grocery store chain is making Indian food to order right in Silicon Valley. There is a gourmet Indian eatery in the Googleplex and on most other tech campuses. I don't have to wait for a box of snacks to come from India anymore.

After several waves of immigration, the Indian population of Santa Clara County now exceeds 117,000. Fremont alone now has more Indians than the city of Los Angeles. Indian-Americans have settled in many other counties all around the San Francisco Bay Area, gaining 53 percent more residents over the 2000–2010 decade, hitting a population of 244,000, and bringing more aspects of Indian culture to the entire area.

The Valley's India Community Center launched in 2003. The Milpitas organization brings together thousands of Indian families for traditional celebrations, yoga classes, summer camps, preschools, and other ways to help new immigrants have a soft landing in their new country.

A half dozen Hindu temples now dot the landscape from Sunnyvale to Livermore. Indian cinema can be seen in its native language on multiple multiplex screens in San Jose, Fremont, Santa Clara, and around the bay in Milpitas, Dublin, and Union City, too. India's music superstars have sold-out arenas in Santa Clara, Oakland, and San Francisco. You can take your pick of which Holi festival and Bollywood hip-hop yoga class to attend.

The Indian food scene has also flourished. For example, Srijith Gopinathan has received rave reviews as the executive chef at Taj Campton Place in San Francisco—the only Indian restaurant in the world with two Michelin stars. In 2020, he opened Ettan in the Silicon Valley, another high-end dining room serving Cal-Indian cuisine.

Another culinary milestone made headlines in 2016: Indian tech entrepreneur Gary Gauba bought the restaurant group that owns Saison, the only three-star Michelin restaurant in San Francisco. We have come a long way from the days when Indians were more commonly known as fast-food franchisees and motel owners.

Just south of the official boundaries of the Silicon Valley, Fremont hosts festivals throughout the year that attract tens of thousands of celebrants, including Indian Independence Day, Diwali, and Holi. There are big parades with dances, music, and food where everyone is wearing traditional dresses and speaking Hindi.

And we can get back home quicker than ever: flights move nonstop from SFO to Delhi in just 16 hours—and soon, a SFO–Bengaluru route will take just an hour longer.

Reunifying the Diaspora

I witnessed the rising influence of Indian-Americans during my four decades in Silicon Valley. One in ten tech workers is now Indian. One in three tech start-ups has an Indian co-founder.

While we had clearly made our mark as founders, investors, philanthropists, and executives, Indian-Americans' influence in other arenas did not appear to be commensurate with our professional strength. I realized Indian-Americans needed to work together to solidify a collective approach to community action.

I founded Indiaspora in 2012 as a way to harness and transform the personal success of Indian-Americans into meaningful impact in our local communities, in India, and around the world. My connections in The Valley's tech, education, medical, political, and nonprofit worlds were a blessing. Together, several hundred leaders from the diaspora pledged to share insight and collaborate on how to move forward in areas of impact.

The results have gone beyond my wildest dreams. We cheered Indian-American Ro Khanna's election to Congress representing the Silicon Valley. We persuaded the US Postal Service to issue a Diwali stamp. We held numerous in-person retreats and online forums across the US and India on a variety of critical issues facing the diaspora. Finally, we have an Indian-American Kamala Harris, entering the White House, bringing more prominence, power, and pride to our community.

The 2020s: Looking Forward

Silicon Valley proved instrumental in driving economic growth to the American economy in the twenty-first century. Cloud, artificial intelligence, blockchain, and a host of new technologies have turned the computing space on its head. Consumers' lives have been revolutionized by smartphones, social media, streaming entertainment, and the sharing economy.

Not one industry or country has been left unchanged by the free flow of information and ubiquitous connectivity. And much of this innovation began with Indian-powered Silicon Valley start-ups.

The Valley is such a vital business center that it warranted a stop during Prime Minister Narendra Modi's US visit in 2017. While dining with tech leaders in San Jose, four of the six CEOs at his table were from India.

The outlook for our diaspora's contributions to the region remains equally bright. On the immediate horizon, we have seen the arrival of more Indian "unicorns"—start-ups with a value of $1 billion. These game-changing companies won't always be born and bred in California; many will be raised in India and then transplanted to California's fertile ground. Companies like Druva, Freshworks, Innovaccer, and Uniphore are a few names that spring to mind.

That's the beauty of Silicon Valley: the hope and excitement of innovation and disruption. There might be no other place on Earth with the power to reinvent itself—and the world around it—with startling regularity.

I moved along the arc of computing from timesharing on mainframes to timesharing in the cloud. And when Kent State University invited me to deliver the commencement address to thousands of graduates in 2018, I was reminded that life *does* come a full circle.

I smile when I see the second generation of Silicon Valley-born Indian-Americans playing an active role in the community. The influence of these bright young individuals is not limited to the technology sector, but proliferates through every profession and industry. After the election of Vice President Kamala Harris, Indian-Americans only have one rung left to climb.

My accidental trip to Silicon Valley turned into a purposeful and wonderful life. I am grateful to have a beautiful family and incredible friends. And I've had a great time coaching, critiquing, and cheerleading the magical place where technology changes the world!

Professors and Academic Administrators: Conspicuous Presence in Temples of Learning

Pradeep K Khosla and Suman Guha Mozumder

Burgeoning Numbers

In the sixties and early seventies, when the semiconductor revolution and internet were in their infancy and search engines like Google were unheard of, the best way to find about the small number of immigrants from India in the US was to look through the faculty listings in university directories. Such listings would almost invariably comprise several names of Indian professors and researchers from various disciplines. In the absence of other means, it was considered a surefire way to track Indians in the USA!

While nobody resorts for obvious reasons these days to telephone-directory search for faculty listings to find out about Indian immigrants, who currently are estimated to number almost 4 million—or 1.2 percent of the US population—Indians since then have branched out to many other professions beyond teaching and research. And the presence of Indian immigrants in the faculties of American universities has continued to remain an important part of the US higher education system. Indian-American academics have been a conspicuous presence in the temples of learning and their numbers are believed to have only grown.

No doubt popular media has from time to time written about how Indian immigrants have excelled in various areas and chronicled their individual success stories, but not much research has taken place about the presence of Indian immigrants and Indian-Americans in academia in the US, their burgeoning numbers and their contributions, although it is commonly believed that a robust body of such successful professionals exists.

An academic's success is difficult to assess unlike those in business and entrepreneurship but there are pointers like the length and duration of teaching careers, membership in and elected fellowship of professional bodies/societies, and publication of research work in peer-reviewed journals, for example. And by all these criteria Indian-American academics pass with distinction.

Foray into Academic Administration

My (Pradeep Khosla) foray into academic administration was more by accident than by design. I imagine many Indian immigrants who have done well in academic administration probably stumbled upon the administrative path as I did. In 1993, when I was being considered for promotion to full professor (six years after starting my assistant professorship), I was pondering the next challenge. And it came about serendipitously as an offer to work at DARPA (Defense Advanced Research Projects Agency) managing programs in robotics, real-time systems, and design and manufacturing. I jumped on this opportunity as it would allow me to have the convening power of the best minds in academia and industry in the country to define research programs and create a national research agenda that was cutting-edge.

During my stint at DARPA, I realized that I enjoyed creating a vision for a research program and also building a team of performers drawn from both industry and academia to accomplish the program objectives. I enjoyed pushing the envelope of technology (like I did in my personal research as a faculty member), but this time it was at a much larger scale. I enjoyed motivating people and pushing the boundaries/limits of what is possible. So, while I was developing my skills at creating and motivating teams, I had to get used to enjoying the success of others and taking vicarious pleasure and pride in their success.

In doing my job at DARPA, I was not only honing my skills at being a successful leader but also realizing that I enjoyed it and would like to pursue that path while also pursuing my research.

This was made possible for me when Carnegie Mellon University offered me in 1996 the opportunity to rebuild a collapsing but prestigious National Science Foundation (NSF) center upon my return from DARPA. This was followed by a department head position (from 1999 to 2004) that allowed me to not only build new areas in the department but also position it for being ranked as top-5 in the country. I also founded CyLab in 1999, which even today is the largest university-based center for cybersecurity research, in addition to revisioning and repositioning Carnegie Mellon Silicon Valley campus.

A Country that Rewards Talent, Hard Work

These successes positioned me for being the dean of the College of Engineering in 2004. The college was ranked twelfth in 2004 and it was ranked fourth in 2012 when I left Carnegie Mellon to assume the position of chancellor of University of California San Diego. The offer to be the chancellor of a top-10 public institution came as a complete surprise (and a very pleasant one!) especially since I had spent my career in a private academic institution rising from a PhD student in 1982 to dean and university professor in 2012 when I left. In fact, when I started my academic career in 1986, I did not believe that it would be possible to witness in my career a person of color who spoke with an accent as the chancellor or president of a top university in the US.

And when it did become possible, I remembered why I had chosen to come to the US instead of going to Europe—this was the country where talent and hard work were rewarded. I am sure that similar thoughts may have inspired many others who immigrated to the US and have moved from pure academics to academic administration.

Untold Story

I have often wondered why there is this lack of literature about Indian academics and their contribution to higher learning. Some of my illustrious colleagues in other equally prestigious institutions have also wondered why the community's high visibility in academia has gone somewhat unnoticed in serious academic deliberations. "Probably someday it will take a PhD thesis by someone to capture this amazing but untold story of Indian immigrants!" a colleague once remarked in a light vein.

Although there is arguably not much academic literature available only on Indian-Americans in academia, and almost certainly there are no hard numbers, nor do they have a representative body like AAPI (for Indian American physicians) and AAHOA (for hoteliers), experts agree that Indian-Americans occupy an important place in the academic world as professors, leading researchers, and academic administrators.

To write about this segment of the population is, however, a challenging task because there are so many of them from diverse fields that it is nearly impossible to decide on an all-acceptable threshold about who all to include and who not to. For example, if one includes Beheruz Nariman Sethna, a professor of business and retired sixth president of the University of West Georgia, arguably the first person of Indian origin ever to become president of an American university, can one leave Abraham Verghese, professor of medicine at Stanford and a renowned author, or for that matter Professor Sital Kalantry, who serves as the faculty director of the Cornell India Law Center that promotes the study of Indian law in the American legal academy? In the following pages, we have included a small sampling of eminent Indian-American academics, certainly not comprehensive, to illustrate the point that the community has undoubtedly carved out a niche for itself in the academic field just like in other areas.

The 1965 Immigration Act and Entry of Indians

After President Lyndon B Johnson signed the Immigration and Naturalization Act into law in 1965, educated Indians started coming in more numbers to the US, sensing opportunities for careers in science and engineering, medicine, and other fields like higher education. Although their presence in the American academia was not as much conspicuous then as it is today, there were many prominent academics of Indian origin on American campuses, including academic and entrepreneur Thomas Kailath, the first Indian-born student to get a doctorate in electrical engineering from MIT in 1961. He became professor of electrical engineering at Stanford University and served as director of the Information Systems Laboratory from 1971 to 1981.

Gayatri Chakravorty Spivak, one of the very few Indian women of that time who came from Calcutta in 1961 to join the graduate program in English at Cornell University, became an assistant professor in the English Department of the University of Iowa in 1965 before receiving tenure in 1970. She is currently university professor at Columbia University, the highest academic rank in Columbia.

Amar Gopal Bose, founder and chairman of Bose Corporation, served with distinction as a professor at the Massachusetts Institute of Technology (MIT) for over 45 years. Bose, however, was born in the US to immigrant parents from India.

Another notable academic from that time is Jagdish Natwarlal Bhagwati, who received a PhD in economics from MIT in 1961 and taught there from 1968 until 1980, before moving to Columbia University where he is currently university professor.

Around the same time, CK Prahalad, one of the world's most influential business thinkers and one of the most beloved teachers at the University of Michigan, began to make his mark in the academic field. Prahalad received a postgraduate diploma in business administration from the Indian Institute of Management (IIM), Ahmedabad, in 1966 and followed that with a PhD in business administration from Harvard Business School in 1975 before joining the University of Michigan in 1977 as a professor.

Similar is the story of Dipak Jain, co-president and global advisor of China Europe International Business School, who joined Northwestern University's Kellogg School in 1986 as an assistant professor and rose to become the Sandy and Morton Goldman Professor of Entrepreneurial Studies and professor of marketing. He remained its dean for eight years from 2001–2009. He stepped down in 2009.

Amartya Sen, who was awarded the 1998 Nobel Prize in Economic Sciences for his contributions to welfare economics and social choice theory and his interest in the problems of society's poorest members, became professor of economics and philosophy at Harvard in 1987 and was appointed Lamont University Professor shortly thereafter.

And a more recent Nobel laureate, Abhijit Vinayak Banerjee, who won the 2019 Nobel Prize in Economics, earned his PhD in economics from Harvard University in 1988 and joined the MIT faculty in 1993 after four years on the faculty at Princeton University and one year at Harvard, joined the league of such illustrious academics.

There are other examples of such academics and scholars.

Venkatraman "Venki" Ramakrishnan, an Indian-born British-American structural biologist who shared the 2009 Nobel Prize in Chemistry, continued to work on ribosomes from 1983–1995 as a staff scientist at Brookhaven National Laboratory, before moving in 1995 to the University of Utah as a professor of biochemistry, and in 1999, the Medical Research Council Laboratory of Molecular Biology in Cambridge, England, where he had also been a sabbatical visitor during 1991–1992 on a Guggenheim Fellowship.

Jagdish Sheth, professor of marketing at the Goizueta Business School of Emory University, had studied and researched at MIT, Columbia, and the University of Pittsburgh.

Raghuram Govinda Rajan, the Katherine Dusak Miller Distinguished Service Professor of Finance at the University of Chicago Booth School of Business, earned an MBA from the IIM, Ahmedabad, before joining the doctoral program at the Sloan School of Management at MIT. Rajan was chief economist and director of research at the International Monetary Fund (IMF) and was the twenty-third governor of the Reserve Bank of India between 2013 and 2016.

Gita Gopinath has been the John Zwaanstra Professor of International Studies and of Economics at Harvard University. She is currently on leave of public service to serve as the chief economist of the IMF.

Raghu Sundaram, who did his BA, Economics in 1982 from University of Madras and PhD, Economics in 1988 from Cornell University, has been dean since 2018 and the Edward I Altman Professor of Credit and Debt Markets at New York University's Leonard N Stern School of Business.

The list of such academics is ever-growing. However, the journey of Indian academic stalwarts to the US dates back even earlier.

Har Gobind Khorana, who had earned his PhD degree from the University of Liverpool in England, moved to the Institute for Enzyme Research at the University of Wisconsin in 1960 as a professor and also co-directed the Institute for Enzyme Research in the Department of Biochemistry. He shared the 1968 Nobel Prize in Physiology or Medicine with Robert Holley and Marshall Nirenberg for their contributions to decoding the genetic code.

Subrahmanyan Chandrasekhar, who got the Nobel Prize in Physics in 1983, joined the faculty of the University of Chicago in 1937 after his graduate studies in Cambridge, England, and PhD in the early 1930s. He had gone to England from India for higher studies.

From Students to Professors

In most cases, people from India who later made a name for themselves in the American academic field are the ones who came to the US mostly as graduate students for research and getting a graduate degree. Over time, many of these students came to be appointed as faculty members either in their alma mater or in other institutions of higher education. There is no precise estimate of the number of Indian-Americans in teaching faculties across the US.

A 2011 survey by the Higher Education Research Institute at the University of California, Los Angeles noted that Asians and Asian-Americans made up 5.4 percent of all undergraduate teaching faculty in the country. Also, in a survey of presidents and chancellors by the American Council on Education, released in 2011, Asian and Asian-Americans made up 1.5 percent of those individuals, according to an Inside HigherEd report in 2013. These statistics provide a telltale sign of the stature of Indian-Americans given that they make up just a little over 1 percent of the population.

Raj Reddy, university professor in computer science and robotics at Carnegie Mellon and a Turing award recipient, was the founder of The Robotics Institute at Carnegie Mellon and a key thought leader in pushing the robotics, AI, and speech recognition revolution in the world. Raj has been a mentor to dozens of students and faculty during his 50 plus-year career and arguably a role model for many people of Indian descent including myself (Pradeep Khosla).

When asked to estimate the number of Indian-American academics in universities in the US, Raj said he believes the overall figure would be somewhere between 5 and 10 percent.

"I do not think there is any firm number available nor would I venture to guess about it. They are so proliferate in various institutions! It is hard to put a number. I can say hundreds for sure, but I don't know if I can say thousands," says Sethuraman Panchanathan, a computer scientist and academic administrator, and the fifteenth director of NSF. Before his NSF appointment, Panchanathan has also been executive vice president of Arizona State University (ASU) where he led ASU's Knowledge Enterprise and was its chief research and technology officer. Panchanathan is the second Indian-American to be serving as the director at NSF. Before him, the position was held in 2010–2013 by Subra Suresh, who had earlier served as dean of engineering at MIT and from NSF had moved to Carnegie Mellon University to take over as its president.

An interesting thing about Indian-Americans is that while the first-generation immigrants came primarily for higher studies in science, medicine, and technology and later took up jobs in academia or as doctors, engineers, or scientists, their children, the second-generation Indian-Americans, even though influenced by their parents' academic success, tend to take up a variety of professions, including in science, engineering, research, or faculty leadership positions. They have pursued successful careers in the arts, politics, business, government, and the military.

Arun Majumdar, the Jay Precourt Provostial Chair Professor at Stanford University, makes a clear distinction between people who came here from India in the sixties, seventies, and eighties, some of whom having a love for research and teaching joined academia, and the second-generation Indian-Americans, who have found career paths in many different fields.

"Unlike their parents, these young people are not naturalized citizens and for all practical purposes are just like any other American. While some of them have joined academia, many second-generation Indian-Americans, although they are equally educated and qualified like their parents, have chosen fields like law, business, politics, and even the army and not necessarily academics," Majumdar, who was nominated by President Barack Obama in 2009 and confirmed by the Senate to become the founding director of the Advanced Research Projects Agency-Energy (ARPA-E), says.

Similar distinctions between first-generation and second-generation Indian-Americans were made by people like Anuradha Luther Maitra, who came to study at Stanford for her PhD in economics in 1972 and later joined the faculty at UC Davis and UC Santa Cruz.

Dipak Jain, who studied at Guwahati University in Assam, and by his admission did not know English very well before coming to the US for a PhD, nor had much international exposure in terms of teaching, agrees on the point of US meritocracy, "The Indians who have come here have all strived for excellence and not mediocrity and people in the US can see through this quality of Indians because America values meritocracy."

Another point experts say works in their favor is that Indian professors often endear themselves to students thanks to their dedication and passion for teaching. "I would say when Indian-Americans teach in their class, they are very keen to know how the students are responding and if they are learning or not. This is in contrast with the approach of many other teachers who believe that their job is to sow the seeds like a farmer, and if students like fertile soil, are good, they will learn. So, I believe Indian teachers feel a lot of empathy for their students and they always want to learn from them as well. That is why they click very easily," Jain observes.

He recalls how at the outset of his teaching career at Kellogg, a group of students once came to his office to point out that he does not know anything about business marketing and was only teaching the course based on a textbook, "I was not upset but took the remark in the right spirit because one needs to get feedback from students."

He, however, does not believe that teaching is something in the Indians' DNA as is sometimes argued. Others like Reddy say that passion for teaching and education is not true only about Indians because there are people from other communities who join academics with equal zest and some of them may now be moving toward academic administration.

Commenting on the success of Indian-Americans, economist Nirvikar Singh, distinguished professor of economics in UC Santa Cruz, once noted, "There is no 'secret sauce'. There are no peculiarly Indian cultural traits. They [Indians] came very carefully selected. They were not coming from poverty.

The simplest policy prescription maybe this: Make sure everyone has access to education."

The career paths of most Indian-Americans, who moved to the US for higher education after receiving basic education in India and eventually moved up the ladder, corroborates Singh's argument about the importance of access to basic education.

Sanjay Subrahmanyam, professor of history, Irving and Jean Stone Endowed Chair at UCLA, was born in New Delhi, and after finishing MA and PhD in Economics from the University of Delhi, received D Litt fom University of Calcutta. He was elected to the American Academy of Arts and Sciences in 2009 and Corresponding Fellow of the British Academy in 2016 .

Akshay Venkatesh, a professor of mathematics at Stanford University, won the 2018 Fields Medal, the highest honor in math. Venkatesh was born in Delhi, India and his family emigrated to Perth in Western Australia when he was two years old.

Equally fascinating is the story of Raj Chetty, the William A Ackman Professor of Public Economics at Harvard University. Chetty was nine when he moved to the US with his family. He was the valedictorian of his high-school class, then graduated in just three years from Harvard University, where he went on to earn a doctorate in economics and, at age 28, was among the youngest faculty members in the university's history to be offered tenure. In 2012, he was awarded the MacArthur genius grant. The following year, he was given the John Bates Clark Medal, awarded to the most promising economist under 40.

Ashutosh Varshney, who was born in India, and is Sol Goldman Professor of International Studies and the Social Sciences and professor of political science at Brown University, previously taught at Harvard (1989-98) and the University of Michigan, Ann Arbor (2001-2008).

However, in the last decade or so, some research shows nearly half the women from India who moved to the US relied on work—not family sponsors—as the path to immigration. Making independent journeys in search of professional opportunities, much like Shyamala Gopalan, mother of Vice President Kamala Harris.

Late Dr Gopalan came to Berkeley, California, in 1958 as an international graduate student with a passion for science. She researched in UC Berkeley's Department of Zoology and Cancer Research Lab. She worked as a breast-cancer researcher at the University of Illinois at Urbana-Champaign and the University of Wisconsin and worked for 16 years at Lady Davis Institute for Medical Research and McGill University Faculty of Medicine.

Lopsided Ratio of Male and Female Scholars

Even though thousands of students from India have come to the US for graduate-level studies and doctoral research, the majority of those students and those who became academics later have mostly been males. There have been notable exceptions though like Gayatri Chakravorty Spivak or Manisha Sinha, the James L and Shirley A Draper Chair in American History at the University of Connecticut and a leading authority on the history of slavery and abolition and the civil war and reconstruction, Sital Kalantry, who came to the US from India at the age of four following her parents and earned her BA in 1994 from Cornell University, master's in development studies in 1995 from London School of Economics and JD in 1998 from the University of Pennsylvania Law School, or Priyamvada Natarajan, an astrophysicist and professor in the Departments of Astronomy and Physics at Yale University. Natarajan came to the US as an undergraduate student, one of the minuscule minority of students, to study as an undergraduate at MIT in 1986.

"The male-female ratio certainly is not 50:50. For women it would be far less," observes Satish K Tripathi, president of the University at Buffalo.

While Indian-American women have succeeded in many different disciplines and have been embraced by academia, they still face obstacles in some ways, mainly in terms of opportunities and recognition. "I think every academic discipline has a kind of 'establishment and in-group' and so breaking into that and having the same kind of opportunities, not just for one's work and leadership is difficult. At the end of the day, we are still brown people. We might have the same educational privilege as the whites but that does not mean we do not face extra obstacles," Natarajan observes.

Immigrant women like Shyamala Gopalan helped challenge gender stereotypes in both India and the US. "The women we interviewed traveled on their own to the US to live, study, and work. While they viewed their journeys as an empowered choice that allowed them to deviate from gendered expectations in India, they also had stories to tell about the gendered and racialized hierarchies in the American workplace," according to a Scroll report. In that interview many Indian women professionals noted that in the US they often face what one respondent called the "discrimination of assumptions" that include the assumptions that Indian women are meek and unable or unwilling to lead, and that they have a secondary interest in their careers.

"My impression is that academia in general in the US has not been that open to women. Everywhere it is a bit of a struggle for us," Natarajan, who did her graduate work in theoretical astrophysics at the Institute of Astronomy, Cambridge University, England, said. She was the first woman to be elected a fellow in astrophysics at Trinity College, Cambridge.

Majumdar also agrees that, generally, the number of women academics of Indian origin in faculties or even the number of grad students in science and engineering is lower than men but the picture may be different in fine arts or social sciences. "This is also true about India where you have a larger fraction of men than women in science and engineering. Naturally, you see there are more men than women coming overseas from India for STEM education."

In a detailed set of studies, although not specifically about Indian-American women, Sapna Cheryan, professor of social psychology in the Department of Psychology at the University of Washington, and her colleagues at the University of Washington, Seattle, noted in a paper, "Why are some STEM fields more gender-balanced than others?" that in the US while over 60 percent of BS, MS, and PhD degrees in biological and chemical sciences are from women, only 25–30 percent of them do computer science, physics, and engineering.

In India, a January 2020 report in *The Hindu* newspaper said the science academies have hardly 10 percent women. The Bhatnagar Prize has gone to 18 women out of a total of 548 so far, and the Infosys Prize to 16 out of a total of 52.

Talking about obstacles, some Indian women academics point out the sexist attitude of some in academia that existed in earlier decades may still be prevalent in the US, and like all other women, Indians may also be affected by it, not more nor less. Even though there are no statistics available, I (Pradeep Khosla) have had personal experiences to support the assertion that women academics have indeed faced hurdles in academia. I offer two examples.

When I was appointed department head in 1999, I was asked to focus on diversity amongst other things. My department had never had more than one woman on the faculty at any time and no woman was ever tenured in its 100 plus-year history. When I stepped down in 2004, I had appointed six women on the faculty including one with tenure. Since then, all of these appointees have done very well in their careers and some are now in academic administration. I experienced something similar at UC San Diego where during my eight years I have appointed five highly-qualified women (including two women of color) to deanships of academic divisions, whereas in 2012 when I got here, no academic divisional dean appointment was ever held by a woman. All of these appointments were an outcome of open competitive searches that consciously avoided subconscious biases.

Nitin Nohria, who retired in 2020 as dean of Harvard Business School (HBS) said in an interview with the university's official news website, *The Harvard Gazette*, that he believed the school had made significant advances on gender equality during this deanship, placing more women in HBS leadership positions, recruiting more women to its faculty and student population.

He expressed optimism that his successor, Srikant M Datar, who assumed the job on January 1, 2021, will need to take up the "unfinished business" of racial and gender equity issues. "Even the gender work is unfinished business, but I think we've made progress. I would in no way declare victory on gender work. That still has a long way to go. But I think the race work, we need to catch up and make progress faster and with more momentum. Now that we have a plan to achieve that, there is clarity on the work that needs to be done."

Although not focused on Indian-American women in faculty, in 1995, the dean of science at MIT established a committee to analyze the status of women faculty in the six departments in the School of Science. It discovered, according to published reports, that junior women faculty feel well supported within their departments and most do not believe that gender bias will impact their careers.

The issue of gender bias has also been looked at by Kingsborough Community College, a public community college in Brooklyn, New York, and part of the City University of New York system. It noted a few years ago that, "There is some evidence that women's advancement opportunities may continue to be influenced by some of the biases that have kept their participation numbers below those of men for the past century.

Pure Academics to University Administrators

After achieving academic brilliance and establishing a professional presence in top institutions, Indian-Americans have now been assuming leadership positions in colleges and universities. In the last few years, a trend seems to have taken hold where many Indian-Americans have assumed leadership roles in top administration, moving from pure classroom teaching to the hallowed chambers of university chancellors or presidents where they presumably can make a greater impact on the academic community of a university system.

I (Pradeep Khosla) believe that many of them, if not all, were influenced by the same kind of thinking and reasoning as I had—that one could make a greater impact on the student community and junior faculty in terms of motivating and inspiring them for success.

Some of those who in recent years have been appointed university chancellors or presidents or vice presidents include Sunil Kumar, who took office as the fifteenth provost of The Johns Hopkins University in 2016. In this role, Kumar is the chief academic officer and second-ranking member of the senior administration, responsible for promoting and coordinating the university's teaching and research mission. Kumar previously served as dean of the University of Chicago's Booth School of Business, as well as the George Pratt Shultz Professor of Operations Management. Prabhas Moghe was appointed executive vice president for academic affairs (EVPAA), the chief academic officer for Rutgers University, in October 2020. Ashish K Jha, a physician and health policy researcher, was named the third dean of the Brown University School of Public Health in 2020. Before joining Brown, he was the KT Li Professor of Global Health at the Harvard TH Chan School of Public Health and director of the Harvard Global Health Institute (HGHI). Others appointed include people like Renu Khator named chancellor of the

University of Houston System in 2008; Vistasp Karbhari, appointed president of the University of Texas at Arlington in 2013; and Kumble R Subbaswamy who became chancellor of UMass Amherst in 2012. Jamshed Bharucha was named president of the famous Cooper Union for the Advancement of Science and Art. Soumitra Dutta was the dean of the Samuel Curtis Johnson Graduate School of Management at Cornell University from 2012 to 2016 and Vijay Kumar was appointed as dean of the School of Engineering at UPenn in 2015. Not to be left out, Satish K Tripathi is the president of the University at Buffalo and was appointed in 2011. The list, needless to say, is by no means exhaustive or comprehensive.

Besides Khator, other Indian-American women have become academic administrators as well. Neeli Bendapudi, who is the eighteenth president of the University of Louisville, was selected for the position of UofL by its board of trustees in 2018 while Latha Ramchand was appointed executive vice chancellor and provost at the University of Missouri (MU), also in 2018.

The trend of internationalization of top academic administration has been noted by the education community many years back. An article in *Inside HigherEd* in 2013 noted that Indian-born academics were seeing their numbers grow in top campus jobs, reflecting internationalization trends over the past 40 years.

Patti McGill Peterson, presidential advisor on global engagement at the American Council on Education and former president of Wells College and St Lawrence University, noted that time that, "Four or five appointments do not make a trend, but it could be a signal on the horizon that this is something to watch and to think about."

Peterson and others said "the selection of such individuals and their growing representation in the candidate pool for such jobs could reflect several trends in higher education, particularly efforts starting 40 years ago to recruit top international talent to fill graduate classrooms and faculty ranks at research universities. Those individuals have been steadily climbing the ranks for years and are now of age to assume top leadership roles."

Ilene H Nagel, head of the education practice at Russell Reynolds Associates, a search firm that assisted on the SUNY-Buffalo and UT-Arlington searches, feels that individuals of Indian descent are often among the strongest candidates in the pool and often have an accomplished record of academic administration.

Lucy Apthorp Leske, vice president, partner, and co-director of the education and not-for-profit practice for Witt/Kieffer, an executive search-consulting firm, was quoted as saying in *Inside HigherEd* that the rising importance of science, technology, engineering, math, and business education and research in modern universities could also be a factor in the recent appointment of Indian-born individuals. Anyone with business, engineering, and scientific backgrounds, people who understand those fields, are moving into top jobs and are in demand by selection boards.

Tripathi, who was appointed the fifteenth president of the University at Buffalo in April 2011, says the fact that such individuals saw an opportunity for graduate work and employment at American universities, and that such individuals are now rising to top leadership jobs, is a testament to the meritocratic nature of the US higher-education system.

A Foot in Two Worlds?

Time was when, like any others in the field, Indians in teaching and higher education devoted most of their time to educating, delivering lectures, attending seminars, and of course, writing those copious scholarly papers, the staple of a typical professor.

Over time, the purely academic mindset of Indian-Americans like other communities seems to have changed as people in academia also venture into entrepreneurship alongside educating. When Bose, the MIT professor, founded Bose Corporation in 1964, he might have been one of only a few such academics who also turned an entrepreneur. Now there seems to have been some shift in the attitude of academics because of which scholarly and entrepreneurial pursuits are not necessarily considered mutually exclusive.

Panchanathan believes Indians, especially the subset of a small group of people from the subcontinent who come to the US, have a lot of risk-taking passion to achieve more and make an impact in society and that passion and spirit sometimes extends in academics as well. The fact that immigrants from India come to the US with just a few dollars in the pocket but with big dreams and ambitions in their minds itself is a testimony to their risk-taking mentality and entrepreneurial spirit.

Kailath, in his stellar career as an academician, inventor, and entrepreneur, is the founder of the Information Systems Laboratory (ISL) at Stanford University, which has played a pivotal technology-transfer role in the growth and success of Silicon Valley and boasts numerous phenomenally successful and influential technology companies that have their roots in the research work done in the laboratory. He has founded several industry-leading high-tech companies, including Integrated Systems (now part of WindRiver Systems), Numerical Technologies, Inc, Excess Bandwidth Corporation (now part of Virata Corporation), Cipher State Inc and Clear Shape Inc. Two of the companies he founded went public.

The modern-day professor, thus, may not be just an intellectual steeped in books, manuscripts, and research papers but at times also in checking company balance sheets. And there may be other reasons for that. According to a report in *Entrepreneur Magazine* in the US, less than 30 percent of faculty members had tenure in 2007, down from 42 percent in 1995. *The Economist* reported in 2010 that 100,000 PhDs were granted from 2005 to 2009 and only 16,000 new professorships were created.

In the past, most professionals with advanced degrees did not seem to have the nerve to get off academia, but slowly things seem to be changing. "Earlier Indian-Americans used to be in academics but now people are also passionate about entrepreneurship in addition to their passion for academics, thanks to a better ecosystem and this will stay I think," Panchanathan notes.

Almost similar is the take of Jain who believes that there is a trend among bright and highly-educated Indians like Sundar Pichai, who did his MS at Stanford University and MBA from Wharton School, or Satya Nadella, an MS in computer science from the University of Wisconsin-Milwaukee and MBA from the University of Chicago Booth School of Business, who tend to make their career in the corporate world rather than sticking to academia. Indians-Americas, however, are not abandoning academics but they are also exploring opportunities in the corporate world and in some cases trying to be both an entrepreneur and academic.

One of the reasons why academics are also venturing into entrepreneurship these days is an enabling ecosystem consisting of start-ups, venture capital, and angel investors, and growing interaction between academics and entrepreneurs, particularly in Silicon Valley.

Stanford University—attended by people like Kailath and Pichai, CEO of Alphabet—has for a long time been an entrepreneurial school, and the research starting in earlier decades there was connected to translational work that would lead to private-sector values and ultimately to what is today called Silicon Valley.

Outside enterprises had interaction with the academia at Stanford because of its R&D work and at the Stanford campus, one could see people coming back and forth and academics interact with entrepreneurs. "When people find something interesting in research, some of them need to find a pathway to commercialize that, and in that cross-pollination, some magic happens sometimes, although not always. The exchange of ideas between the private sector people and academia is important," observes Majumdar who also worked as vice president for energy at Alphabet Inc's Google before returning to Stanford faculty.

He says that for Indian-Americans moving to academic administration jobs should be seen as a natural progression for people who excel in what they do, especially in the leadership category.

Majumdar's observation could not be more apt as Indian-Americans over the last half century have moved up the career ladder gradually, not only in academics but in several other fields, including leadership positions in business, and in politics like Kamala Harris.

An important achievement of the community in academia has been the entry of the crème de la crème of Indian scientists, engineers, and medical professionals into the three honorific societies—the National Academy of Sciences (NAS), National Academy of Engineering (NAE), and National Academy of Medicine (NAM). Each has about a total of 2,200 to 2,400 members who are elected and these academies are often referred to as Hall of Fame for sciences, engineering, and medicine.

Among many others of Indian descent, Arun Majumdar, Raj Reddy, Pradeep Khosla, Vijay Kumar, and Thomas Kailath have been members of the National Academy of Engineering and the American Academy of Arts and Sciences. Among others who were inducted into the academy in 2020, include University of Illinois at Urbana-Champaign computer science professor Sarita V Adve, Renu Khator and Indira M Raman, a professor in the Department of Neurobiology at Northwestern University, where she holds the Bill and Gayle Cook Chair in Biology and held the Charles Deering McCormick Professorship of Teaching Excellence. Membership of such prestigious national bodies, in addition to their long and storied faculty careers, points out not only to their academic brilliance but is also a testament to the enduring contribution of Indian-Americans to higher education in America.

Success Drivers of Indian-American CEOs: Fostering a New Wave of Corporate Leadership

Raj L Gupta

After five decades of immigration to the US, an extraordinary number of Indians have reached the summit of influence in their professional fields—and the corporate world is no exception. In 2020, Indian-American CEOs collectively employed more than 3.6 million people worldwide and accounted for $1 trillion in revenue and $4 trillion in market capitalization.

Be it IBM's Arvind Krishna, Berkshire Hathaway's Ajit Jain, or Novartis's Vasant "Vas" Narasimhan, the Indian-American executive is at the forefront of America's economic progress and job creation.

Given the prevalence and stellar reputation of Indian talent in the executive suite today, it is hard to believe that I was the only Indian in the corporate office of the organization I was then working with in 1971.

I joined Rohm and Haas after earning my MBA—an uncommon goal for Indians in the early 1970s—and then invested 39 years of my life in the Philadelphia Chemical Company. I worked on three continents for 13 bosses in 17 jobs, and rose to become chairman and CEO in 1999. During my decade as CEO, I am proud to have led the corporation to become the second-best performer in the S&P 500 Index.

During my career, I have also had the privilege of serving on the board of directors of 29 organizations, eight nonprofits, seven private firms, and 14 public companies, including DuPont, Tyco, Hewlett Packard, and the Vanguard Group. I have served as executive chair, non-executive chair and have chaired nominating and governance, executive compensation, and audit committees at a number of companies.

The bottom line? I know the characteristics of a successful corporate leader. I have felt the weight of authority that a CEO feels when running a multinational corporation. As a board member, I have participated in many searches and know that selecting the right top executive is our most important job.

And given my decades of experience in governance, I believe Indian-Americans are poised to become an even greater force in the executive suite.

Do we Indians possess a genetic trait that makes us successful CEOs? No. Would I recommend an Indian for an executive position over a better-qualified non-Indian? Never.

But I *do believe* Indian immigrants have a cultural background, work ethic, and life experience that makes them highly capable of successfully navigating their way up the corporate ladder.

After speaking with other Indian CEOs quoted in this chapter and considering a review of my own life and career experience, I believe there are six differentiators that give Indian immigrants a solid base on which to build a successful CEO career. I expound on them later in the article.

"*It is inspiring to see so many leaders of Indian heritage playing a significant role in business and in society. Our culture and our values are a common starting point. But it's what we do with the opportunities presented to us that makes the difference.*"—Ajay Banga, president and CEO, Mastercard

The Rise of the Indian-American CEO

Indian immigration to the US had its share of enablers—some organic and others, accidental. President Lyndon B Johnson's landmark Immigration and Naturalization Act of 1965—heralded as one of America's biggest success stories of the Cold War era—gave the country's famed corporations the ability to attract skilled labor. It put an end to the long-standing national-origin quotas that favored certain ethnic communities over people of color.

It was somewhat coincidental that this period also marked a boom in technical and medical education in India. Innumerable graduates from reputed institutions like the Indian Institute of Technology (IIT) became available for these global corporations and other centers of excellence.

In the immediate decades following India's independence, the country's brightest trained minds migrated to the farthest corners of the world for two main reasons. First, the well-educated Indian represented the early globalization wave that broke new cultural and geographical barriers; and, second, despite the need for a technically skilled workforce to drive the new nation's growth, there was a perceptible lack of opportunities and professional incentives that matched their capabilities.

The Indian-American population has grown significantly in the past 50 years, now known as the most affluent ethnic group in the US. Historically, Indians in the US worked in medicine, science, technology, engineering, and mathematics-related jobs. Some, like the Patel community from Gujarat, took to the hotel industry and, over time, grew to dominate it. Others became entrepreneurs in Silicon Valley after the digital revolution of the 1980s.

The evolution of Indian-Americans in all professions took a good decade before one started to see a rise up the ranks in academia (medicine, science, and engineering in particular) and as entrepreneurs (start-ups, small businesses, restaurants, and motel owners). The rise in business leaders in other industries took longer, mostly moving from technical roles to broader responsibilities.

Former President Barack Obama once quipped in reference to Indian-Americans, "Whenever I'm asked about Indians taking away our jobs, I want to say, 'You know what? They've just created 50,000 jobs'."

This validation, coming from a shrewd politician, and master communicator like President Obama, did not surprise me in the least. While India earned the reputation of being the "back-office of the world"—a reference to its highly-skilled workforce, engaged in outsourced activities on the payroll of global firms—President Obama's impassioned appeal pointed out the unprecedented rise of Indian CEOs in America's leading corporations and their rapid growth.

Rajat Gupta's appointment as managing director of McKinsey & Company in 1994 marked the first Indian-born CEO taking the helm of a multinational corporation. In 1997, Ramani Ayer became the first Indian CEO to head a Fortune 500 financial firm, The Hartford. In the latter half of the 1990s, Indian-Americans reached top executive positions at US Airways Group, Quest Labs, and, as noted earlier, my appointment to lead Rohm and Haas.

By the 2000s, Indian-Americans had become the stars of America's corporate sky. Indra Nooyi was appointed CEO of PepsiCo in 2006; before that Sunil Kumar was named ISP CEO in 1999; Vikram Pandit became CEO of Citigroup in 2007; Francisco D'Souza was named president and CEO of Cognizant Technology Solutions in 2007, Shantanu Narayen took over as CEO of Adobe Systems in 2007; Sanjay Jha was appointed co-CEO of Motorola in 2008; Deven Sharma was announced as president of Standard & Poor's in 2010; Ajay Banga was named president and CEO of Mastercard in 2010; and Rakesh Sachdev became Sigma-Aldrich CEO in 2012. In the past decade, even more Indians took the CEO helm, including Vasant "Vas" Narasimhan at Novartis and Niraj S Shah at Wayfair.

The never-ending rise of the software and technology industry brought up many Indian chief executives as well. Hyderabad-born Satya Nadella walked into the big Microsoft-CEO shoes once worn by Bill Gates. Sundar Pichai now leads Alphabet, the parent company of Microsoft's rival Google, where three of its 13-member management team executives are Indian.

Arvind Krishna made worldwide headlines when he was named CEO of IBM in 2020. Other notable tech CEOs from the diaspora include Sanjay Mehrotra of Micron, George Kurian of NetApp, Nikesh Arora of Palo Alto Networks, Sandeep Mathrani of The We Company, and Dinesh C Paliwal of Harman International Industries.

The pattern continued in companies like Cisco, where Padmasree Warrior was CTO; Intel, where Vinod Dham invented the famous Intel

Pentium processor; and Ajay Bhatt, who became the chief client platform architect. Bhatt had also co-invented USB along with several significant standards in graphics and computer architecture, holding 31 US patents. It is not surprising, then, that the distinction of becoming the first chief technology officer of United States went to an Indian-American, Aneesh Paul Chopra, who served from 2009–2012.

Success Drivers of Indian-American CEOs

After decades of living and breathing corporate governance, I know that an Indian surname is no guarantee of executive prowess. At the same time, the prominence and success of diaspora CEOs pushed me to review the differentiators that seem to provide Indian immigrants with a competitive advantage in the executive suite.

Differentiator 1. Family Values

Like many corporate leaders, my training for CEO-hood began at home in Uttar Pradesh (UP). My parents had a full house—six children in seven years—yet they did not rule with iron fists. They gave us plenty of opportunity to study and to play as long as we lived by their values: Be honest, respect others, work hard, try your best, and don't worry about the outcome.

Operating within these value-based parameters, my siblings and I developed a healthy spirit of competition. When my older sister finished high school as the only one with a first division in the whole school, I vowed that if she could do it so could I. I finished sixth out of over 100,000 students in the whole state of UP.

Because our parents gave us freedom and authority, we developed the confidence and desire to succeed. If they had pushed and micromanaged us, the opposite would likely have occurred. The same dynamic holds true in the corporate world: Leaders crave opportunity and trust from their managers to tackle opportunities as they see fit.

"*It's the uniqueness of our experiences that have the potential to ignite creativity and drive innovation. I've found that our common goals truly serve as the key to unlocking the strength of diversity's direct contribution to successful business outcomes.*"—Bob Patel, CEO, LyondellBasell

It is critical to let people find their own passion and direction. When it became our turn to parent, my wife Kamla and I gave our daughters complete freedom to pursue their chosen career and lifestyle. They each took a completely unique path and both have become incredibly successful. Watching my daughters build their lives and careers has been a profound learning experience for me both as a parent and as a corporate leader.

Another leadership lesson learned at home? Watching Kamla deftly manage years of motherhood, numerous household moves, and decades of maintaining connections with family and friends around the world. Despite my best efforts, I have never learned to successfully multitask as well as my wife.

Differentiator 2. Higher Education

Regardless of religion, all Indians believe in the power of higher education. Their lifelong commitment to learning is another aspect that sets them apart from many native-born Americans. Even though the parchment received by all graduates reads "MBA", the immigrant student has typically had to be more dedicated and log more years of study to earn it.

By the time immigrants of the 1960s and 1970s arrived for their first day of work in corporate America, they would have already completed years of intense study. Each student would have already competed for a spot at a preeminent Indian university, finished their undergraduate studies, and matriculated from at least one graduate degree program in the US before gaining employment with an American company. (And, of course, all these degrees don't reflect the street smarts acquired by years of traveling hundreds of miles from home to college and then thousands of miles to America for school.)

My commitment to learning was typical of most Indian CEOs. After high school, I was proud to get admission into the 1967 class of IIT Bombay as one of the 1,500 students chosen from 200,000 applicants for the five IITs. The meritocratic nature of the IIT entrance process helped spread India's educational opportunities to many different groups and is often credited as one of the main drivers of the country's growth as a global power.

My father had been a civil engineer but I decided to study mechanical engineering—a field I considered more exciting. Once in the halls of IIT, I was surrounded by many elite students talking about their hopes to study and work in *America*—not England as had been the destination for prior generations. US universities and corporations had cemented their reputations as being among the world's best. After graduation, more than half of our class headed for America.

"*When I arrived in the US as a university student, I was awestruck by the wonders of this country, but also found myself longing for the familiar sights and sounds of home. Through the years, I have never lost that sense of wonder—realizing there is far more that connects our two cultures than separates us. This deep connection between India and the US makes us natural collaborators. Our working together enhances the global economy, promotes geopolitical stability, and makes each of our nations richer, both literally and figuratively.*"—Punit Renjen, CEO, Deloitte Global

Differentiator 3. Technological Savvy

Many Indians living in the US today were beneficiaries of the visa programs for students or high-skilled professionals that allowed them to stay and work in America. And most young diaspora members arrived at US universities to continue their medical or engineering education.

I was no exception: My first US destination was Cornell University and a MS in Operations Research. Kamla and I had married just prior to our move so we had each other to help soften our landing in New York. It was around this time that I realized my skills were more pragmatic than technical.

During my first job at Scott Paper Company, I began taking night classes at Drexel University in Philadelphia. After receiving my MBA in 1971, I accepted a financial analyst position with Rohm and Haas, and ended up spending most of my career there.

Though it was uncommon for early Indian immigrants to pursue business degrees in the US, a notable trailblazer had actually set a precedent in 1964: Dr Amar Gopal Bose founded the company which is today the most famous audio manufacturer in the world. At a time when stethoscopes and seminars were preferred over profits and products, the Indian-origin founder of Bose Corporation stood out from the crowd. A former professor at Massachusetts

Institute of Technology (MIT), Bose created his eponymous company with initial funding from angel investors. It currently employs more than 10,000 people with revenue exceeding $3 billion annually.

It's not surprising that Indian CEOs have both a broad and deep perspective into innovation-driven businesses that are driving the global economy today. India's IITs and commitment to technological know-how has helped the nation produce many sophisticated CEO minds who may lead a business, medical, academic, or manufacturing organization but started their education by studying engineering.

"*The intersection of technology and business has been my passion since my formative years in India and through my professional career in the US. Strong cultural values, a deep grounding in math and science, and a lifelong learning orientation were instilled in me by my parents that I have never forgotten, and am thankful for my heritage. In turn, encouraging STEM education has been my ardent interest to pay forward to future generations.*"— Steve Sanghi, chairman and CEO, Microchip Technology

C-suite executives need to consider problems at a very high level but cannot ignore the day-to-day machinations that will bring their vision to life. I definitely feel that my background in mechanical engineering and computer science helped me approach my work at Rohm and Haas as more of a generalist, rather than a specialist.

Indian-Americans now regularly feature as top innovators in the technology segment, especially, those under the 35-year-old age bracket. Sonia Vallabh, Maithilee Kunda, Dinesh Bharadia, and Jagdish Chaturvedi are the four Indian-American innovators under 35 on the MIT Technology Review list.

Differentiator 4. Adaptability

As an executive at Rohm and Haas, I was fortunate to first participate and then support their Leadership 3000 program, which ran between 1988 and 2008. It identified the employees who displayed the most potential and then created a customized leadership development experience to transform them into top executives.

A 2021 *Management and Business Review* feature about Leadership 3000 extolled its methods, "It was not about the newest methods in leadership development but about the most *enduring*." Indeed, a *Harvard Business Review* article called Rohm and Haas one of a handful of "stealth CEO factories"—20 percent of the program graduates went on to become CEOs.

Leadership 3000 worked because it placed highly-talented candidates in roles with expanded authority and encouraged them to think like CEOs. It's no surprise that most of the program's graduates experienced at least one posting overseas as an expatriate director. Adapting to a foreign culture as an expat requires a variety of business and interpersonal skills; leading a successful division is even more challenging.

"*When I think of the Indian heritage that links so many of the leaders in the world, the first word that comes to mind is culture. Culture transcends from heritage to how a community or team does things, and when you have a culture in a company that strives to make an impact on the world with passion and energy, it is the most rewarding aspect of business.*"—Samir Kapuria, President, NortonLifeLock

Here's where I believe Indian immigrants could have a head start against other candidates. We first-generation executives grew up in India in a multicultural environment of different races, religions, and social settings. The heritage, culture, social norms, ethical values, and the belief systems are all associated with the Indian subcontinent. It is an amalgamation of several cultures and has been influenced by a history that dates back to the Indus Valley Civilization.

We had to figure out how to operate in that complex framework and succeed in a way that led us to come to America for university—and then negotiate operating in a new, complex framework. I believe "adaptability" is a critical characteristic for leaders so perhaps it is not surprising that first-generation Indian-Americans and other immigrants have the constitution necessary to lead multinational companies.

"*I am grateful for the gift of India's diverse culture,* sanskar, *or values, and the unconditional love from my parents and family. My family has been fortunate to live the life of global nomads, living across India, South Africa, Thailand,*

China, and the United States. These experiences have shaped my conviction on the goodness of humanity, and the spirit of inclusiveness and cooperation across societies. It is a privilege to be part of this group of leaders, as we do our part in helping people live better, healthier lives, across the world."—Steve Sanghi, chairman and CEO, Microchip Technology

Differentiator 5. Temperament

A big part of leading a company is being sure you're being followed. Climbing the corporate ladder for nearly 30 years taught me that doing a good job is not enough to command respect from your subordinates. A good leader must consistently deliver more than expected and demonstrate that he or she is always thinking of the company at large—not just engaging in self-promotion and trying to be the "smartest person on the block".

To be a good CEO, confidence is essential but overconfidence is disastrous. I like to say that arrogance and complacency are the worst combination in a leader. I believe Indian values are the reason why diaspora CEOs operate not only effectively but respectfully.

On November 7, 2007, I faced the greatest challenge of my career. At the behest of the majority shareholding family, I had orchestrated a $15 billion sale of Rohm and Haas to Dow Chemical Company. Unfortunately, as the deal was being finalized, the beginnings of what would become a massive financial downturn hit the global economy and the deal began to crumble. Over the next 18 months, I worked tirelessly to resurrect the sale and please the shareholders. I credit my Indian temperament to keeping relationships intact throughout the process.

My counterpart at Dow Chemical, Andrew Liveris, was a notoriously fiery Australian personality. He was known in the media as a very vocal, blunt, and aggressive businessman. Yet throughout the renegotiation process, we never had a single shouting match. He knew me well enough to not cross any boundaries with me and I never had to raise my voice.

"*Indians spoke in different languages, dressed differently, followed different religions, ate different kinds of food, but, were of the same temperament.*"—Milind Pant, CEO, Amway

Differentiator 6. Mentors and Networks

Though I was the only Indian in the office when my career began, I later realized the significance of the inclusive environment and level-playing field that I experienced at Rohm and Haas. I was never made to feel that I had barriers to overcome because I looked different.

It's tough to tell what makes some executives CEO and some not—regardless of their ethnic background. But the presence of a skilled mentor and connections to a professional network can make a huge impact on leadership potential.

This is especially true for immigrant or minority employees who might subscribe to a self-reasoned argument that they can't get to the top because they're different. It's easy to put in place a preconceived idea that there is a bias in the company against those who don't "look like them".

I'll never forget one mentor who set me straight early in my career, pointing out the uselessness of self-imposed barriers to my own success. Having an honest coach on my team definitely helped make the difference between winning and losing.

While working 15 years in Europe for Rohm and Haas, I never saw another Asian face in a business meeting. Another mentor reminded me to forget about the history of India and the English, "You need to get over the idea that white men are at the top."

Another mentor invited me for a glass of wine when I was leaving to head up Asia. "Raj, I have two pieces of advice for you. One, you are far too respectful of authority. You have great ideas and need to share them. And two, you are wishy-washy in person. You sit silently in a meeting and then come back to tell me in private what you should have said in the meeting. You're going to cheat yourself and cheat the company if you don't speak up."

"*It's outstanding to see a tremendous set of role models from the Indian diaspora and the impact they are having in their arenas. The more notable impact they have is as leaders, who role model tolerance and support diversity in all its forms: perspective, attitudes, orientation, identification, and appearance. Only when we seek to understand, will we be understood, and find the compassion needed to stamp out injustice and realize the best version of ourselves.*"—Laxman Narasimhan, CEO, Reckitt Benckiser

There are many examples of productive mentoring and network impact among Indian immigrants. In Silicon Valley's technology industry, which is a closely-connected network and a fiercely-competitive environment, Indians succeeded by playing by the rules of engagement. They supported each other to the extent of providing seed funding to others of their community and offering mentorship. Many became visible, vocal role models for those who followed. Some early tech entrepreneurs and venture capitalists like Vinod Khosla, Vinod Dham, Kanwal Rekhi, Venktesh Shukla, MR Rangaswami, and Gurbaksh Chahal, have become legends for their ability to mentor and create networks of Indian tech executives.

Today, new cross-industry organizations aim to rally Indian-Americans to become a stronger voice by connecting professionals across generations and industries. Founded in 2012, Indiaspora united Indian leaders from diverse backgrounds and inspired them to bring about positive social change. In 2020, the nonprofit released a first-ever list honoring executives of the Indian diaspora who lead global corporations. A compilation such as this quantifies and underscores the power and influence of Indians in the boardroom.

The Next Generation

As we look ahead from 2021, we struggle to imagine the post-pandemic world. Even before Covid-19, globalization was in trouble. The open system of trade that had dominated the world economy for decades had been damaged by the financial crash and the China–US trade war. The pandemic has made the situation worse because of stringent measures of nationwide lockdowns witnessed in many countries, including those in the European Union.

As economies reopen, activity will recover, but the world of unfettered movement and free trade will not immediately resume. The pandemic will politicize travel and migration by enforcing stringent regulations. This inward-looking lurch will enfeeble the recovery.

"*The 2020 Business Leaders list is testament to the strength of the Indian diaspora, which in many ways, was the product of globalization. That world order is now under threat, with increasing nationalism one of the downsides coming out of the pandemic. My hope is that in a fractured world, bridges can continue to be built, and our young people have the same opportunities that [the] previous generations had.*"—Piyush Gupta, CEO, DBS Bank

Yet America's companies appear to be in good hands. There's no doubt we see an increasing number of Indians leading companies in America and around the world. And we hope that more of these leaders will be women.

Will we see as many second- and third-generation Indian-Americans step into the CEO role? Perhaps. The young members of the diaspora who I meet on university campuses today are brilliant. They are making headlines in a variety of areas, from spelling bees to robotics to medicine.

The difference with today's young Indian-Americans is that many do not have the multicultural experience of growing up in India and moving to the US. They don't have the same motivations, challenges, and adaptability that were must-haves for first-generation immigrants.

That said, the first wave of Indian CEOs has helped pave the way for a more inclusive and successful C-suite in the future. I believe the authenticity of Indian-Americans is what has put us in good stead despite challenges along the way. My hope is that the future generation of Indian-Americans can similarly become an exemplar for the larger society they live in.

Leading Meaningful Change: Building a Culture of Philanthropy among Indian-Americans

Deepak Raj and Ashish Shah

The philanthropy ecosystem in the US is evolving rapidly. Charitable giving is no longer the exclusive realm of billionaires at the top of the pyramid and retail "micro-donors" at the bottom. A very large and sophisticated "middle of the pyramid" is developing that is made up of intermediaries, catalysts, and passionate changemakers. This new middle tier is focused on creating scalable and sustainable impact by expanding the philanthropic ecosystem and making it more accessible and transparent to a growing stream of potential donors.

And a lot of today's changemakers are Indian-Americans.

Members of the diaspora are moving rapidly to fill in all levels of the ecosystem pyramid. They have applied success strategies and best practices from their professional careers to the business of charitable giving—and achieved new levels of impact.

Though historic activity may have lagged, we believe Indian-American philanthropists are now ahead of the curve, with their levels of giving growing significantly and visibly, and leading to meaningful change in twenty-first century giving.

A Generous Group

America is one of the most philanthropic countries in the world. In 2019, US charitable giving hit $450 billion according to the latest Giving USA report. While corporate and foundation donations are also on the rise, individual donations make up the vast majority of giving, rising 4.7 percent to $310 billion.

The Indian-American community has tremendous philanthropic potential, and we see the decade of 2020 as a very important time for elevating its level of giving. There are more than four million people of Indian origin who live in the US, a community that has one of the highest median household incomes of any immigrant group. Our community includes successful entrepreneurs, prominent CEOs, physicians and healthcare professionals, noted academicians, and other professionals. We are a young, growing, well-educated, and socially aware group.

All these factors should arguably make us uniquely predisposed to giving generously, but a survey of giving habits and trends of the Indian diaspora conducted by Dalberg and Indiaspora in 2018 highlighted that we may not be making philanthropic contributions at our full potential. While Indian-Americans are great at donating time and volunteering, we lag behind when it comes to donating money, compared to the rest of the American population.

The survey found that Indian-American volunteering hours are twice the US average. However, the estimated donation rate of Indian-Americans is 1.5 percent of income per year, compared with the American donation rate of 4 percent per year—a gap that increases with income. The result? A "giving gap" of $2–$3 billion between current giving and what the diaspora would give if they matched the US average rate.

One of the key goals of Indiaspora, a US nonprofit organization focused on amplifying the voice of the global Indian diaspora, is to double diaspora philanthropy in the coming years as part of their philanthropy and social impact work.

Understanding the Gap

The giving gap exists not because Indians are not generous or are less passionate about social issues. We believe Indian-Americans have been less active philanthropically so far for the following four reasons:

Timing and Priority

The number of Indians immigrating to the US rose exponentially during the 1970s and early 1980s—and the population has increased steadily since. A majority of the initial Indian-American population arrived in the US either to study or work, and so the first couple of decades in America were focused on finding good employment opportunities or setting up their businesses, accumulating wealth, and bringing their families to America. During this time, even if philanthropy was on their to-do list, it was not a top priority because the focus was on settling down and working hard to succeed.

However, this community of first-generation Indian-Americans is now settled, matured, and has become increasingly successful over the years and is at a much different stage in their life. Now, they can focus on ways to give back and become more active with their philanthropic activities. Whether it is supporting their local community in the US, or giving back to India, people are looking for opportunities to engage and learn more on how to make the most impact with their time, money, and abilities.

The second and third generations of Indian-Americans born in the US are already thinking about ways in which they can effectively use their resources to give back and/or become a changemaker by working in the development sector and inspire social change. These younger Indian-Americans who are well-educated and financially secure are looking for opportunities to engage in philanthropy much earlier and with a longer view of strategic impact.

Trust-deficit and Donor Skepticism

It is fair to assume that a majority of first-generation Indian-American donors are a little skeptical toward organizations they are giving to, which results in a significant trust deficit for this category of donors. They are anxious about their giving and a lot of their anxiety relates to fundamental questions like *"Am I giving to the right organization?"*, or *"Will my giving actually make any impact?"* This mainly stems from either their own experiences and assumptions, or the overall poor donor self-perception of the impact and deployment of philanthropic giving. This ultimately creates doubt and damages their ability to give to their full potential.

Remittances to India

It is important to note that in determining the giving gap, the study did not include the total amount sent to India by the diaspora via remittances. A World Bank report found India to be the top recipient of remittances in 2018 with its diaspora sending $79 billion back home, and more than $10 billion of this being sent from the US. In the Indiaspora study, remittances were excluded because they are not considered philanthropic giving. However, these funds still comprise a major part of the diaspora's informal giving to family and friends, which could explain some of the diaspora's giving gap.

Giving to Religious Institutions

Religious and faith-based giving to temples, gurdwaras, mosques, etc. is another key area where the Indian diaspora has made considerable donations. For example, the BAPS Swaminarayan Sanstha has over 100 centers in North America. For the Indian community, especially those who came as part of the first and second waves of immigration in the late 1960s, 1970s, and early 1980s, these religious institutions were more than places of worship. They were more of an intrinsic part of their identity for different Indian-American groups and a place to congregate and feel a sense of community. These religious institutions provided a place where they could feel at home and celebrate their cultural heritage, festivals, and traditions. Hence, while donating substantial sums of money to help build a temple or a mosque may not be considered or reported as "true" philanthropy, it continues to remain an important personal priority for a subset of the community that believes in giving to religious institutions.

Encouraging Outlook: Inspirational Examples and Innovative Initiatives

Individual philanthropy is specific and unique to the donor. Every donor thinks about giving in a way that aligns with their personal journey, philosophy, and goals. A donor can be a micro-donor or a large donor. The donation can help a local community or an organization in India. Funds can be sent directly to the beneficiary organization or via a social impact fund. One philanthropist might give to a social cause and another to a university.

How, to whom, and in what manner we give is not important as long as we give to a cause that we care about and celebrate the joy of supporting.

There are hundreds of inspiring examples of diaspora giving. Here are nine distinct examples that highlight the diversity of alliances, new initiatives, opportunities, and success stories that showcase the trendsetting nature of Indian-American philanthropy today—and signal a very encouraging outlook for its impact going forward.

India Philanthropy Alliance (IPA): Uniting Nonprofits for Leverage

On October 2, 2019, the 150th anniversary of Mahatma Gandhi's birth, 11 nonprofit organizations in the US announced the formation of the India Philanthropy Alliance (IPA), a collaborative to further advance humanitarian and developmental goals in India through increased engagement. These philanthropic and charitable organizations mobilize people and funding in the US (and elsewhere) for development and poverty-reduction programs in India. Each of these organizations has a presence in the US for mainly donor cultivation, fundraising, and outreach, but their programs focus on India. The organizations that were part of IPA at the launch included Akanksha Fund, American India Foundation (AIF), Arogya World, CRY America, Dasra, Ekal USA, Foundation for Excellence (FFE), Indiaspora, Magic Bus USA, Pratham USA, and VisionSpring.

The IPA's mission is to enhance collaboration among organizations working to advance the development agenda in India. One of the key reasons to create IPA was that prior to forming the coalition, India-focused organizations operated in their own silos and did not share information on best practices or trends of diaspora giving. It felt like everyone was trying to get a slice of the giving pie and not work to grow the diaspora giving ecosystem in the US. The need though was to work together to foster a more robust and better-recognized culture of giving among Indian-Americans and, over time, increase the scale and impact of philanthropy benefiting India. This is precisely what IPA hopes to achieve in the coming months and years. The time is right for building a more robust culture of philanthropy among Indian-Americans and we are positive that efforts of the IPA will help accelerate social progress in India.

Since its launch, IPA has added two more organizations to the alliance and we expect this number to grow as more organizations find out about IPA's objective and impact. The 13 organizations currently part of the IPA collectively raise more than $135 million annually in philanthropic donations, including more than $60 million in the US. Their most generous donors are Indian-American entrepreneurs and professionals as well as companies doing business both in the US and in India. Together, these organizations have cumulatively impacted more than 70 million people with their evidence-based programs spanning education, health care, livelihood support, and other essential services. To help India meet its Sustainable Development Goal commitments, the organizations that are part of the alliance will work more closely together in their constituency-building efforts in the US and in their work in India.

ChaloGive: Crowdfunding for Smaller Donors

ChaloGive is an online giving campaign to provide the Indian diaspora living in the US a platform to come together and support a cause that they care about. Run during the week of Gandhi Jayanti from October 2-8, every year, ChaloGive is part of Indiaspora's philanthropy initiative to use crowdfunding and engage with the Indian diaspora looking for an opportunity to learn and support some of the best charitable organizations in India and their local community.

The focus is on participation by giving during the ChaloGive week—it does not matter how much is donated. The goal is for the community to come together during that week and celebrate the joy of giving by donating to an organization of their choice. The idea of ChaloGive is in some sense similar to Giving Tuesday in the US or Daan Utsav in India, because each of these events are looking to engage and empower the individual donor and create a movement that inspires social change through the joy of giving.

The initial success of the ChaloGive campaign is an encouraging sign for Indian nonprofits looking to fundraise online and connect with potential US donors. As nonprofits in India explore and expand online fundraising options, the Indian diaspora is a great pool to tap into because it is looking to engage and give back, has high disposable income, and has strong cultural and emotional ties to India. Many of these potential donors grew up in India, still have close family there, and often turn to the country for their charitable giving.

Also, a high percentage of Indian-Americans work for big tech companies, many of which encourage a strong giving culture among their employees with generous matching programs that can help further amplify the impact of their giving. Indian nonprofits, however, need to ensure that their online fundraising campaigns have clear and transparent goals, and provide a simple and compelling giving experience.

Nonprofits in India should be encouraged and excited because the next several years seem very promising for online giving from the US to India and this new stream of donors and funds can really help boost the scale of their programs, interventions, and impact.

Private Foundations: Achieving a Personal Mission

Private foundations established by successful and wealthy Indian-American leaders and families are emerging as a new force in diaspora philanthropy. In addition to providing personal fulfillment and deepening social consciousness, a private foundation allows the donor to really focus on a mission and cause that matters to the individual. The giving can be very strategic and targeted to advance the objectives defined by the foundation's goals, and this helps in being focused on specific giving areas and not being distracted by requests to give to other causes and entities.

The Wadhwani Foundation is a perfect example. Founded in 2000 by Silicon Valley entrepreneur Dr Romesh Wadhwani, the organization focuses on accelerating economic development in emerging economies by driving job creation through large-scale initiatives in entrepreneurship, small business growth, innovation, and skilling. The Wadhwani Foundation launched the Rs 200 crore ($26 million) Wadhwani Sahayata initiative in early 2020 to help distressed small and medium enterprises (SMEs) in India impacted by the economic crisis as a result of Covid-19 and to support the public health ecosystem by investing in technological innovation and skilling programs.

Deepak Chopra's AAM Foundation runs the Freedom Employability Academy (FEA) project that aims at improving the employability skills of youth from low-income backgrounds in India. The FEA runs an educational program for ages 15–27 and has educated over 100,000 students so far. The FEA curriculum has been developed after consulting with global experts and involves building English language skills, developing personal skills, and fostering a passion for learning.

There are several other examples of Indian-American leaders who are using their time, money, skills, and networks to create tremendous opportunity through their foundation's work.

Sunil Wadhwani's WISH Foundation seeks to improve the health of the poor in India and other developing countries by scaling up innovative approaches to health care, thereby building an equitable, innovation-led ecosystem that makes quality health care accessible to the poor.

Bharat Desai and Neerja Sethi's Desai Sethi Foundation is committed to building sustainable social enterprises to improve the lives of underserved individuals through education, entrepreneurship, and wellness.

Another example of a charitable foundation involved in innovative work at scale is the Vijay and Marie Goradia Foundation that is focused on improving health and educational outcomes in India.

As more diaspora members and their families become steeped in philanthropy and think about ways in which they can get more focused and strategic about their giving, we will start to see a rise in private foundations that will enable streamlining their personal goals and structure their giving.

Ecosystem Changemakers: Rewriting the Philanthropy Rulebook

When we think about the Indian-American diaspora in philanthropy, it is important to think not only about philanthropists and donors, but also about the entire philanthropy ecosystem. This includes nonprofit organizations, philanthropy partners and intermediary organizations, crowdfunding and fundraising platforms, social sector advisory and consulting firms, impact investing partners, and so on.

The Indian-American community is very well represented in leadership positions in these organizations. They are making an impact every day as they try to excel in their professional careers in philanthropy, whether it is working at a foundation, a nonprofit organization, in the field as an implementation partner, or a research and grant-making organization, and so forth.

Some examples of Indian-American changemakers include the following individuals. This is by no means a comprehensive list but just a handful of examples of diaspora leadership across different philanthropy roles:

- Ankur Vora: Chief strategy officer at the Bill and Melinda Gates Foundation, a leader focused on the foundation's overall strategic opportunities, risks, and trade-offs.
- Dr Rajiv Shah: President of The Rockefeller Foundation, a global institution with a mission to promote the well-being of humanity around the world.
- Dr Geetha Murali: Chief executive officer of Room to Read, an organization that seeks to transform the lives of millions of children in low-income communities by focusing on literacy and gender equality in education.
- Premal Shah: Cofounder of Kiva, an international nonprofit and crowdlending platform, founded in 2005 in San Francisco, with a mission to expand financial access to help underserved communities thrive.
- Sachi Shenoy: Cofounder and chief impact officer at Upaya Social Ventures, an organization that identifies, invests, and helps scale early-stage businesses with the greatest potential for job creation in the world's most vulnerable communities, thereby creating jobs that lift families out of extreme poverty.
- Sampriti Ganguli: Chief executive officer at Arabella Advisors, a certified B Corp founded to provide strategic guidance for effective philanthropy ensuring their clients increase their philanthropic impact.

These leaders are building great organizations and creating collaborative partnerships through their passion and professional contributions. Whether it is engaging with a new stream of potential donors, or providing tools or subject-matter expertise to help philanthropists make their giving more strategic, or thinking of new ways and models to help nonprofits scale, these changemakers are effectively growing the philanthropy landscape for all stakeholders.

Giving Pledge and LivingMyPromise: Recruiting the World's Wealthiest

The Giving Pledge is a commitment to philanthropy that requires the world's wealthiest individuals and families to commit to giving the majority of their wealth to philanthropy or charitable causes, either during their lifetimes or in their wills. This pledge was created in 2010 by Bill and Melinda Gates and Warren Buffett following a series of conversations with philanthropists around the world about how they could collectively set a new standard of generosity among the wealthiest of the global community.

Signatories fund a diverse range of issues, including poverty alleviation, refugee aid, disaster relief, global health, education, women empowerment, medical research, criminal justice reform, environmental sustainability, and arts and culture. Many Indian-American leaders and families have signed the pledge, including Romesh Wadhwani, Vinod and Neeru Khosla, Manoj Bhargava, and Aneel and Allison Bhusri.

There are several others who are also part of the Giving Pledge such as Azim Premji, Kiran Mazumdar-Shaw, Rohini and Nandan Nilekani from India, Drs BR and CR Shetty, Mohammed Dewji, Shamsheer and Shabeena Vayali, Sunny and Sherly Varkey, and PNC and Sobha Menon of the Sobha Group. Given the rising profiles of several Indian-Americans in the US across industries and professions, we expect The Giving Pledge to include more Indian-Americans in the coming years.

Like The Giving Pledge, LivingMyPromise is bringing a similar opportunity to upper- and middle-class Indians with a net worth of more than 1 crore rupees ($140,000) to come forward and promise to donate a minimum of half of their wealth to charity while they are alive or in their will. The goal is to create a community of like-minded individuals who would like to do more, and also inspire millions of others to "re-benchmark" their levels of giving.

LivingMyPromise is inspired by millions of people across all income levels who give generously, and often at a great personal sacrifice, to make the world better. The campaign aims at helping shift the social norms of philanthropy toward giving more, giving sooner, and giving smarter. It is not restricted to people living in India. Anyone of Indian origin who has a net worth of Rs 1 crore or more including all assets can sign up to LivingMyPromise irrespective of citizenship.

LivingMyPromise is working on engaging with the Indian-American community and we hope and expect it will get a lot more traction in the US in the coming years. We expect to see an increase in promises and participation for LivingMyPromise from the Indian-American diaspora.

Give Where You Live: Directing Aid to Local Communities

Increasingly, Indian-Americans want to contribute to their local communities to express gratitude for the support they've received near home. HungerMitao (Remove Hunger) is a striking example of how the Indian community in the US stepped up to give back locally. In the spirit of "give where you live", HungerMitao, a movement founded by Raj and Aradhana (Anna) Asava of Texas, focuses on raising awareness about hunger in the US, improving engagement, and channeling resources and contributions of Indian-Americans in the fight against hunger.

"Contributing toward unfulfilled needs in the community we live in is critical for us to properly integrate. That is exactly what HungerMitao set out to achieve," said Anna Asava.

The current Covid-19 pandemic has pushed an alarming number of families in the US into financial and food insecurity and placed a tremendous strain on the food banks across the country. In response, HungerMitao has enabled more than 15 million meals for Feeding America and its network of food banks.

"With over 53 million food-challenged people across the US, we are unifying the resources and efforts of the four million-strong Indian-American community to fight hunger, thereby affecting transformational change in our adopted land," added Raj Asava.

Higher Education: Giving to Universities

Donations to American universities grew by 6 percent to a record $43.6 billion in 2017, according to the Council for Aid to Education. More than $19 billion of these charitable funds were given by individuals. Indian-Americans are the most educated ethnic group in the US. As a community, Indian-Americans embody the ideal of hard work and have even been named the most entrepreneurial ethnic group in America.

Quality higher education is of extreme importance to Indian-Americans. In 2018, Indiaspora embarked to quantify that importance with the establishment of the Indiaspora Monitor of University Giving. The study aims at highlighting Indian-Americans' past philanthropic actions so that the group's commitment to higher education can become even stronger in the future.

The first release of data from the Indiaspora Monitor of University Giving found that Indian-Americans donated more than $1.2 billion to 37 American universities and colleges from 2000 to August 2018. Fifty different donors made the 68 donations that were analyzed. A total of 47 percent of the gifts in the database are from repeat donors who had also given $1 million or more to either the same or a different university. Clearly, the diaspora is supporting the educational institutions that gave them a leg-up in America.

Grammy-nominated artist Chandrika Tandon gave $100 million to New York University's engineering school. She remarked that the engineering school's "entrepreneurial spirit" made her want to donate, highlighting one of the values important to women of color striving for professional success in the US.

Response to Covid-19: Teaming Up for Greater Impact

There is nothing left unsaid about the Covid-19 pandemic's devastating impact on public health, the global economy, and the overall functioning of society. Over the course of this pandemic and lockdown, it has become increasingly clear that Covid-19 is a much larger humanitarian crisis than merely one of health, particularly in India. The need and urgency for support present a tremendous challenge as well as a huge opportunity for all of us who have the means to give back generously. To that end, we have come to witness remarkable support by the global Indian diaspora. One can argue that perhaps never before has there been such a coming together of this community.

Indiaspora recently released a report highlighting the diaspora's response to Covid-19 that identified around 60 nonprofit organizations who have repurposed or increased their efforts in response to the pandemic. The response has been across the board with efforts to help both in the US and in India. Actions taken range from providing meals, dry ration and hygiene kits, personal protective equipment (PPE) such as masks and gloves to both frontline health workers and individuals, e-learning platforms for kids, health care, and legal resources. Across India, endeavors by the diaspora have largely centered around helping migrant workers and day laborers.

ChaloGive, Indiaspora's annual online giving campaign discussed earlier in the chapter, raised close to $1.2 million and enabled over eight million meals in the US and in India earlier this year. The campaign focused on addressing food insecurity and supporting the most vulnerable communities in the US and in India. The campaign's goal of raising $1 million was achieved in just nine days, which confirms that the community was eager and looking for ways to give back.

With no clear end in sight, we know that the impact of this pandemic is going to be felt for several months, and even years, in personal and professional arenas and civil society in general. Progress made in the development sector over the past several years has suffered a huge setback, and has prompted leaders of the philanthropic ecosystem to come together and adopt strategies that call for extraordinary and urgent measures to address the ongoing crisis. The desperate need of the development community presents an incredible opportunity for bold and innovative philanthropy. As funders, we have an opportunity and responsibility to pause, reassess, and restructure ourselves in a way that allows us to be flexible in our support to the development sector.

While we acknowledge that we have a long way to go to reverse the devastating impact of the pandemic and that we must not let this momentum slow down, we must also acknowledge and celebrate the Indian diaspora banding together with such energy and intent to support Covid relief efforts in India and their local communities.

Diaspora in Need: Supporting the "Invisible Minority"

While Indian-Americans are often referred to as the most successful ethnic group in the US, a study by Devesh Kapur and Jashan Bajwa of Johns Hopkins University identified a small but expanding group of immigrants from India who are struggling in their adopted homeland.

An analysis of US Census data of 2018 found 6.5 percent of Indian-American households live below the poverty line that equates to more than a quarter-million members of the diaspora living in need. Many of these individuals are not citizens, making their challenges even more intense.

This presents an opportunity for diaspora philanthropy to work with nonprofit organizations to rally around impoverished Indian-Americans with localized support to help them get on their feet and on the road to success. We are beginning to see discussions in the philanthropy community around some potential options that could help Indian-Americans struggling with poverty. Some ideas and strategies include focusing on countries where poverty is most concentrated, or working with specific vulnerable communities such as children and victims of domestic violence.

Leading the Way

Philanthropy is changing.

Whether its donations target an Indian metropolis or a local American town, aim for financial or social impact, or build personal or networked relationships, the community is proving that they are able to tackle a diverse set of needs with a wide variety of approaches. And recent increases in intensity and giving prove that it is truly a transformative moment for Indian-American engagement.

We believe the diaspora has stepped forward to serve as the model for twenty-first-century philanthropic leadership.

All the Presidents' People: Trust in the Corridors of Power

Arun Kumar

Long before Joe Biden showed "the audacity", as Kamala Harris says, to select a woman—that too of Indian descent—as his vice president, successive tenants of the White House have looked at Indian-Americans to get things done. Biden's choice of the daughter of an Indian mother and a Jamaican father was indeed designed to woo four constituencies at once—blacks, browns, women, and immigrants—and change the very complexion of the 2020 US presidential race. But from Republican Ronald Reagan to Democrat Biden, US chief executives from either side of the political divide have offered top government jobs to Indian-Americans for their accomplishments and potential and not for the color of their skin or the country of their origin. Harris's historic selection as Biden's running mate, in fact, epitomizes why the Indian diaspora of four million people, constituting just one percent of America's population, has come to exercise an influence far beyond its numbers in the US polity.

The first black and Indian-American woman to rise to America's second-highest office has often recalled what her Chennai-born mother Shyamala

Gopalan told her growing up: "Don't sit around and complain about things, do something." That "is what drives Harris every single day", says her official biography. And that's also what drives a typical child of an Indian who has come to this land of opportunity chasing the American dream.

As Nikki Haley, the first Indian-American politician to get cabinet rank as US ambassador to the UN under Trump, says, "I think Indians are so good at everything they touch." Speaking at the annual summit of the US–India Strategic Partnership Forum in September 2020, she asked Indian-Americans to "brag about their achievements and not hide behind their traditional humility and shyness". Indian-Americans don't have to really brag now. Their accomplishments speak for themselves. They as a community are most affluent, most educated, most philanthropic, and least dependent on government aid, as Haley claims.

Obama Years

But it wasn't until the historic election of Democrat Barack Obama, son of a white mother and a Kenyan father, in 2008 that Indian-American professionals started finding their trusted place in the corridors of power. Seeking to nurture what he called "one of the defining partnerships of the twenty-first century", Obama first chose then Indian Prime Minister Manmohan Singh as the guest of honor at his first state dinner in 2009. He then placed many from the community, wrought in the mold of Singh—"a self-effacing technocrat", as he describes him in his memoir *A Promised Land*—in key positions to build a strategic relationship with India.

Obama picked Richard Rahul Verma, 52, a Canadian-born Indian-American lawyer to serve as America's man in New Delhi from 2014 to 2017, making him the first person of Indian descent to do so. Verma had earlier worked as assistant secretary of state for legislative affairs at the State Department from 2009 to 2011 under Obama's Secretary of State Hillary Clinton. Before that, he served as the senior national security advisor to then Senate Majority Leader Harry Reid from 2002 to 2007. Verma currently serves as vice chairman of The Asia Group, a strategy and capital advisory group based in Washington, DC. The youngest of five children, Verma, with degrees in law and industrial engineering began his career in the US Air Force as an air force judge advocate, serving on active duty from 1994 to 1998.

As his point of contact for India in Washington, Obama chose Nisha Desai Biswal, an immigrant from India, as assistant secretary of state for South and Central Asian affairs. The first South-Asian-American to hold the pivotal position from 2013 to 2017, she oversaw the US–India strategic partnership during a period of unprecedented cooperation, including the launch of an annual US–India Strategic & Commercial Dialogue (S&CD). With a BA in international relations from the University of Virginia, Biswal is currently the president of the US–India Business Council (USIBC) and senior vice president for South Asia at the US Chamber of Commerce.

Obama chose yet another Indian-American, Arun M Kumar, 68, to lead America's trade and investment promotion efforts as assistant secretary of commerce for global markets and director general of the US and Foreign Commercial Service (USFCS). Leading a team of 1,600 professionals in over 100 US cities and 78 world markets, Kumar played a key role in strengthening commercial ties between India and the US during his three-year tenure from 2014 to 2017. Working with then Commerce Secretary Penny Pritzker, he helped establish the US–India S&CD placing commerce and business at the center of the US–India relationship. A renewed US–India CEO Forum and the launch of the US–India Innovation Forum led to India–US engagement across a spectrum of activities from ease of doing business to US participation in the development of smart cities. Born in Kerala, Kumar came to the US in 1978 to earn an MBA at MIT. Chairman and CEO at KPMG India since February 2017, Kumar also founded and led the firm's US–India practice from 2007 to 2013.

Obama again chose physician and health economist Rajiv "Raj" Shah, 47, as the sixteenth administrator of the US Agency for International Development (USAID) in 2010. Before his five-year stint there, he worked for a year as chief scientist and undersecretary of agriculture for research, education, and economics. Son of immigrant parents from Gujarat, Shah holds degrees in health economics and medicine. As a graduate student, he created Project Impact for South-Asian-Americans, a nonprofit organization through which he raised small dollar donations for his new community service organization. Shah came to government service from the Bill and Melinda

Gates Foundation where he served in a range of leadership roles, including director of agricultural development, director of strategic opportunities and chief economist. He currently serves as the president of the Rockefeller Foundation.

Trump Times

If Obama appointed the largest number of Indian-Americans in his administration, his Republican successor Donald Trump was the first to give a cabinet position to a person of Indian descent, Nikki Haley, as US ambassador to the UN. Born Nimrata 'Nikki' Randhawa to an immigrant Punjabi Sikh family from Amritsar, Haley too has many firsts to her credit. She was the first female governor of South Carolina (2011–2017), the first Asian-American female governor, the youngest governor in the US and the second governor of Indian descent after Bobby Jindal of Louisiana. First elected to the South Carolina House of Representatives in 2004, she served three terms. In 2010, during her third term, she was elected governor of South Carolina and reelected in 2014. Confirmed by the US Senate in a 96-to-4 vote as ambassador to the UN, she stepped down on December 31, 2018 amid reports that she was eyeing a presidential run in 2024.

Trump chose another Indian-American health policy consultant, Seema Verma, 50, as administrator of the Centers for Medicare & Medicaid Services. She is the founder and previous CEO of SVC Inc, a health policy consulting firm, which has worked with state insurance agencies and public health agencies in preparation for the implementation of Obama's signature Affordable Care Act.

Verma has a bachelor's degree in life sciences and a master's in public health from the Johns Hopkins School of Public Health.

To head the US Federal Communications Commission (FCC), Trump tapped Ajit Varadaraj Pai, 47, making him the first Indian-American to hold that office. Born to Indian immigrant parents, Pai studied social studies at Harvard University before earning a law degree from Chicago Law School. Joining the FCC as a lawyer in its Office of General Counsel in 2007, he was nominated to be a commissioner in 2011 by Obama on the recommendation of Republican Senate Majority Leader Mitch McConnell. A proponent of repealing net neutrality in the US, he voted with the majority of the FCC in December 2017 to reverse the decision to regulate the internet under Title II of the Communications Act of 1934. Pai has announced his plans to leave the FCC on January 20, 2021, when Biden becomes president, over one-and-a-half years before the expiry of his term.

To lead the National Science Foundation, the foremost US agency supporting fundamental research and education, Trump chose Indian-American engineer-scientist Dr Sethuraman Panchanathan. A graduate of the Indian Institute of Science (1984) and IIT (1986), Panchanathan was the second Indian-American to head the prestigious 70-year-old foundation. Another Chennai-born IITian, Dr Subra Suresh was nominated to the post with a six-year term by Obama in 2010, but left after three years. With a budget of nearly $8 billion, the NSF is said to fund approximately 24 percent of all federally supported basic research conducted by the US colleges and universities. A physics undergrad of Chennai University's Vivekananda College, Panchanathan is a fellow of a host of prestigious scientific bodies including the National Association of Inventors. He is also the founder of the Center for Cognitive Ubiquitous Computing (CUbiC) for designing technologies and devices to help people with disabilities ranging from impaired vision to stroke and autism.

Leading the transition to Biden at the Pentagon is Indian-American Kashyap 'Kash' Patel, a Trump loyalist who was installed there after Trump fired Defense Secretary Mark Esper days after losing the November 3 presidential election. Patel, a senior director of counterterrorism at the National Security Council, was named chief of staff to acting Defense Secretary Chris Miller after the incumbent quit following Esper's firing. Patel previously worked for Devin Nunes, the top Republican on the House Intelligence Committee, and as a staffer played a key role in helping Republicans discredit the Russia probe. He was one of the authors of the so-called Nunes Memo that accused the Federal Bureau of Investigation (FBI) and Justice Department of bias against Trump. Hailing from Gujarat, Patel's parents immigrated to the US from East Africa by way of Canada during the 1970s. A law graduate, he worked in Miami as a federal public defender before joining the Justice Department in 2014.

Biden–Harris Transition

With polls predicting their victory for months, the Biden–Harris team had been preparing to "hit the ground running from day one". Given his 47 years in public life, eight of them as Obama's vice president, Biden was quick to assemble his transition team. Drawing upon Obama's talent pool of Indian-Americans, he named as many as 20 of them to his transition's agency review teams, including three as leaders, to start what some critics have called "Obama's third term".

Later "building an administration that looks like America"—the most diverse in US history—Biden picked "smart as hell" Neera Tanden, a controversial but inspiring choice to head the powerful White House Office of Management and Budget. If confirmed by the Senate, Tanden, 50, who currently heads left-leaning think tank Center for American Progress, would be the first Indian-American cabinet member in a Democratic administration. Like Harris, Tanden, a controversial close confidante of the Clintons, credits her rise to her India-born single mother, who kept the family afloat using food stamps to eat and housing subsidy vouchers to pay rent. "I'm here today thanks to my mother's grit, but also thanks to a country that had faith in us, that invested in her humanity, and in our dreams," she said on her nomination recalling the family's struggle after her parents divorced when she was five. Now, it's her turn "to help shape those budgets and programs to keep lifting Americans up, to pull families back from the brink", said Tanden. "To give everybody the fair chance my mother got, and that everyone deserves."

Introducing Tanden as a "a brilliant policy mind with critical practical experience across government", Biden noted, "She will be in charge of laying out my budget that will help us control the virus, deal with the economic crisis, and build back better." Tanden currently serves on the New Jersey Restart and Recovery Commission, and previously served as senior advisor for health reform at the US Department of Health and Human Services developing policies and provisions of Obama's signature Affordable Care Act.

A science graduate with a law degree from Yale Law School, Tanden also worked as director of domestic policy for the first Obama–Biden presidential campaign, and in a variety of other roles in the government and on the campaign trail. Tanden, who also worked on Hillary Clinton's 2016 presidential campaign, courted controversy over her critical tweets about the Republican leadership, including one referring to Senate Majority Leader Mitch McConnell as "Moscow Mitch".

Biden tapped Vivek Murthy, "a son of Indian immigrants, who raised their children to always believe in the promise of America", to "help restore faith in this country as a place of possibilities". Murthy, 43, who served as "America's Doctor", as the surgeon general is called, under Obama, missed getting a cabinet position by a whisker, due to perceived lack of experience running a large government department. After toying with the idea of making him health secretary, Biden gave Murthy his old job back—but with expanded responsibilities—to "be a key public voice on our Covid response, to restore public trust and faith in science and medicine."

Describing himself as the "grandson of a poor farmer in India", Murthy vowed to bring to his expanded role an approach learnt at his immigrant parents' clinic decades ago. "As a child, I saw how they took the time not just to diagnose illnesses, but to ask about their patients' families and lives, happily poring over photos of children and grandchildren taken from wallets, listening deeply to people's stories and struggles, often running well over the appointment time," Murthy recalled. "That is the kind of doctor I have always tried to be," he said vowing to take the same approach as "America's doctor".

Biden, who in his very first picks had made Murthy one of three co-chairs of his Covid task force, lavished high praise on his nominee calling him "a trusted national leader on health care". "During his tenure, he took on some of the most pressing public health issues we face—from the opioid crisis to threats to America's mental health," he recalled.

Born in Huddersfield, Yorkshire, to immigrants from Karnataka, India, Murthy's family moved to the US in 1978 when he was one-year-old. Raised in Miami, Murthy has a BA from Harvard and MBA and MD degrees from Yale. While a Harvard freshman in 1995, Murthy co-founded VISIONS Worldwide, which he led for eight years. The nonprofit organization focused on HIV/AIDS education in the US and India. In 1997, he co-founded the Swasthya Community Health Partnership to train women as community health workers in rural India. He also founded TrialNetworks, a technology company dedicated to improving collaboration and efficiency in clinical trials and Doctors for America, a nonprofit mobilizing physicians and medical students to improve access to affordable care.

Joining Murthy as members on transition's Covid advisory board were two other Indian Americans—Atul Gawande, a surgeon and author, and Dr Celine Gounder, 43, an infectious diseases specialist at New York University's Grossman School of Medicine.

Another Indian who missed out on a cabinet position was Professor Arun Majumdar, director of the Precourt Institute of Energy at Stanford University. Currently heading Biden's transition team for Department of Energy, he was widely tipped for the post of energy secretary. A mechanical engineering graduate from IIT, Bombay, Majumdar did a three-year stint at the energy department under Obama, including 15 months as the acting under secretary of energy. Named as the first director of the Advanced Research Projects Agency-Energy (ARPA-E), he helped make the laboratory for cutting-edge research in the field of energy a model of excellence and innovation. Before joining Stanford, Majumdar was the vice president for energy at Google, where he created several energy technology initiatives, especially at the intersection of data, computing, and electricity grid. A member of a number of prestigious academies, including National Academy of Sciences, Majumdar came to the US in 1985 to earn a doctorate at the University of California, Berkeley.

By January 20 inauguration day, Biden had named nearly two dozen Indian-Americans for key jobs in his administration, including 13 women, two of them from Kashmir, the largest number of desis to be roped in ever during transition. It was in keeping with his promise made during a virtual celebration of India's August 15 Independence Day to "continue to rely on Indian-American diaspora, that keeps our two nations together, as I have throughout my career".

The appointees included veteran diplomat Uzra Zeya, who quit her State Department job in 2018 denouncing Trump administration's alleged racial and sexist bias, as undersecretary for civilian security, democracy, and human rights, Wharton-trained strong consumer advocate Rohit Chopra, as director of the Consumer Financial Protection Bureau and Vinay Reddy, second of three sons of Indian-American parents, to translate his vision into words.

An alumnus of Miami University and the Ohio State University College of Law, Reddy had also worked as deputy speechwriter for the Obama reelection campaign in 2012. After leaving the White House, he worked as vice president of strategic communications for the NBA. Reddy studied in Ohio's public schools from kindergarten through law school.

To help restore "faith in government by speaking honestly and directly to the American people", as Biden put it, he included Gujarat-born Vedant Patel in his White House communications team as assistant press secretary. Currently senior spokesperson of the Biden inaugural, he was a part of the Biden campaign as regional communications director. A graduate of the University of Califonia-Riverside and the University of Florida, he has previously also worked as communications director to Indian-American House member Pramila Jayapal. "I took the leap with Joe Biden when he announced because I believed in his vision for what this country could be," tweeted Patel, "so honored to be part of this team…."

To "help connect the White House to the American people in new and innovative ways", Biden and Harris included Kashmir-born Aisha Shah as partnerships manager in the White House Office of Digital Strategy. An advancement specialist for the Smithsonian Institution, she served as a digital partnerships manager on the Biden–Harris campaign. Previously, she worked as an assistant manager on the corporate fund of the John F Kennedy Center for the Performing Arts and as a strategic communications specialist at Buoy, an integrated marketing firm that specializes in social impact communications.

To help "lift all Americans out of current economic crisis—and build a strong, inclusive, and more resilient economy for the future", Biden included Harvard and Yale graduate Bharat Ramamurti in his economic team. Born in Massachusetts, Ramamurti will serve as deputy director for financial reform and consumer protection, on the National Economic Council (NEC). Managing director of the corporate power program at the Roosevelt Institute, Ramamurti also served as a top economic advisor to Senator Elizabeth Warren's 2020 presidential campaign. "We have much to do to get through this crisis and create a stronger and fairer economy—and I'm excited to get to work alongside this great team," he tweeted.

Again "building an administration that looks like America", Biden named Gautam Raghavan, an openly gay trailblazing Indian-American as deputy director of the office of presidential personnel. India-born Raghavan has served in multiple positions at the White House and on Capitol Hill in the past decade. Before joining the Biden transition last year, he served as chief of staff to Jayapal. Previously, Raghavan served as an advisor to the Biden Foundation, and as vice president of policy for the Gill Foundation, one of the oldest and largest private foundations dedicated to the cause of LGBTQ equality. During the Obama–Biden administration, Raghavan served in the White House as the liaison to the LGBTQ community as well as the Asian American and Pacific Islander community. He also served in the White House Liaison Office for the US Department of Defense and as outreach lead for the Pentagon's "Don't Ask, Don't Tell" working group. A Stanford University graduate, he lives in Washington, DC, with his husband and their daughter.

In one of his first White House appointments, Biden named Indian-American Mala Adiga, whose family emigrated from India's Karnataka state, as policy director to First Lady Jill Biden. A graduate of Grinnell College, the University of Minnesota School of Public Health, and the University of Chicago Law School, Adiga served as a senior advisor to Jill Biden and a senior policy advisor on the Biden–Harris campaign.

To lead the transition's Office of National Drug Policy team, Biden chose Rahul Gupta, who had gained national recognition for his work as public health commissioner for West Virginia leading the state's opioid crisis response since 2015. Son of an Indian diplomat, India-born Gupta also launched a number of pioneering public health initiatives, such as the Birthscore program to identify high-risk infants, in the state. Currently working at March of Dimes, a leading mom and baby health firm, Gupta is also adjunct professor in the Department of Health Policy, Management and Leadership in the School of Public Health at West Virginia University.

Leading the Office of Personnel Management team is Kiran Ahuja, CEO of Philanthropy Northwest, who had served as the chief of staff to the director in the agency from 2015 to 2017. India-born Ahuja assumed that position after serving for six years as the director of the White House Initiative on

Asian Americans and Pacific Islanders. She has also been a lawyer with the US Department of Justice and a founding director of the National Asian Pacific American Women's Forum. Ahuja currently serves on the board of directors for Asian Americans/Pacific Islanders in Philanthropy (AAPIP), the United Philanthropy Forum and the Wing Luke Museum.

Biden and Harris also named Indian-American Maju Varghese as executive director of their Presidential Inaugural Committee to plan the festivities surrounding their swearing in on January 20. A lawyer by training, Varghese, the son of immigrant parents from Thiruvalla, Kerala, had also steered the Biden–Harris campaign. Earlier, as Obama's special assistant he had organized the president's January 2015 historic trip to India to be the chief guest at the annual Republic Day parade.

The Pioneers

But desis, as South Asians in America call themselves, were not on the radar of White House before the eighties. By then, many Indian professionals coming from IITs and other prestigious Indian institutions had gradually established themselves after changes in immigration laws in 1965 opened doors to them.

It was only in August 1986 during the presidency of Republican Ronald Reagan that Dr Jan Pillai, a professor of law at Temple University, became the first person of Indian origin to get a senior-level job in the federal government. Founder and honorary chairman of the National Association of Americans of Asian Indian Descent (NAAAID), Pillai was appointed acting director for regulatory analysis at the Federal Energy Regulatory Commission (FERC).

It was "the first major appointment for the Asian-Indian community to the senior levels of the federal government", as then Republican Senator Bob Dole noted in a press release. "The administration and FERC made the right choice in recognizing Jan. He will bring credibility, initiative, and a high level of professionalism to the FERC office," stated Dole, who ten years later lost the presidential race to Bill Clinton.

A year later, Reagan appointed Dr Joy Cherian as commissioner of Equal Employment Opportunity Council (EEOC), recalls Dr Thomas Abraham, founder president and current chairman of the Global Organization of People of Indian Origin (GOPIO). In terms of political appointment, this was the first major sub-cabinet-level appointment on a federal level, he says, noting Dr Cherian went on to serve under three presidents—Reagan, George HW Bush, and Bill Clinton.

As commissioner, Dr Cherian was able to sensitize discrimination based on national origin to other commissioners, says Abraham.

Finally, EEOC included discrimination under national origin in the employment area as a cause for relief along with other causes for discrimination, he noted calling it a "major contribution" of the Indian-American community in the domestic American policy.

Two other appointments under Reagan's successor, George Bush Sr, were Bharat Bhargava as assistant director of Minority Business Development Authority (MBDA), and Dr Sambu Banik as executive director for the Presidential Commission on Mental Retardation.

Clinton Era

Although Democrat Bill Clinton imposed economic sanctions on India after India's peaceful nuclear explosion at Pokhran in May 1998, relations between the two were on the mend again with Clinton's March 2000 visit to India. The Clintons also cultivated many well-heeled members of the Indian community, so much so that during the 2016 Democratic Party presidential primaries, Obama's campaign took a jab at his rival Hillary Clinton, calling her the Democratic senator from Punjab.

But there were only a handful of Indian-American appointees in the Clinton administration, old-timers recall. One of his first appointments was that of Dr Arati Prabhakar as director of the National Institute of Standards and Technology (NIST). The first woman to head NIST, she held that position from 1993 to 1997. In 2012, Obama named her as the head of DARPA, the US Defense Advanced Research Projects Agency, a position she held until Trump took over on January 20, 2017. Prabhakar, whose family immigrated to the US from New Delhi when she was three, became the first woman to earn a PhD in applied physics from the California Institute of Technology (Caltech) in 1984.

Another Clinton appointee was Neil Dhillon, who was nominated deputy assistant secretary of government affairs at the Department of Transportation in 1993. Clinton later officially recognized him as the top Asian-American appointee in a White House ceremony. He also named Dr Rajen Anand as deputy director of the Center for Nutrition Policy and Promotion (CNPP) at the US Department of Agriculture in 1995. Promoted to executive director in 1997, he held that position until 2001. In 2009, Obama renamed Anand as head of the agency with a mission to improve the nutritional status of all Americans by linking research to the dietary needs of the consumer. Under his leadership, the CNPP released the 1995 and 2000 editions of Dietary Guidelines for Americans, produced a new Thrifty Food Plan, which sets the cash allotment for food stamp recipients, and developed a Healthy Eating Index. With doctorates in human physiology, nutrition, biochemistry, and veterinary medicine, Anand was a professor of physiology for 30 years, including six years as department chair, at California State University, Long Beach.

Bush Age

Indian-American journalist Fareed Zakaria, in his book *The Post-American World*, has described Republican George W Bush Jr as "the most pro-Indian president in American history". Indeed, during his eight-year tenure, India–US relations blossomed with the 2008 landmark India–US civil nuclear deal reversing three decades of American nonproliferation policy being the high point of their strategic partnership.

Bush tapped Mumbai-born, India-educated scholar Ashley J Tellis to provide expert advice in negotiating the nuclear deal as senior advisor to the undersecretary of state for political affairs. Before that, Tellis, who was senior policy analyst at the RAND Corporation and professor of policy analysis at the RAND Graduate School, was commissioned into the foreign service to serve as senior advisor to the US ambassador in New Delhi. Tellis, with BA and MA degrees in economics from Bombay University and an MS and PhD in political science from Chicago University, also served on the National Security Council staff as special assistant to Bush and senior director for strategic planning and Southwest Asia. He currently holds the Tata Chair for Strategic Affairs and is a senior fellow at the Carnegie Endowment for International Peace.

Bush also named a few other Indian-Americans to key roles starting with a young 30-year-old Rhodes scholar, Piyush "Bobby" Jindal, as assistant secretary of health and human services for planning and evaluation in March 2001. But a very ambitious Jindal, now 49, after serving as the principal policy advisor to the secretary of health and human services for less than two years, returned to Louisiana to run for governor in 2003. He narrowly lost the 2003 race, but won in 2007 and was reelected in 2011 in a landslide, winning more than 65 percent of the vote. Jindal was the first Indian-American governor, and the only one until Nikki Haley was elected governor of South Carolina in 2010. He also made an unsuccessful bid for the Republican nomination in the 2016 presidential election.

In 2004, he was elected to the US House of Representatives, becoming the second Indian-American in Congress. He was reelected in 2006. To date, he is the only Indian-American Republican lawmaker. Earlier, in 1995, Jindal was appointed secretary of the Louisiana Department of Health and Hospitals. Four years later, at the age of 28, he became the youngest president of the University of Louisiana System. Son of Punjabi parents, who immigrated to the US in 1971, six months before his birth, Jindal graduated from Brown University in 1992 at the age of 20, with honors in biology and public policy.

During the 2007–2008 financial crisis, Bush gave Neel Tushar Kashkari, 47, the key responsibility of overseeing the Troubled Asset Relief Program (TARP) as interim assistant secretary of the treasury for financial stability from October 2008 to May 2009. A Wharton School graduate, Kashkari worked initially as an aerospace engineer before becoming an investment banker, covering the information technology security sector for Goldman Sachs. A Republican, Kashkari unsuccessfully ran for governor of California in 2014. He became president of the Minneapolis Federal Reserve in November 2015, succeeding Narayana Kocherlakota.

Washington-born attorney Karan Krishna Bhatia, whose family hails from Uttar Pradesh, served for six years in the Bush administration, including as deputy US trade representative from 2005 to 2007. Earlier, he worked as assistant secretary of transportation for aviation and international affairs from 2003 to 2005 and deputy undersecretary of commerce for industry and security from 2001 to 2003. Bhatia returned to the private sector in 2008 to lead government affairs for General Electric. He currently leads global public policy and government relations for Google.

Another Bush appointee was Gopal Khanna, who in 2002 became the chief technology officer of Peace Corps. With a BA from Christ Church College, Kanpur, India, Khanna was president and CEO of ITC, a Minneapolis-based technology solutions firm, before his appointment to the Peace Corps.

What the Future Holds

Indian-Americans have come a long way from those early days when, as GOPIO's Abraham points out, most political appointments were through individual contacts with community organizations doing little in "promoting our candidates". But Kamala Harris's nomination and subsequent victory has brought about a tectonic shift in America's political landscape spurring organizations like US–India Political Action Committee (USINPAC) and IMPACT into action. USINPAC has set up a website to help "the best and the brightest from our community", as Chairman Sanjay Puri put it, get into the new Biden–Harris administration with about 4,000 positions to fill.

IMPACT, which raised a 10-million-dollar war chest for 2020 elections, has compiled a "Brown Book 2.0" with over 350 resumes of desis with qualifications ranging from master's to doctorates, including 77 with more than 10 years of experience in government.

But longstanding Washington watchers also discern a dramatic change in Indian-American aspirants to public office coming as they do in many shades. There are some like Jindal, who since childhood has chosen to be called "Bobby", after a character in *The Brady Bunch*. He is seen by many "as a man who has spent a lifetime distancing himself from his Indian roots", as the *Washington Post* wrote in a June 2015 article. Then there are those like Nikki Haley who are proud of their Indian heritage and want to "carry the legacy of their parents' generation forward" by going out to "share what we know we can be good at—from business to education to health care, and everything in between". Yet others like Harris are somewhat ambivalent about their Indianness. To be sure, she credits her India-born mother for her rise all the time, but apparently finds it more politically expedient to project her black or, sometimes, the larger South Asian identity. And then there are many like Neera Tanden, who have made it through sheer grit and determination surviving a tough childhood on food stamps and government housing subsidy. But they all have one thing in common—a laser-focused ambition to "do something" like Harris—coupled with education, hard work, and an unshakable faith that "you can be anything in America," as Jindal's parents told him.

Shedding traditional shyness and humility, the Indian-American has emerged from the shadows to take the centerstage in public life. And with Kamala Harris smashing the glass ceiling, sky is the limit!

At the Center of Excellence: Seminal Contributions in the World of Science

Mayank Chhaya

Indian-Americans have been at the center of America's globally consequential pursuit of excellence in science and technology for so long that they have now become a cliché in the best possible sense of the word.

The stereotype of Indian-Americans choosing the career paths of just being doctors and engineers has long been proved overblown. In the past couple of decades, they have expanded their footprint far beyond traditional career choices. The dominance of Indian-Americans in Silicon Valley, both as inventors and entrepreneurs, has been well recorded and applauded. But it is in serious and substantive scientific pursuits that they have been making seminal contributions to America, which continues to be the preeminent scientific power even as China is knocking at the door.

"We have a tremendous Indian population in the United States and many of the people you are talking about are working on the vaccine too," Trump said in May 2020 in reference to a question about many Indian-Americans working on the development of the vaccine and in the battle against the coronavirus.

"Great scientists and researchers," he said in reference to the scientific and research talent of the Indian-American community, many of whom are engaged in cutting-edge research in the medical sciences, biopharma start-ups, research institutions, and universities.

From pioneering the theory of loop quantum gravity to engineering oil-eating bacteria, from monitoring a rover on Mars to interpreting the genetic code and its function in protein synthesis, Indian-American scientists have for decades straddled an astonishing range of breakthroughs in pure and applied sciences.

Three Nobel Prize Winners

It is a measure of their standing in their chosen fields that at least three of Indian-American scientists are Nobel Prize winners in physics, chemistry, and medicine, and several others with major honors attached to their names.

The tallest of all, arguably, was the late Dr Subrahmanyan Chandrasekhar, the 1983 winner of the Nobel Prize for Physics—shared with Dr William Fowler—"for his theoretical studies of the physical processes of importance to the structure and evolution of the stars". Chandra, as he was popularly known, was recognized for his work in what the Nobel Prize committee described thus: "Stars in the universe form from clouds of gas and dust. When these clouds are pulled together by gravitational force, energy is released in the form of heat. And when a high enough temperature is reached, reactions among the atomic nuclei in the star's interior begin. Beginning in the 1930s, Subrahmanyan Chandrasekhar formulated theories for the development that stars subsequently undergo. He showed that when the hydrogen fuel of stars of a certain size begins to run out, it collapses into a compact, brilliant star known as a white dwarf."

According to the Nobel citation, he was recognized for his work in the 1950s that "showed how these nuclear reactions also account for how various elements are formed. These processes have created the elements that make up our earth and other heavenly bodies in the universe".

Chandra happened to be a nephew of the celebrated Nobel Prize-winning Indian physicist Chandrasekhara Venkata Raman (CV Raman), who was awarded the Nobel Prize for Physics in 1930. Raman was awarded for his groundbreaking work in the field of light scattering. The phenomenon was subsequently called Raman Scattering. The year Raman won the Nobel, his nephew Chandra finished his Bachelor of Science in physics at Presidency College, Chennai. A month later, he was granted a government of India scholarship to study at Cambridge, England. On his way by ship, he made some calculations about what is known as the "white dwarf", stars which have burned up their fuel. Scientists of the time had assumed that when a star burned all its fuel, it would go cold and become a "white dwarf" star. However, Chandra's calculations revealed something extraordinary. His calculations showed that a "white dwarf" that was much heavier than the Sun could undergo an eternal collapse.

This is how Chandra recalled the beginning of his life in America in his Nobel Prize biography, "I took my PhD degree at Cambridge in the summer of 1933. In the following October, I was elected to a prize fellowship at Trinity College for the period 1933-37. During my fellowship years at Trinity, I formed lasting friendships with several, including Sir Arthur Eddington and Professor EA Milne.

While on a short visit to Harvard University (in Cambridge, Massachusetts), at the invitation of the then Director Dr Harlow Shapley, during the winter months (January-March) of 1936, I was offered a position as a research associate at the University of Chicago by Dr Otto Struve and President Robert Maynard Hutchins. I joined the faculty of the University of Chicago in January 1937. And I have remained at this university ever since."

His association with Chicago and the University of Chicago remained until his death on August 21, 1995, spending nearly six decades of exceptionally productive and diverse work in various branches of physics.

Notwithstanding Dr Chandrasekhar's standing as one of the foremost physicists/scientists of the twentieth century, another brilliant mind from India won a Nobel Prize a decade and half before he did. It was Dr Har Gobind Khorana, who won the Nobel Prize in Physiology or Medicine in

1968 jointly with Robert W Holley and Marshall W Nirenberg "for their interpretation of the genetic code and its function in protein synthesis".

Twelve years younger than Chandra, Khorana was born on January 9, 1922 in Raipur in what is now Pakistan in a poor family. His early university education was at the University of Punjab in Lahore. Dr Khorana also received a government of India fellowship which made it possible for him to travel to England and study for a PhD degree at the University of Liverpool.

After some job- and country-hopping, which first took him to Vancouver, Canada, then back to India for a while, he eventually came to America in 1960 when he joined the Institute for Enzyme Research at the University of Wisconsin. By the time he arrived in America, his interest in both proteins and nucleic acids at that time had already struck roots for about a decade, and that work led him to win the Nobel Prize.

Dr Khorana's work in the 1970s beyond the Nobel Prize was wide-ranging, including synthesizing the first artificial copy of a yeast gene and mutations in a particular protein that lead to night blindness.

The third Nobel Prize winner from the community is of a relatively recent vintage in 2009 when Dr Venkatraman Ramakrishnan was awarded jointly along with Thomas A Steitz and Ada E Yonath "for studies of the structure and function of the ribosome".

Dr Ramakrishnan divides his time between the United Kingdom and the United States. His has been an interesting disciplinary shift from being a physicist to a biologist to a chemist.

Dr Ramakrishnan's early interest was in mathematics and physics but he said he recognized that he perhaps did not have it in him to become a top-tier mathematician or a physicist. After his graduation from the Ohio University as a 19-year-old, he shifted his focus to biology and went to the University of California in San Diego.

"Making a fundamental breakthrough in physics is very difficult. Back in the mid-1970s, there were really no major conceptual advances. Meanwhile, every issue of the *Scientific American* that I read had a report about some major breakthrough in biology," he said during a lecture at the Tata Institute of Fundamental Research in Mumbai in January, 2020. Even though he considers himself "a failed physician", his change of discipline to molecular biology and chemistry paid off eventually winning him the Nobel Prize.

In Contention for Nobel

While there are those like Dr Ramakrishnan who believe that physics has hit a sort of a dead-end in the past few decades, there are also those who have pursued new fundamental areas with extraordinary passion. One physicist whose name stands out and is often considered to be in the contention for a Nobel Prize is that of Dr Abhay Ashtekar, a theoretical physicist and the 2018 winner of the prestigious Einstein Prize given by the American Physical Society (APS).

Over four decades after he began his scientific engagement with gravitational science, Professor Ashtekar was honored by the APS "for numerous and seminal contributions to general relativity, including the theory of black holes, canonical quantum gravity, and quantum cosmology".

Ashtekar is currently professor of physics, Evan Pugh Professor, holder, Eberly Chair, and director of the Institute for Gravitation and the Cosmos at Pennsylvania State University.

It is a measure of Dr Ashtekar's standing that Sir Roger Penrose, regarded as one of the foremost physicists of our time and the winner of the 2020 Nobel Prize in Physics at the age of 89, has described the Indian-American scientist's work in loop quantum gravity in his bestseller *The Road to Reality* thus: "I must say that both the Ashtekar variables and the later description in terms of loop variables strike to me as powerful and highly original developments in the quest of quantum theory of gravity.... In fact I have little hesitation to say that these developments are the most important ones in the canonical approach to quantum gravity that started roughly half a century ago by (Paul) Dirac and others." Elsewhere, he has called loop quantum gravity the most promising approach he has seen to quantum gravity.

Dr Ashtekar developed a passion for physical sciences while he was in high school in India. "At first, I knew only Marathi literature, my mother tongue, and was the medium of instruction until I was 11. Then I was exposed to Hindi and English literature and realized how deeply literature is tied to specific cultures. What is considered great in one language or context could well be mediocre in another. At the same time, I learned Newton's laws and universality of gravity—what makes the apple fall on earth also makes the planets go around the sun. This was stunning by itself," he said.

What he found most remarkable was that, unlike art and literature, which are "so tied to human conditions", Newton's laws transcend both. "It was striking to me that the same Newton's laws are taught and admired in India as in China, Japan, and the West."

After receiving his PhD in 1974 from the University of Chicago, Ashtekar went on to hold influential positions in France, Canada, and India. His biography on the National Academy of Sciences, to which he was elected a member in 2016, describes him as someone "best known for initiating the Loop Quantum Gravity program by introducing new variables to simplify Einstein's equations, for analyzing the very early universe using Loop Quantum Cosmology, and for his contributions to the study of the asymptotic structure of space-time and gravitational waves in full non-linear general relativity".

Asked whether physicists in India are producing world-class research, Ashtekar said, "There are extremely talented physicists in India who are making first-rate contributions to pure physics in areas I have first-hand acquaintance with. I am particularly pleased by the 'LIGO-India' project that is now placing India firmly in the front ranks of international efforts. The Inter University Centre for Astronomy and Astrophysics in Pune, in particular, will play an important role in the major discoveries that will be made with the international network of gravitational wave observatories between five and ten years from now. In this area India is ahead of China, for example.

"My colleagues in other areas of physics, on the other hand, tell me that this is not the case in their field; that there is a lot of good research but not enough 'great' research that gets published in the most visible journals," he said.

One of the fundamental questions at the heart of physics has been the near fetish-like fixation among the scientific community to unify quantum mechanics and general relativity. The question that is not asked nearly enough is—why can't something of the scale of the universe have several operating systems as it were?

Dr Ashtekar's answer was typical of a rational, open-minded physicist. "I think that's quite possible but so far one is driven by the success of what one has had before. We had no reason, for instance, to believe that the apple falling on the earth follows the same law as the moon going around the earth and the earth going around the sun, so on and so forth. One could have just said well, that's just a different phenomenon. So why can't we just live with it? But we have been extremely successful so far that there is one unified description of nature and various things are part of it. That happened when general relativity was born a little over a hundred years ago. Newton's theory was toppled, and our notions about space and time changed completely but it is not as if we just discarded what we had. We just expanded our horizon to encompass more phenomena. So it is not that general relativity is valid for black holes but is not valid on earth. The apple falling on earth is also following the same law as the black holes are following. The same thing is true of quantum mechanics. So the point is that so far there is a strong indication, there is a flow of logic and argument that says that there are fundamental laws and every time we find them we broaden our scope. It is not that there is some law somewhere and some other law somewhere else. And that is what is really driving this, it is this experience that is driving this great search but as you said it could be."

The Superbug Superhero

From loop quantum gravity to oil-eating bacteria is quite a leap but Indian-American scientists have taken that as well. Among those pursuing this field, perhaps the most notable has been the late Professor Ananda Mohan Chakrabarty, known as the "superbug superhero".

During the many interactions that I had with him, Dr Chakrabarty was always passionate about the need to seek new frontiers constantly. "Science is about never sitting idle because it is just a never-ending quest," he would say. For him that quest began in 1971 while working at the General Electric Research and Development Center. Working on a method of genetic cross-linking, he ended up with a way to transfer genes that would help degrade oil; hence the name "oil-eating bacteria".

What was extraordinary about this particular bacterium was that it was capable of eating up two-thirds of hydrocarbons found in a typical oil spill at a much faster rate, about one or two orders of magnitudes, than previously existing strains of oil-eating microbes. In a sense, Dr Chakrabarty's bacteria used fuel oil as their nutrient.

"This was to me applied science at its best. I understood the implications quickly but then it was a long legal fight," he said.

The long legal fight that he referred to, in fact, became a very significant precedent in America. As described by the University of Illinois, Chicago (UIC), where he was emeritus distinguished professor of microbiology and immunology, "By 1980, the eight-year-long process to patent the evolved strain of Pseudomonas ended in the US Supreme Court. The then-novel problem of patenting a living cell led to the famous 1980 US Supreme Court decision in the case called 'Diamond v Chakrabarty', which opened the door for subsequent patenting of recombinant microbes as well as higher organisms."

In June, the Smithsonian Institution in Washington, DC hosted a multi-speaker conference on the fortieth anniversary of this ruling that began with a brief oral presentation by Chakrabarty. The Chakrabarty patent was of immense importance for the growth of biotechnology companies.

The university tribute also noted this, "Chakrabarty's fame as the name on the first patent for a recombinant microbe led to a second career as an expert and lecturer on legal issues of patenting and intellectual property rights of biological significance. He sat on many American and international committees and taught in workshops for American and international judges on these matters. For his achievements in genetic engineering technology, he was awarded the prestigious civilian Padma Shri by the government of India in 2007. He was for many years a global roving ambassador for UIC."

His work in this area was published in research journals and books, presented in meetings, and developed by start-up companies.

By the time he died at the age of 82 on July 10, 2020, Professor Chakrabarty had put six decades into scientific research on the cutting edge of his chosen field. "We Indians seem to have a particular knack to grapple with these challenges. It is a pity that doing science in India has always been so hard.

That explains why so many Indians distinguish themselves abroad, especially here in America in a vast diversity of field, including far away from earth," he said.

NASA PLANETARY SCIENTIST

Speaking of Indian-Americans doing science far away from earth, for NASA planetary scientist Ashwin Vasavada, work on average is about 225 million kilometers away.

Sometimes it moves as far as over 400 million kilometers. It is a good thing Dr Vasavada does not have to travel to Mars where NASA's most ambitious mission to date, the $2.5 billion Curiosity mission, is digging rock and soil samples.

With a BS in geophysics and space physics from University of California, Los Angeles, and a PhD in planetary science from California Institute of Technology, Dr Vasavada is now in the midst of what could potentially upend our definitions of life. As someone engaged in the geologic studies of Mars with regard to surface properties, volatiles, and climate history, he is at the cutting edge of finding out whether Mars ever had or has habitable environments capable of supporting microbial life.

As the deputy project scientist on the Mars Science Laboratory (MSL) mission with its Curiosity rover at the Jet Propulsion Laboratory, Pasadena, he helps lead an international team of over 400 scientists.

Dr Vasavada is among the new young generation of Indian-American scientists doing exciting work. A son of Gujarati parents, who came to America in the 1950s, Dr Vasavada very nearly chose a career in music over science, but in the end, his parents persuaded him otherwise.

Asked what has been the most exciting find or high for the Curiosity rover, Dr Vasavada said, "Curiosity determined that Mars once was a habitable planet. It explored the site of an ancient lake, where the water was fresh and abundant, and other chemicals necessary for life were present. Since then, we've spent a year driving toward Mt Sharp, a 5-km high mountain. Along the way we've found more and more evidence for rivers and lakes in the ancient past. Everywhere we look, there are sandstones deposited by flowing water, and pebbles rounded by rolling in streams."

In terms of the eventual colonization of Mars, whenever that might happen, how would we look back at the Curiosity and Opportunity missions? "In one sense, we'll look back to Curiosity and Opportunity as the pioneers that preceded us. On Earth, our early explorers were other humans. In our exploration of the solar system, we send robots like Curiosity ahead of us. In another sense, we'll look back at these robots as scientists aiming to understand whether life ever existed on Mars. By the time we colonize Mars, it will be too late. The moment the first human sets down on Mars, we likely will no longer be able to detect traces of Mars life apart from our own contamination," he says.

Growing up as an Indian-American child, he says he had two alternate goals, "To be involved in space exploration, and to be a musician. I wandered back and forth between them, and tried to pursue both in college. But I think my parents eventually won, and convinced me to pursue science."

To the question of what drew him to geophysics and planetary science, not the two most preferred career choices for the Indian-American community, he says, "Growing up in the USA of the 1980s, space exploration was an inspiration. There's a whole generation of scientists and engineers who were inspired by the Space Shuttle, and the exploration of the Moon and planets. At the same time, perhaps growing up in a smaller town with few other Indian Americans allowed me to consider other career options than just medicine! Honestly, I follow my own Indian father's tradition. He didn't become a doctor like his own father."

He has been involved with the Mars Curiosity mission since March 2004. "Amazingly, there has never been a dull moment. There certainly is a lot of waiting for the payoff. But every step is challenging and interesting, from selecting the payload, designing the spacecraft, testing and rehearsing operations, launching, landing, and of course exploring Mars."

For him, one of the unexpected consequences of his work on the Mars mission is how his Indian values have influenced his work. "Probably most significantly it is the Indian values that brought me to this career level. One wonderful result of this mission has been a rediscovery of my heritage. I've received many emails from Indians around the world who have seen my name on this mission. And I've had the chance to talk with several Indian journalists and with Indian college students. It makes me proud to feel that I can represent Indians and Indian-Americans in this way."

Observational Cosmologist

From Mars as part of our solar system and therefore our universe, Indian-American scientists have also been involved in ideas which may seem bizarre. For instance, as cosmic discoveries go, not much can get bigger than possibly detecting another universe. Observational cosmologist Dr Ranga-Ram Chary has been in science headlines lately for a discovery that may well turn out to point at an alternate universe, apart from the one that we live in.

After studying data of a period of the universe barely 270,000 years after the big bang some 13.7 billion years ago, Dr Chary says it is hard to imagine that there is not another universe. A researcher at the US Planck Data Center in Pasadena, California, Dr Chary, who grew up in Delhi, has detected a glow in certain regions of the nascent universe that is 4,500 times brighter than what theory predicts. One very likely explanation of the glow is that it could be light from a neighboring universe leaking into our own.

The era of the universe that Dr Chary studied by using a detailed map of the cosmic microwave background (CMB) created by the Planck telescope is called recombination. It was a time when electrons and protons combined to create hydrogen and, in the process, emitted light. While that light would be necessarily faint, Dr Chary found spots that were markedly brighter, prompting the possibility of another universe.

The idea of multiple universes beyond our own has found considerable scientific traction in recent years, but it is perhaps the first time a real visual sign of an alternate universe has been detected by this 1995 alumnus of the Regional Engineering College (now called National Institute of Technology), Trichy, India. He earned his PhD in astronomy and astrophysics from the University of California, Los Angeles, in 1999.

Dr Chary's paper describes his work thus: "The properties of our observable universe have recently been characterized in unprecedented detail through analysis of the cosmic microwave background fluctuations, a relic of the hot big bang. The fine-tuning of parameters in the early universe required to reproduce our present day universe suggests that our universe may simply be a region within an eternally inflating super-region."

To the overarching question as to whether there is another universe, Dr Chary says, "Based on what we know about the properties of our universe, and the need for inflation and vacuum energy, it is hard to imagine there isn't. Otherwise, it suggests a very dramatic fine-tuning of parameters."

Asked if his finding suggests an eerie glow indicating matter leaking into our universe from a neighboring one, that is, whether the glow is statistical or visual in the sense that one can see it, he says, "It is visual."

The glow, which is 4,500 times brighter than what is theorized, was seen despite the CMB, which normally drowns out light. Is that an accurate description? "Not just the CMB, but the galaxy and individual sources," he says.

The existence of alternate universes requires extraordinary proof. In his assessment, "We have one very strong piece of evidence…the regions which are above 5 sigma. So at least two, may be three regions." (*5 sigma is a measure of scientists' confidence level that refers to the probability value of a finding at one in about 3.5 million. In simplistic terms, it would be that hard to find something and having found it, its probability increases.*)

Does he ever pause to consider that the existence of alternate universes has the potential to completely upend human certitudes? "It is humbling to imagine that our vast universe is just a chance quantum fluctuation among a multitude of others. But not entirely surprising since we're an ordinary planet around an ordinary star in an ordinary galaxy. So why should our universe be special?" he wonders.

If there are indeed other universes, they throw up many questions one of which would be to wonder if they too originate from the same source as our universe and popped up as bubbles or there is a possibility that they might have come into being separately. "There is no 'source'. The bubbles are forming out of vacuum energy as space expands. So each bubble is seeded separately at a different time and expands at a different rate. Some may be so dense they just collapse on themselves on a short timescale while others may keep expanding," he explains.

If the latter is possible, does that reinforce the idea that the big bang was a local occurrence that did not necessarily change the expanse outside?

"Yes, each bubble may have its own big bang when its time started," he says.

A Growing List of Achievers

The list of Indian-American scientists is a long and distinguished one, and it keeps strengthening every year. Perhaps the most important measure of that is the Presidential Early Career Award for Scientists and Engineers which was founded by President Bill Clinton and continues as a practice. For instance, the recipients for 2019 included 15 Indian-Americans from across America. They were Sanjay Basu, Stanford University, Department of Health and Human Services; Piya Pal, University of California-San Diego, Department of Defense; Padmini Rangamani, University of California-San Diego, Department of Defense; Dhruv Batra, Georgia Institute of Technology, Department of Defense; Subbian Panayampalli, National Center for Emerging and Zoonotic Infectious Diseases, Department of Health and Human Services; Vivek Agarwal, Idaho National Laboratory, Department of Energy; Gaurav Bahl, University of Illinois-Urbana-Champaign, Department of Defense; Prashant Jain, University of Illinois-Urbana-Champaign, NSF; Yogesh Surendranath, Massachusetts Institute of Technology, Department of Defense; Bharat Jalan, University of Minnesota-Twin Cities, Department of Defense; Sandeep Mallipattu, Stony Brook School of Medicine, Department of Health and Human Services; Priya Rajasethupathy, Rockefeller University, Department of Health and Human Services; Sohini Ramachandran, Brown University, Department of Health and Human Services; Meenakshi Madhur, Vanderbilt University, Department of Health and Human Services and Nitya Kallivayalil, University of Virginia, NSF.

The preponderance of the Department of Defense (DoD) in this list can be explained by the fact that a great deal of research and development in America begins as part of the DoD and then percolates into civilian applications.

It is a testament to that diversity of roles Indian-American science and technology professionals play that Sethuraman "Panch" Panchanathan, a computer scientist and engineer, was appointed the fifteenth director of the National Science Foundation (NSF) in 2019 by President Donald Trump. He was unanimously confirmed by the US Senate on June 18, 2020. The NSF is an $8.3 billion independent federal agency and the only government agency charged with advancing all fields of scientific discovery, technological innovation and science, technology, engineering, and mathematics (STEM) education.

In that capacity, Panchanathan has a remarkable oversight and view of science and technology in America. He is regarded as a leader in science, engineering, and education with more than three decades of experience. He has a distinguished career in both higher education and government, where he has designed and built knowledge enterprises, which advance research innovation, strategic partnerships, entrepreneurship, global development, and economic growth.

Rise of Women Scientists

The story of Indian-Americans in high sciences is a continuing one and there is every expectation that the community will continue to be a source of world-class names, some of whom will go on to win top-notch recognition, including the Nobel Prize. However, as Dr Ashtekar, himself a prospective winner in physics, points out, "You do science as a quest for something deeper, to answer profound questions. If some prizes come along the way, that's fine. If not, your rewards are far more profound."

Speaking of scientific vindication, in 1999 as a graduate student at Cambridge University, Priyamvada Natarajan made quite an extraordinary prediction about cosmic winds and black holes. She said cosmic winds driven by black holes could potentially carry gas and other star-making material thousands of light years away from their host galaxies. It was quite a prediction to make then and now, two decades hence, a research group led by astronomer Mark Lacy of the National Radio Astronomy Observatory in Virginia recently reported the observation of just such a wind flowing away from a type of supermassive black hole known as a quasar, according to Dr Natarajan's official webpage at Yale.

Now as a Yale professor of astronomy and physics, Dr Natarajan is one of the growing number of Indian-American women scientists whose range of contributions to sciences is no less wide-ranging and impressive than their male colleagues.

Born in Coimbatore, Dr Natarajan did her undergraduate study at the MIT and has degrees in physics and mathematics from there. She has been known for her work investigating the nature of dark matter and dark energy.

In an illustration of how science still remains male-heavy in terms of at least the public profiles of male scientists if not necessarily the quality of their work, Dr Natarajan in a conversation with the well-known theoretical physicist and author Dr Brian Greene said, "I would personally be more comfortable if there were a few more heroines around. There is always that that niggles me. Greatness does not stick to our kind [women scientists] as easily."

Notwithstanding the odds being stacked against them, Indian-American women scientists have made their presence felt across a wide spectrum not just in pure science and physics such as Dr Natarajan but even in applied science such as space. Two names that jump out as astronauts are those of Kalpana Chawla and Sunita Williams. Dr Chawla was selected as an astronaut candidate in 1994 by the National Aeronautics and Space Administration (NASA). Nearly three years later, in November 1997, she became the first Indian-American woman to travel to space aboard the space shuttle Columbia on flight STS-87.

She studied aeronautical engineering at Punjab Engineering College before immigrating to the US. She did her master's degree from the University of Texas and later joined the University of Colorado to get a doctorate in aerospace engineering. She was awarded her doctorate in 1988.

Williams became only the second part-Indian (she is part-Slovenian) to become an astronaut. She had her first space journey to the International Space Station in 2006 when she had accumulated 29 hours of spacewalk and over 195 days in space.

Other notable Indian-American scientists working with NASA are Dr Madhulika Guhathakurta, a NASA astrophysicist, Dr Anita Sengupta, an aerospace engineer, and Dr Sharmila Bhattacharya, a payload scientist.

There are other younger trailblazers, such as Deepika Kurup, 22, an inventor and scientist working on water purification. Born in Nashua,

New Hampshire, Kurup, whose alma mater is Harvard, plans to study neurobiology. In 2015, she was named as one of *Forbes* 2015 30 Under 30 in Energy. In 2012, she used a photocatalytic compound for water purification which won her the Discovery Education 3M Young Scientist. Employing that disinfectant method, she was able to reduce the amount of total coliform from 8000 colony-forming units to 50.

In a compelling example of the diversity of scientific pursuits among Indian-American women professionals, Dr Sangeeta Bhatia investigates applications of micro- and nano-technology for tissue repair and regeneration. According to her biography on the Koch Institute for Integrative Cancer Research at MIT, Dr Bhatia is "a biomedical researcher, MIT professor, and biotech entrepreneur who works to adapt technologies developed in the computer industry for medical innovation. Trained as both a physician and engineer at Harvard, MIT, and Brown University, Bhatia leverages 'tiny technologies' of miniaturization to yield inventions such as human microlivers that model human drug metabolism and liver disease, as well as responsive nanoparticles and nanoporous materials that can be engineered to diagnose, study, and treat a variety of diseases, including cancer. She applies ideas from computer technology and engineering to the design of miniaturized biomedical tools for the study and treatment of diseases, in particular liver disease, hepatitis, malaria and cancer."

It says, "Research in the Bhatia laboratory is dedicated to leveraging miniaturization tools from the world of engineering to improve human health. Using micro and nanotechnologies, also called 'tiny technologies', the lab aims to interface living and synthetic systems to improve medical diagnostics, as well as drug delivery, tissue regeneration, and disease modeling. In particular, Professor Bhatia is working to develop nanotechnology for the diagnosis and treatment of cancer, and to improve therapies for liver disease."

Yet another example of how Indian-American women scientists may be engaged in a much greater diversity of scientific work is Dr Anita Goel, who is both a physicist and a physician. She has done pioneering work in nano biophysics with a focus on molecular mechanics behind the reading and writing of information in DNA. She has a PhD in physics from Harvard University and also holds an MD from the Harvard–MIT Joint Division of

Health Sciences and Technology. She was mentored by two Nobel laureates, for chemistry Dudley R Herschbach and for physics Steven Chu. Her page at Harvard describes her work thus: "Dr Goel has a deep passion for fundamental science, especially elucidating the physics of living systems at the nanoscale. Her work in applied science harnesses these fundamental insights to develop nanotechnology platforms such as those for portable disease detection and nanosystems for novel energy harvesting and biocomputing applications."

America's Enabling R&D Ecology

If there is an underlying theme to the stories of these scientists working across such a remarkably broad spectrum, it is that given half a chance people of Indian origin tend to scale heights which are often out of reach for them in India. There is no one explanation to explain why Indian scientists and technologists do so well in America, but one of the most significant reasons is the research and development ecology in America that allows them to pursue what might seem like outlandish ideas in India. In a country where ordinary people invent and patent tools and techniques that do not even figure in everyday discourse elsewhere in the world, it is not surprising that much grander ideas find support, both in terms of institutional finance and scientific and technological infrastructure.

Perhaps nothing illustrates this unique strength of America than the example of Gitanjali Rao, who at barely 15 is already a much feted and awarded inventor, author, and passionate promoter of STEM. She has been interested in solving problems using science and technology since the age of ten. When Flint, a city in Michigan, began experiencing a seriously hazardous contamination of its water in 2014 because of its high lead content, Rao got to work and eventually developed a device called Tethys based on carbon nanotubes. Carbon nanotubes are cylindrical carbon molecules which are particularly sensitive to chemical changes making them very effective at detecting contamination. This device sends data about the quality of water using Bluetooth. In 2017, Rao won the Discovery Education 3M Young Scientist Challenge and was awarded $25,000 for her invention which consists of a 9-volt battery, a lead sensing unit, a Bluetooth sensor, and processor. Hers is an inspiring example of a young inquisitive mind employing all the modern tools and technology to solve a problem. For instance, she learned about carbon nanotubes on the MIT website.

In December 2020, she was declared "Kid of the Year" by *Time* magazine putting her on its cover. The well-known actress Angelina Jolie interviewed her as part of that story. "I was like 10 when I told my parents that I wanted to research carbon nanotube sensor technology at the Denver Water Quality Research Lab, and my mom was like, 'A what?' It was just that changing factor of, you know this work is going to be in our generation's hands pretty soon. So, if no one else is gonna do it, I'm gonna do it," Gitanjali told *Time*.

If that illustrates the freedom to pursue scientific and technological ideas in America at any age, the same Gitanjali has now also created an app called Kindly, which detects signs of cyberbullying.

Perhaps one constructive consequence of the Covid-19 pandemic is the renewed respect for science and technology, and that could usher in a whole new era of inventions where Indian-Americans would have the opportunity to shine and excel. And nothing proves it more than recognitions like the Presidential Early Career Awards for Scientists and Engineers, the highest US honor for young professionals, that invariably has in its ranks a clutch of young Indian-American names.

Physicians of Indian Heritage: America's Healers

Ajay Ghosh

"Unsung Heroes"

It was an amazing sight to behold. In April 2020, at the peak of the Covid-19 pandemic, a fleet of nearly 200 loudly-honking police vehicles, fire brigade trucks and private cars did a unique drive-past the home of Dr Uma Madhusudana, an Indian-American physician, in a heartwarming gesture of gratitude and recognition for her work in treating Covid-19 patients and saving lives in South Windsor Hospital in Connecticut.

Dr Madhusudana, who graduated from JSS Medical College, Mysuru, was hailed as one of the area's "unsung heroes", as physicians and healthcare workers put their own lives to risk during the pandemic to help others. The contributions and dedication of Indian-American physicians to their profession, especially during the pandemic, have come more than ever to be recognized across the United States.

"Indian-American physicians are bearing the brunt of this pandemic in the US," said Dr Joseph M Chalil, a cardiologist and professor at several universities in the United States. "Not a day goes by without hearing about many of them getting infected with coronavirus, with some losing their lives, because of their disproportionate share in the healthcare field. This pandemic is hitting close to home for me and my colleagues."

Describing Indian-American physicians as "the real heroes", Dr Anupama Gotimukula, president-elect of AAPI said, "Thousands of Indian-American physicians are struggling with Green Card backlog and are on temporary visa plans. Due to their vulnerability, they work in critical and challenging places serving and caring for Covid patients. Many have become positive in the process, some have died, some are in ICU, and some are recuperating at home. These are the true saviors and unsung heroes saving the lives of so many Americans. We are proud of the services of Indian-American physicians in this country."

History of Indian-American Physicians

India has a long medical history and Indians have been known for their advanced knowledge in medicine, surgery, and natural ways to treat illnesses. Steve Raymer, an associate professor of journalism at Indiana University in Bloomington, wrote in *Yale Global Online* in 2004 about the development of medicine in ancient India and how, around 600 BC, more than a century before the Greek physician Hippocrates came to be regarded as the "father of modern medicine", Atreya and Sushruta were some of the early names in medicine in India, with the *Sushruta Samhita* a highly regarded Sanskrit text in medicine and surgery. Indian healers were known to have developed a code of ethics that required them to maintain patient confidentiality and were enjoined to lead a life dedicated to caring for the sick.

Two thousand and six hundred years later, physicians of Indian origin are renowned around the world for their expertise in medicine, surgical skills, clinical expertise, and qualities of caring and compassion.

Among the many groups of professionals of Indian origin who came to the United States in the early 1960s and 1970s, Indian doctors stand out as one of the most respected and influential group of people with a standing in American society that few other ethnic groups have been able to match.

Early Immigrants

According to historians, the first documented physician of Indian origin who landed on the shores of the United States in 1883 was Dr Anandibai Joshi, a woman with a pioneering zeal to serve her country. Overcoming social opposition, with financial contributions from well-wishers across India, including the British Viceroy of India who contributed Rs 200 to a fund for her higher education, Joshi began her voyage on April 17, 1883, from Calcutta (now Kolkata), chaperoned by two female acquaintances, and reached New York in June 1883. Soon, she found admission to the Woman's Medical College of Pennsylvania, Philadelphia.

In a letter of application to the college, she stated: "[The] determination which has brought me to your country against the combined opposition of my friends and caste ought to go a long way toward helping me to carry out the purpose for which I came, i.e., to render to my poor suffering countrywomen the true medical aid they so sadly stand in need of and which they would rather die than accept at the hands of a male physician. The voice of humanity is with me, and I must not fail. My soul is moved to help the many who cannot help themselves."

The college offered Joshi a scholarship of $600 per month for three years. She chose the topic "Obstetrics among the Aryan Hindoos" for her specialization. At the convocation held on March 11, 1889, Joshi received a standing ovation when the college president said, "I am proud to say that today should be recorded in golden letters in the annals of this college. We have the first Indian woman who is honoring this college by acquiring a degree in medicine. Mrs Anandi Joshi has the honor to be the very first woman doctor of India." Soon after, Dr Joshi returned to India and continued her practice until she died of tuberculosis.

The Story of Dr Subbarow

Since the return of Dr Joshi to India, there is not much of a recorded history of Indian-American physicians until the arrival of Yellapragada Subbarow, another pioneering Indian physician and biochemist who discovered the function of adenosine triphosphate as an energy source in the cell, developed methotrexate for the treatment of cancer, and discovered a broad spectrum of antibiotics including tetracycline and chlortetracycline.

"You have probably never heard of Dr Yellapragada Subbarow. Yet because he lived you may be alive and well today, because he lived you may live longer," wrote Doron K Antrim in *Argozy,* an American magazine in the 1950s. Methotrexate has been proved to be one of the best US Food and Drug Administration (FDA)-approved drugs, as it is cheap and effective in managing cases of psoriasis and Sezary syndrome along with many off-label uses.

Dr Subbarow is reported to have to his credit some of the biggest contributions in several fields of science—biochemistry, pharmacology, microbiology, oncology, and nutritional science. These continue to be applied to numerous experiments, which are relevant to science even today. Born in 1895 in a Telugu family in the West Godavari district of Andhra Pradesh, he came to the United States after completing his medical degree from the Madras Medical College. Being encouraged by a visiting American doctor, John Fox Kendrick, he was inspired to attend Harvard School of Tropical Medicine in Boston for postgraduation. He was ineligible for a scholarship because his Indian degree did not meet Harvard's standards. The same was true when he tried getting an internship at Boston Hospital. He supported himself by working as a night porter, cleaning urinals and bedpans of patients, and doing other odd jobs in his spare time.

After earning a diploma from the Harvard School of Tropical Medicine in June 1924, he managed to join Harvard Medical School, where he worked with Dr Cyrus Fiske, and the duo developed the Fiske–Subbarow method for the estimation of phosphorus in body fluids and tissues. His discovery and publications on the Fiske–Subbarow method of phosphorous estimation paid off, and he was awarded a PhD degree in June 1929 at Harvard.

According to *Hektoen International Journal*, "Subbarow did not receive a Nobel Prize, but his discoveries entitle him to be called the father of targeted cancer chemotherapy. He worked initially in the laboratory of Cyrus Fiske at Harvard Medical School, and later as director of research at the Lederle Laboratories. He first invented a method for measuring phosphorus, the Fiske–Subbarow method, which led him to discover two critically important phosphate-containing molecules, phosphocreatine and adenosine triphosphate (ATP)."

Academic Discriminations

Although it was common for a scientist of his talent to use research assistants and collaborate with peers in the lab, Harvard directed he work alone. Although he made advances in phosphorus compounds connected to RNA synthesis, he was not allowed to publish his results. In 1935, he had to disown the extent of his role in the discovery of the color test related to phosphorus, instead giving the credit to his co-author, who was being considered for promotion to a full professorship at Harvard.

Denied tenure and tired of his second-class status at Harvard, in May 1940 he accepted an offer to become Lederle's associate director of research at their Pearl River Lab in New York. Aureomycin was his last gift to mankind, as he left the world in 1948 at the young age of 53 years.

The discrimination experienced by Dr Subbarow came to be experienced by those who followed him later on, after the US opened its doors to immigrants from South Asia in 1965. The US President Lyndon B Johnson's signing into law the Immigration and Naturalization Act of 1965 (also known as the Hart–Celler Act), lifting the national-origin quotas system and issuing visas based on preferred skills or family reunification, opened the doors to the skilled immigrants from South Asia, and with that began the influx of physicians of Indian origin.

The Influx

They came by ship and later on by air seeking greener pastures across the US. The going was not easy for those who came and began establishing their practice in several parts of the nation, bringing with it several professional and social challenges.

"It was tough and challenging for pioneer physicians to establish a practice and find suitable job opportunities. Faced with instances of overt as well as subtle discrimination in residency recruitment and license reciprocity, physicians of Indian origin organized themselves in several states to fight the unfair treatment," Dr Ranga Reddy, chair, AAPI History Task Force and past president of AAPI, recalls.

Realizing the need to support one another to overcome the challenges of discrimination, they began to form associations or medical groups in some of the states where they were sizable in number. "It was first in the state of Michigan that physicians from India formed an association called Michigan Association of Physicians of Indian Origin (MAPI) in 1976. Various other organizations such as Indian Medical Association of America Inc (AMAI) of Washington, DC, India Medical Association of Illinois (IMA, IL), Chicago, and Indian Medical Association of New England (IMANE), Boston, were founded around the same time," said Dr Ranga Reddy.

Identifying and contacting the prospective members, who were scattered across the length and breadth of the country, was a huge challenge. The absence of internet and e-mail services and the skeletal telephone services existing at that time made it even harder to locate each of them. Often one had to wait for days and weeks to confirm via postal mail to correspond and receive responses from fellow physicians.

"In 1980, as the president of the Indian Medical Association of America, Inc, I had communicated my intention—to various presidents and the leaders of the existing city, state and national specialty associations of Indian physicians in the US—of creating a federation of all associations under an umbrella body," recalls Dr Navin C Shah, co-founder and past president of AAPI.

In 1981, Dr Shah obtained a list of Indian-origin physicians from the American Medical Association (AMA). He then "reached out to multiple association leaders from New England, Ohio, Iowa, Michigan, Alabama, Kentucky, Washington, DC, Cleveland, Chicago, Flint, Battle Creek, Grand Rapids, and also the national associations of psychiatry, radiology, surgery, and urology for their participation in this enormous task."

Later on, Dr Ujamlal Kothari, MAPI president in Detroit, Dr Shah, and several others spearheaded the movement for the creation of an overarching federation of state-level Indian-American medical associations. They had one aim: helping Indian physicians to come together to address their problems and bring to the attention of state and national bodies in organized medicine and the federal government the concerns and challenges faced by their growing numbers.

Leaders of associations from various states met at Dr Kothari's residence and unanimously agreed to form a national association comprising of all the states, specialties, and alumni associations. A steering committee was set up to organize a national meeting in August 1982 with Dr Kothari as chairman, and Dr Jagan Kakarala, Dr Ratnakar Kini, Dr Bhimsen Rao, and Dr Bhanu Shah as members. As those few pioneering leaders struggled together to form an alliance, little did they realize then that their efforts would lead to a phenomenal organizational success story!

Birth of AAPI

The first national-level meeting took place in Detroit in August 1982, giving birth to what has come to be the largest ethnic medical association in the United States, the American Association of Physicians of Indian Origin (AAPI).

In choosing the name for the organization, there had been series of discussions. "We did not want to call it as a group of doctors," says Dr Shah. "Physician sounded more professional as 'doctors' was colloquial, rather a term used by a common person. We wanted to stress on qualified physicians of Indian origin. This was in my mind and the other leaders present at the AAPI formation agreed with me."

Dr Shah proposed Dr Kothari, the senior most among them, for the post of president, and Dr Kothari in turn proposed Dr Shah for the post of vice president. "We both were elected unanimously. Dr Kothari proposed the name of Dr Jagan Kakarala for secretary-treasurer to run the office from Detroit. I feel very fortunate to be part of this historical event," reminisces Dr Shah, recounting the historic events with a sense of pride and achievement.

"On September 9, 1982, I issued the first report of the formation of AAPI to all the medical associations of Indian origin. On August 17, 1982, *India Abroad*, the weekly newspaper widely read by Indian-Americans, reported about the formation of the national association. In October 1982, Dr Kothari and I issued an appeal through the ethnic media, urging all existing associations to join AAPI," Dr Shah continues.

AAPI, in its early period, played an essential role in three vital areas: supporting foreign medical graduates (FMGs) against discrimination;

obtaining equality with US medical graduates (USMGs); and providing service to the motherland (India) in the field of health care and medical education.

Since the medical field's opening up to foreign-trained physicians, Indian-American physicians have continued to constitute as one of the largest of all immigrant physicians in the US. According to AMA, which keeps track of all licensed physicians, in the early 1990s, there were 32,000 physicians of Indian origin—about a fifth of 179,000 foreign-trained physicians. The latter had graduated from schools in over 100 different countries.

Why Do Indian Doctors Stand Out?

What makes the physicians of Indian origin stand out? Dr Ravi Kolli, a psychiatrist in Pittsburgh, Pennsylvania, practicing for several decades, says, "This is due to the selection bias of more motivated and focused students from India, pursuing opportunities that tend to bring here a relatively better cohort of doctors. So those who emigrate to US tend to outperform others in general. Also, they have to be on their 'A game' to overcome some structural barriers which also promote their resilience and efficiency."

However, Dr Kolli laments some aspects of Indian medical training that lacks uniformity or standardization due to uneven resources and lack of transparency. But emphasis on clinical skills and experience in India rather than over-dependence on technology and testing give them an edge.

Physicians who came from India and other countries were originally labeled foreign medical graduates (FMGs), a name which was seen as discriminatory in nature. It required "strong lobbying efforts" by the International Association of American Physicians (IAAP) to change the name to international medical graduates (IMGs).

IMGs had experienced discrimination in several areas, including residency positions, jobs, promotions, hospital privileges, licensing, reciprocities, and other areas related to medical practice. These were subtle and often could not be established in a court of law or appeals at human resources departments. Hospital authorities, county, state medical societies, and even the AMA did not take adequate steps to ensure fair treatment to IMGs.

There was also a dual standard in obtaining a medical license. It favored the USMGs and discriminated against the IMGs. As there was no unified federal-level licensing requirement, those who came from India and other nations needed to comply with several state and local requirements for residency and jobs. Many states required additional years of training, ranging from one to three years above and beyond that required of USMGs. Some federal agencies and medical institutions routinely announced job positions only for USMGs, openly discriminating against qualified IMGs. In 1982, the AMA passed a resolution which put the responsibility on qualified IMGs to prove that the medical school from which they graduated was as good as American medical schools.

AAPI Leads the Way for Other IMGs

Doctors from other countries found common ground and were happy for a more organized AAPI to lead the way. The fourth annual convention of AAPI was held in Washington, DC, in June 1986. This was co-hosted by AAPI, the American College of International Physicians, Association of Pakistan and Islamic Physicians, Filipino Medical Association, and South American Physician Association.

Lobbying with Congressmen and Senators and their staff, educating them about issues affecting IMGs was a significant task with its members testifying strongly in favor of forming a section within the AMA for IMGs to address their unique issues. The group presented a list of the injustices against IMGs to the AMA president, Dr John Coury. Despite repeated representations, the AMA's House of Delegates rejected the IMGs' plea.

It was at this time IAAP acquired the services of US Senator Vance Hartke, a Democrat from Indiana, and Kern Smith, formerly with the Kennedy administration, as lobbyists to represent their legislative interests in Congress, and submitted draft legislation against discrimination against IMGs (AS 1868-Sen Moynihan, HR 3773-Rep Solarz, and HR 3241-Rep Bates). These Bills prohibited discrimination against IMGs in licensing, reciprocity, jobs, promotions, residencies, hospital privileges, and other medical practice aspects. They contained built-in penalties against states and institutions that practiced discrimination against IMGs.

Dr Navin Shah, along with other IAAP leaders and Rep Stephen Solarz, a pro-India Congressman, testified in favor of the Bills in the House of Representatives. The AMA, while opposing the Bills, boycotted the hearings. According to Dr Shah: "I presented over 50 documented cases of discrimination against IMGs in training and practice and also listed the numerous contributions of the IMGs in the US health care system, especially in the rural areas across the nation." IAAP recommended that the US government create a central repository of IMGs' documentation that should be used for licensing, reciprocities, hospital privileges, and all other medical practice areas, which are on the principle of uniformity in licensing and reciprocity laws. IAAP suggested similar qualifying examinations for both IMGs and USMGs to eliminate the two-tier system for residents in training. Forty-six lawmakers co-sponsored the three Bills in Congress.

In December 1988, Rep Jim Bates introduced a Bill in the House to have a study by the Government Accounting Office (GAO). The AAPI provided the GAO with the numerous cases, which had then grown to 78 in number, detailing the cases of discrimination. By 1989, there were four Bills—two in the House and two in the Senate—HR 1134-Rep S Solarz, HR 6140-Rep J Bates, S 8790-Sen Lieberman and S 304-Sen Moynihan. A total of 91 lawmakers from both the Democratic and the Republican Parties opposed discrimination against IMGs.

On April 29, 1989, as the sole spokesperson for IMGs, Dr Shah was invited to participate in a roundtable conference that was chaired by GAO officials. Among the invited were representatives of Human Health Services, Federation of State Medical Boards (FSMB), AAMC, AMA, NBME, ECFMG, and Sen Hartke. It was the first time that the IMGs actually got to meet with the leaders of organized medical services. During the day-long deliberations, mainly three areas were discussed: education, examination, and experiences of IMGs.

"Due to overwhelming support in the US Congress for the IMGs, in 1989 the AMA, for the first time created an office to address the issues and concerns of IMGs," said Dr Shah. This was seen as a major victory.

In May 1990, the GAO report "Requirements Different for Graduates of Foreign and US Medical Schools in Medical Licensing by Endorsement" cited the two-tier examination and licensing system and admitted that IMGs had to undergo additional years of training and had to produce more documents of their medical education as compared to USMGs. The GAO supported a single exam for both IMGs and USMGs and a central repository for IMGs' documents. In September 1992, the Congress passed legislation prohibiting discrimination against IMGs, and President George H Bush signed the legislation into law, banning discrimination and enabling all IMGs to take similar licensing examinations as the USMGs.

However, in the following years, IAAP failed to take advantage of the tremendous efforts and support from almost 100 US lawmakers and the positive GAO report toward realizing the pending legislation in Congress. "The momentum was lost as IMGs were hampered by their loose coalition, in-fighting, and lack of effective and dedicated leadership. The detailed history of the IMGs' struggle is well-documented in the book, *Fight for Equality*, by Shawn McMahon (2005)," adds Dr Shah.

AAPI's Growing Influence and Recognition

AAPI's mission has grown and its horizons expanded over the past four decades. Each president under his/her leadership worked hard to enhance the programs and its reach, serving both the US and India. Known to be the largest ethnic medical organization representing over 80,000 practicing physicians and over 40,000 medical students, residents, and fellows of Indian origin in the US, "AAPI has made its presence felt across the nation through the many roles it plays and the noble causes and programs it supports both in the US and India," says the current AAPI president, Dr Sudhakar Jonnalagadda.

India today provides the largest number of IMGs to the US, according to a study conducted by the *New England Journal of Medicine*. Indian-Americans constitute a little more than 1 percent of the country's population, but they account for 9 percent of the American doctors and physicians. Given that a physician of Indian origin serves every seventh patient in this country and every fifth patient in rural and inner cities across the United States, the reach and influence of Indian-American physicians go well beyond the fast-growing Indian-American community.

BEGINNING OF VITAL RECOGNITIONS

Indian-American physicians began to be professionally appreciated for their contributions to larger American society, and state and national leaders began recognizing them as a capable and influential cohort that needed to be courted.

After years of sitting on the political sidelines, Indian-Americans—affluent, educated, and doubling in number every 10 years—were starting to flex their muscles in Washington. Indian physicians were lobbying at the state and federal level, quizzing presidential candidates, and working closely with the 167-member Indian Caucus—a group of US Congress members friendly to India and Indian-Americans.

At the third annual convention in Chicago in May 1985, Dr Harrison L Rogers, president of AMA, a body that was earlier shunning foreign-trained doctors, was the chief guest. At the tenth convention organized at AAPI's birthplace in Detroit in July 1992, Vice President Dan Quayle was the chief guest. House Speaker Newt Gingrich was the chief guest at the twelfth convention in Atlanta in 1994 where Dr Deepak Chopra attracted a large crowd for his inspirational talk.

It was indeed a very proud moment for AAPI at the thirteenth annual convention in Chicago in June 1995 when President Bill Clinton addressed the gathering of 5,000 people and praised Indian-American physicians' contributions. Indian-American doctors were now mainstream. The eighteenth convention in New York, in June 2000, had the then First Lady Hillary Rodham Clinton as guest of honor.

Earlier, the first legislative conference of AAPI in 1998 under the presidency of Dr Ranga Reddy had been a huge success with dozens of lawmakers in attendance. Rep Frank Pallone (New Jersey) introduced the Patient's Bill of Rights based on AAPI's position paper and commended AAPI on the floor of Congress. A diabetes study among Indians in America based on the studies and recommendations by AAPI was undertaken. Congress, in a landmark action, directed the Center for Disease Control to allot $500,000 to the study. March 29 was also declared as "AAPI DAY".

A white paper outlining demands and concerns was submitted to the dozens of lawmakers who had addressed the delegates. Some of the issues outlined in the white paper included increasing residency slots; passing hate crime laws; reducing the Green Card backlog; reforms to the Stark Law to improve physician–patient health care; and insurance companies' ability to sell health plans across state lines.

Dr Vivek Murthy, US Surgeon General

When President Barack Obama nominated Dr Vivek Murthy to be the US Surgeon General in 2014, Indian-origin physicians lobbied hard for it, and they flew into Washington from various parts of the country, for the confirmation of Dr Murthy by the US Senate.

Said Dr Sampat Shivangi, who was the chair of AAPI's Legislative Affairs Committee for 10 years: "Our biggest achievement has been to lobby with the US Senate members, especially among the Senate Republicans to vote to confirm Dr Vivek Murthy. But for our frequent visits and lobbying efforts, we would not have had an Indian-American as the US Surgeon General." This was aptly described by Dr Jayesh Shah, AAPI president at the time, as "cementing the reputation of physicians of Indian origin that has spread across America".

As the Surgeon General, Murthy was the leading spokesperson on matters of public health and operational head of the 6,500-strong US Public Health Service Commissioned Corps, one of the seven uniformed services that include the army, navy, air force and marines. As "America's Doctor", Dr Murthy created initiatives to tackle the country's most urgent public health issues, choosing areas of focus that were raised by people during his inaugural listening tour. He focused his attention on chronic stress and isolation as problems with profound implications for health, productivity, and happiness. Partnering with the Veterans Health Administration, he led a convention that brought together leading thinkers, researchers, and practitioners to identify scientifically proven ways to cultivate emotional well-being and fitness to help people thrive in the most challenging circumstances.

"Murthy was an inspiring surgeon general who brought a unifying message about prevention to communities across the country," said Dr Shivangi.

President Joe Biden nominated Dr Murthy to the US Surgeon General post in December 2020. While announcing the nomination Biden described Dr Murthy as a "renowned physician" who could help guide Americans safely out of a still ranging coronavirus pandemic.

Giving Back to India

"Members of AAPI have both collectively and individually been engaged in addressing the huge healthcare-related needs of our motherland, India, for several decades, by organizing, supporting, partnering, and collaborating with local groups in India and making a difference in their villages, cities or states," said Dr Jagan Ailinani, a past president of AAPI.

Since its inception, AAPI has been in the forefront organizing services and leading efforts to streamline healthcare needs in India. Dr Apparao Mukkamala organized a group of Indian-American physicians to start a medical school and hospital, NRI Academy of Medical Science, in Vijayawada, Andhra Pradesh, in 1993. The entire state of Andhra Pradesh was covered by state-of-the-art ambulances with matching grants from AAPI and the government.

AAPI both funds and runs dozens of free health clinics and medical camps across India. Its members continue to provide funds to numerous programs including the Rotary International polio project; the government's rural health initiatives; and supply of clean drinking water to millions of villagers in Andhra Pradesh, Gujarat, Punjab, and Rajasthan.

Dr Sanku Rao co-founded the Global Association of Physicians of Indian Origin (GAPIO) to bring together all the physicians of Indian origin around the world to improve the quality of healthcare and to offer access to healthcare in underserved areas in India. In addition to the regular educational, philanthropic and legislative programs impacting healthcare delivery, Indian-American physicians are continuing to work on several projects, ranging from sanitation to cancer treatment to supporting research-based alternative and indigenous systems of medicine.

The annual Global Healthcare Summit (GHS) has come to be known for the critical role Indian-American physicians play in India in important areas of health delivery, policy issues, and in initiating numerous health-care programs in collaboration with the central, state and local governments, and many non-governmental organizations across the country. Dr Jonnalagadda explained, "The upcoming GHS 2021 in Visakhapatnam will be history-making as AAPI plans to strengthen on the past initiatives and plans newer ventures benefitting the larger Indian population."

Recognition by India

As the contributions and achievements of Indian-American physicians expanded steadily, the government of India also recognized their services. At the annual convention of AAPI in Chicago in 2012, Indian consul general in New York, Riva Ganguly Das, said, "We have watched how AAPI has grown over the years and how we want other NRI groups to emulate the success model of AAPI," stating that the government of India "values our relationship with AAPI and the many initiatives and contributions you have made for the people in India."

Indian Ambassador Arun Kumar Singh, addressing the AAPI convention in San Antonio, said, "All of you, in a sense, are permanent ambassadors here. You have an understanding of the US. You have an understanding of India and Indian society. So based on this understanding and the network you have, you will be in a position to take forward this relationship in different areas."

The 2018 GHS in Mumbai was a joint exercise with GAPIO and was inaugurated by President Ram Nath Kovind. The GHS in Kolkata in 2019 was inaugurated by Vice President Venkaiah Naidu who acknowledged AAPI's initiatives in traumatic brain injury guidelines, training of first responders, and engaging local authorities to address significant causes of road fatalities.

On September 22, 2019, AAPI leaders presented a memorandum to Indian Prime Minister Narendra Modi offering to play critical role in the implementation of Ayushman Bharat during one of the biggest public events attended by over 50,000 people from across the nation at the NFL stadium in Houston, Texas, which was jointly attended by Modi and President Donald Trump.

"I am proud of the achievements and contributions of the Indian-origin physicians across the world in the battle against Covid-19," said Prime Minister Modi, who was the chief guest at the first-ever Virtual

Global Summit of AAPI on June 27, 2020. "I have closely followed your contributions, sacrificing your life to save that of others. Some have made the ultimate sacrifice of giving up your own lives at the service of others. You will be remembered forever."

In his address, Indian Ambassador Taranjit Singh Sandhu described Indian-American physicians as the "real heroes, who have risked your lives and have been out to assist others." There is widespread recognition of their contributions in the US, he added. "Lawmakers in the US appreciate your contributions."

Appreciating them for their philanthropic work in India, he said, "India and the US are strategic partners," and pointed to the collaboration between the two nations on cutting-edge medical research in the healthcare sector and science.

Touching People's Lives

Indian-American physicians have gone beyond their call of duty to meet the diverse needs of the larger American community, by dedicating their time, resources, and skills during national disasters and family crises. One of the cherished goals of Indian-American physicians has been to educate and prevent childhood obesity, which has more than doubled in children and quadrupled in adolescents in the past 30 years.

AAPI childhood obesity awareness program is now run in 100 schools all over the US. They are among the first to reach out to serve local communities during national calamities with many volunteering to organize free medical camps for those who lack healthcare insurance.

The contributions and dedication to their profession, especially during the pandemic, have come to be widely recognized. Dr Jagdish Gupta, an internist and gastroenterologist, says, "It's our going beyond, being available to our patients, often at the cost of our family time" that distinguishes the Indian-American physician. "We are known to be altruistic and service-oriented. We get attached to our patients; we go out of our way and make ourselves available to them all the time, thus becoming closer to them."

He recalled his close association with a Holocaust survivor who he had treated for 20 years in Brooklyn, NY. At the age of 88, on her deathbed, she made a request for her doctor, and Dr Gupta came and spent the last few moments with her, holding her hands and supporting her as she breathed her last. "This was one of the many such touching moments that stand out and drives me to serve my patients," Dr Gupta, who has practiced medicine in the US for 48 years, says.

Dr Manju Sheth from Boston shares some heartwarming responses from the community, "One of my elderly patients told me that I have become part of her family. Two of my patients organized a prayer service for me when I injured my shoulder, and they saw me struggling with a wrapped arm. It is strange that the worst situation can bring out the best in people."

Dr Vandana Agarwal, an oncologist in Pomona, California, recalls the treatment she had offered to a "complicated case" of leukemia. "She was my patient in the second trimester of pregnancy and was discovered to have acute promyelocytic leukemia, which was successfully treated with chemotherapy and resulted in the delivery of a male baby after a two-month stormy course in ICU. It was gratifying to see this patient being finally discharged home with her baby. She was grateful to me for 'saving her life'."

These are only a few of the stories of true compassion, expertise, skills and knowledge, patients across the US have come to admire Indian-American physicians for.

Frontline Covid Educators

Several Indian-American physicians have been in the forefront of educating people in the US and across the globe during the pandemic. The popular face of CNN on healthcare and medical issues, Dr Sanjay Gupta is the global channel's multiple Emmy-award winning chief medical correspondent. A practicing neurosurgeon, he has been named as one of the "Ten Most Influential Celebrities" by *Forbes* magazine.

Dr Amesh Adalja, a senior scholar at the Johns Hopkins Center for Health Security, became another popular face on major media outlets with his insightful attempts to explain the disease and ways to mitigate its impact. Another familiar face on numerous TV networks for his easy-to-understand analysis has been Dr Ashish K Jha, recognized globally as an expert on pandemic preparedness and response as well as on health policy research and practice.

Dr Kavita Patel, Nonresident Fellow at Brookings Institution, is another expert who has come to be recognized as a credible voice on the pandemic. She has played a critical role in development and evaluation of policy initiatives connected to health reform and connected economic issues.

The importance and high esteem with which physicians of Indian heritage are held by their patients is self-evident, as they occupy critical positions in the healthcare, research and administrative policy positions across America. They have made their mark in respected institutions from Harvard Medical School to Memorial Sloane Kettering Cancer Center to the Mayo Medical Center.

They Make Us Proud

Hundreds of them qualify to be featured here, but for lack of space, we will limit to mentioning a few names who perhaps, in my reckoning, stand above the rest. Dr Abraham Verghese, a Linda R Meier and Joan F Lane Provostial Professor and Vice-Chair for the Theory and Practice of Medicine at the School of Medicine at Stanford University, devoted his life for helping young AIDS patients for which in 2016, he received a National Humanities Medal at the White House from President Barack Obama.

Dr Mathai Mammen, an Indian biochemist, researcher, is the global head of R&D for the Janssen Pharmaceuticals Companies of Johnson & Johnson. Under his leadership, the Theravance team of 200 scientists created three approved products (Breo®, Anoro®, Vibativ®), with several others in the pipeline. US–India Chamber of Commerce noted "Dr Mammen's mission is to make meaningful medicines that impact the lives of patients, their families and communities."

Dr VK Raju has devoted over four decades in a crusade to eliminate preventable blindness in areas plagued by poverty and poor access to medical care. Through his West Virginia Ophthalmology Foundation he has been serving 2.5 million people in over 30 developing countries and the US, and performed 340,000+ vision-saving surgeries, with 30,000+ surgeries performed on children alone.

Dr Sharad Lakhanpal, a practicing rheumatologist in Dallas, Texas, and the first and only Indian and non-American to become president of the American College of Rheumatology (ACR) in its 85-year history, and was made a Master of the ACR, the highest honor bestowed by it for lifetime achievements. He serves on the prestigious President's Council at the George Bush Presidential Center and Library in Dallas, Texas.

Dr Navin C Nanda, a distinguished professor of medicine and cardiovascular disease at the University of Alabama, and an author of over a dozen medical books and over 500 original scientific publications, is considered as the "Father of Modern Echocardiography". Among others, he was recently honored by the government of India as the "Icon of the Century in Cardiology and Echocardiography in the World".

Dr Dattatreyudu Nori is a world-renowned radiation oncologist and was named one of the top doctors in America for the treatment of cancers in women by the women's magazine *Ladies' Home Journal.* A professor and executive vice chairman of the Radiation Oncology Department at The New York-Presbyterian Hospital/Weill Cornell Medical College in New York City, Dr Nori is one of the world's leading authorities in the subspecialty of brachytherapy, which improved the quality of life of men with prostate cancer.

An expert in the field of mind–body healing, Dr Deepak Chopra is a world-renowned motivational speaker and best-selling author on alternative medicine. He founded the Chopra Center for Wellbeing in California, oversaw the creation of several affiliated clinics and became well-known among celebrities. *Time* magazine dubbed Chopra "the poet-prophet of alternative medicine" and called him one of the top 100 heroes of the century.

A physician, biologist, hematologist, oncologist, and author, Dr Siddhartha Mukherjee is best known for his 2010 book *The Emperor of All Maladies: A Biography of Cancer* that won notable literary prizes, including the 2011 Pulitzer Prize for General Non-Fiction and Guardian First Book Award, among others. A three-part documentary series based on the book, directed by Barak Goodman and executive produced by Ken Burns, debuted on PBS stations in March 2020. He is an assistant professor of medicine at Columbia University Medical Center.

Acknowledgment

I am grateful to several doctors, in particular Dr Ranga Reddy, Dr Navin Shah and Dr Joseph Chalil, who helped me put together this inspiring story.

From Stereotypes to Household Names: A Cultural Shift and New Role Models

Vikrum Mathur

When one discusses American entertainment, media, and pop culture today, it is hard to imagine not seeing an Indian face. From film to television, news media to modeling, late night to primetime, online to stage, Indian-American entertainers have come a long way in establishing themselves and becoming household names. If you talk to anyone about artists of Indian ethnicity who have made a mark in the US, names such as Aziz Ansari, Mindy Kaling, Kal Penn, or M Night Shyamalan instantly come to mind. These are indeed prolific names in the pantheon of the entertainment world—names so celebrated due to their excellence and contributions to their craft, that they are recognized globally.

This list of entertainers, however, is not limited to these well-known names, and continues to grow year on year. Former Miss America Nina Davuluri and choreographer Joya Kazi also exemplify not only achievement in the arts but also the diversity of talent Indian-Americans have.

The journey to reach this seminal moment in entertainment history is not a road to be taken for granted. It has been a quest wrought with many struggles and barriers, and each of the artists that we celebrate today has worked incredibly hard to overcome those obstacles. The obstacles are not only those of opportunities—it has been a battle for proper representation as well and these artists have fought hard to shed stereotypes that permeated for decades.

Since the 1940s, this has been the saga of individuals with ambition, passion, and drive, of those who dare to dream and live to excel, and ultimately of an entire community seeking artistic release.

The Early Years

It is often forgotten that Indians have been appearing on American screens for the past 80 years. The earliest person that achieved worldwide popularity on the silver screen in the US was none other than a young man by the name of Sabu Dastagir, better known as Sabu.

Sabu's foray into films was nothing short of luck and circumstance. Reports say that the young man, originally from Mysore, was spotted by filmmaker Robert J Flaherty when he worked as a 'mahout' (caretaker of elephants) for the *maharaja* of Mysore, leading to his getting cast in the film *Elephant Boy.* This led to several successful films for Dastagir in which he played the lead role, such as *The Jungle Book, The Thief of Baghdad*, and *Arabian Nights*. He continued to act steadily in films until his sudden death from a heart attack at the age of 39 in 1963. While Sabu became an international star, his roles represented an enduring problem which would take decades to upend—stereotyping.

Sabu was regularly portrayed as the poor, loincloth- or turban-wearing earnest young man who had an affinity for animals or the mystical. At the time, this was the perception that permeated in the West—India as an exotic country with magical qualities, snake charmers, poverty, and dense jungles with various animals. As this depiction proved to be successful and fed the appetite of global audiences, any portrayal of Indians on screen began to follow this formula. However, after the death of Sabu, there was no global Indian star that emerged in quite the same way for many years.

As time went by, interest in things Indian continued to entice Hollywood. Films were being written featuring Indian characters, but rather than casting Indian actors who could suit those roles, Hollywood stuck to 'brownface' with films such as 1968's *The Party* starring Peter Sellers. In the early eighties, casting of Indian actors in major films had an uptick, but the issue of stereotyping remained. In the 1983 James Bond epic *Octopussy*, veteran Indian actor Kabir Bedi was cast as one of the main villains. However, his character was portrayed as a largely silent and sneering stereotypical exotic Indian villain. This portrayal manifested itself even more controversially in *Indiana Jones and The Temple of Doom* in 1984. Legendary Bollywood villain Amrish Puri was cast as the evil leader Mola Ram in this highly-anticipated movie, but was shown as a Goddess Kali worshipping, heart-tearing, cult leader who beats children.

Such stereotypes of the "Exotic East" continued even into the early 2000s. In 2003, in the film *The Guru*, an Indian immigrant is shown looking for work and ends up becoming a professional sex guru. The film makes abundant jokes about Indian eroticism and even has our leading man wear a turban. While some films like *Monsoon Wedding* in 2001 and *Bend It Like Beckham* in 2002—both by Indian-origin filmmakers Mira Nair and Gurinder Chadha—gained international popularity, Indians were still considered "niche" as far as Western cinema was concerned. Luckily as the mid-2000s came, this completely changed.

Hollywood Goes to White Castle: The Rise of Kal Penn

In the early 2000s, Kalpen Suresh Modi, better known as Kal Penn, was a young, working actor from New Jersey stuck in the rut of middling roles in various teen comedies. His first film, the cult flick *American Desi*, had been a bona fide hit in the independent film circuit, with Penn making a mark in a supporting role as the rap-loving Ajay. Penn, a UCLA acting graduate, continued to struggle to find a big break and continued to receive scripts and auditions that were offensive, asking him to speak in South Asian accents or playing up certain standard Indian stereotypes.

However, in a rare move for a major Hollywood production, Penn was cast in the role of Taj Mahal Badalandabad in the 2002 comedy hit

Van Wilder. Playing a strong sidekick role opposite Ryan Reynolds, the success of the film put Penn on the mainstream acting map, though still with limitations. Penn's character was the stereotypical Indian—accented, shy, and sexually repressed, and these attributes served as the butt of jokes surrounding the character. Penn followed the film with more supporting roles in movies such as *Malibu's Most Wanted, Love Don't Cost a Thing*, and *Dude, Where's the Party*. And then came *Harold and Kumar Go to White Castle*. This was released in 2004 with limited fanfare, a largely unknown cast, limited marketing and the only big name being the director, Danny Leiner. While Penn played the playful Kumar Patel, John Cho played his shy Korean-American friend Harold. The stoner comedy easily surpassed its low budget at the box office, found massive success on video/DVD, and became a cult film which spawned a franchise with two more films.

For the first time on American screens, leading men of ethnic origin were portrayed as mainstream. There were no accents, no turbans, and no stereotypes of any kind. The film was just a simple comedy about two young men figuring out their lives, loves, and goings-on in America in a crazy adventure revolving around a desire to eat a White Castle burger at the restaurant of the same name.

Penn became an instant star and opportunities started pouring in. In 2006, Penn was cast as the lead in director Mira Nair's adaptation of Jhumpa Lahiri's touching novel *The Namesake*, alongside acting veterans Irrfan Khan and Tabu. The film became a critical and theatrical hit. For Penn, it was a milestone because the film showed him in a lead dramatic role apart from his usual teen comedies.

He followed the film by playing the main role in *Van Wilder: The Rise of Taj*, reprising the role of Taj Mahal Badalandabad from the first film. He also played one of the sidekick villains to Kevin Spacey's menacing Lex Luthor in Bryan Singer's *Superman Returns*, marking the first time an Indian-American played a key role in a big blockbuster superhero film. Penn also found success with *Harold and Kumar Escape from Guantanamo Bay* and *A Very Harold and Kumar 3D Christmas*.

Penn, not to be an actor to be stuck in stereotypes, also found good roles and much appreciation on television during this same period. He played strong roles on shows such as *24, How I Met Your Mother, Designated Survivor* and *House*.

Penn broke barriers for Indian-American actors with the success of his various roles and opened a whole new avenue for Indians who nursed an ambition to pursue a career in the entertainment world. If not for his portrayal of Indian characters as a regular part of society, Indian-American actors may still have had to struggle to find quality parts.

The Dawn of Night: The Amazing Success of M Night Shyamalan

The year was 1999 and a horror-thriller film released that audiences had no idea would become one of the most iconic films of all time. At once both touching and terrifying, the film became one of the biggest hits of the year, with a dialogue from the film, "I see dead people", becoming part of film lore. The credit for the success of the film *The Sixth Sense* could be attributed to the film's talented young writer-director M Night Shyamalan.

M Night, born Manoj Nelliyattu Shyamalan, grew up in a comfortable life in Pennsylvania. Manoj became bitten by the cinema bug at an early age, idolizing filmmakers such as Steven Spielberg, and dreamt of becoming a filmmaker at a time when Hollywood had no prominent Indian-American filmmakers. The ambitious young man subsequently took a chance and enrolled at NYU's famed film school to pursue his dreams. While at the school, Shyamalan made his first feature, *Praying with Anger*, where he served quadruple duty as director, producer, writer, and actor, followed by *Wide Awake*, a dramedy.

While neither film catapulted him to fame, Shyamalan's creative juices continued to flow. Known as a writer of light comedies and children's films, such as the much-loved *Stuart Little,* Shyamalan sought to change direction with the latest script that he wrote, a supernatural thriller called *The Sixth Sense.*

Getting the film made proved to be quite challenging for the young filmmaker. Shyamalan, then 25 years old, was deeply attached to the script and was adamant that in order to get the film made, studios had to adhere to specific asks on his part. Most notably, he wanted to be able to direct the film, and sell it at a minimum of $1 million, driven by a passion to make sure that either the film gets made in the way that he envisioned it, or not get made at all. The key force behind the purchase of *The Sixth Sense* was none other than the production head of Disney at the time, David Vogel, who purchased the script for over $2 million, a price higher than what Shyamalan had pitched.

After the sale of the script, and the studio meeting his demands, Shyamalan had all of the clout necessary to make the film that he set out to make. Shyamalan was able to cast superstar Bruce Willis in the film, which added to the movie's commercial potential and marketability.

With low expectations, the film released in August of 1999 and instantly became a surprise blockbuster, as audiences resonated with the film's themes of loss, fear, and redemption. Unlike most horror movies, the movie had a deep emotional core, stirring performances, and an original story. Of particular renown is the movie's famous twist at the end, which forced some audiences to watch the film multiple times in a new way. The amalgamation of these factors is what contributed to the iconic nature of the film, and the credit went entirely to M Night. In fact, the famous twist ending was to become a key hallmark of M Night's subsequent movies.

Following the mammoth success of *The Sixth Sense,* Shyamalan had a new set of pressures—dealing with a growing brand name. *The Sixth Sense* had been the top movie at the box office for five weeks and, as *The Atlantic* noted, "At the time, that financial run was practically unheard of; the only parallel in recent memory is the smaller (but similarly consistent) moneymaking power of *The Greatest Showman.*" Accolades and awards also touched the film, where it earned a whopping six Oscar nominations including Best Picture, Director, Supporting Actress, and Actor.

Shyamalan's next venture was a slight pivot, a superhero thriller entitled *Unbreakable.* Once again, he took on writing and directing duties, and cast Bruce Willis in the lead role in the film alongside Samuel L Jackson. *Unbreakable* released in 2000 and was a worldwide box office success, which continued to cement Shyamalan's status as a filmmaker to reckon with.

In 2002, Shyamalan signed Mel Gibson and Joaquin Phoenix for his next project, a supernatural suspense thriller called *Signs,* which also received critical acclaim and box office gold. He was on a hot streak of success and critical acclaim, but as in the case of most good things, what goes up must also come down. *The Atlantic* wrote, "Shyamalan himself began to cultivate an air of mystery and quickly became one of the rare directors who can sell a movie on their name alone." He was, perhaps unfortunately, dubbed "the next Spielberg" by *Newsweek* on the release of his 2002 film *Signs*. Though he's made several other hits, the phenomenon of *The Sixth Sense* proved difficult for him to move past. His next three thrillers, *The Village*, *Lady in the Water*, and *The Happening* all became critical and commercial disappointments.

Following these failures, Shyamalan tried to change gears with two sci-fi adventures, *The Last Airbender* and *After Earth*, but once again Shyamalan tasted failure. At this juncture, he was at crossroads to come up with something good fast or risk becoming a one-time wonder. Luckily for him, his comeback was right around the corner.

In 2015, Shyamalan wrote and directed *The Visit*, a horror-comedy made in the found footage format. The film proved to be a huge success when it released, and was widely touted as a "back to form" for Shyamalan. The film was certainly fresh with great performances, but what really made it stand apart was its focus on comedy and horror together. Audiences laughed and felt scared at the same time, producing the blend of two distinct genres that are in fact opposites of each other. Shyamalan once again became a director of repute with widespread acceptance of *The Visit* and not too long after, he wrote and directed his next film, a psychological thriller, *Split*, starring James McAvoy in 2017. The film proved to be an even bigger success than *The Visit*. Buoyed by the love for *Split*, Shyamalan penned and directed a sequel, *Glass*, in 2019 which was also a huge money spinner, though critical reviews were mixed.

As of 2020, with his last three movies becoming blockbusters, Shyamalan proved that he is a talent here to stay.

Mindy Kaling: The Girl from Massachusetts

Mindy Kaling was born Vera Mindy Chokalingam in 1979 in the state of Massachusetts to parents who were immigrants from India. As time went by, Mindy began to recognize an unusual talent that she possessed—the ability to write, present, and weave together stories in a manner which was relatable and entertaining. As *Variety* noted, "Even as a young kid, Kaling loved to tell stories. After school, she would spend afternoons at her mother's practice, where she would be cordoned off in a room where patients' blood was drawn. She'd amuse herself by writing single-page plays involving fantastical situations such as a haunted house populated by ghosts, werewolves and goblins. She realized she was funny when something she created would get her mother to laugh."

Upon completion of her studies, Kaling began to pursue a career in the arts. She moved to New York and, given her talent for telling stories, wrote a one-act play, *Matt and Ben.* Telling the story of the friendship between actors Matt Damon and Ben Affleck, the satirical play became a huge success, and became the main turning point in Kaling's career. Legendary writer, producer, and showrunner Greg Daniels had been in attendance at a performance of the play and loved Kaling's performance and writing so much that he hired her for a new sitcom he was developing about a gaggle of crazy personalities working through the mundane day to day of an average American office. That show would become *The Office.*

Upon being hired on *The Office*, it did not take long for actors, co-workers, and executives to realize the uniqueness of Kaling's talents as she was one of the youngest hired writers on the show, and initially the only woman and person of color. As *Variety* said, "Kaling quickly distinguished herself not only with her ability to compose killer jokes but also with her talent for story…Kaling gravitated toward stories based in conflict—the kind of squirm-inducing, awkward and hilarious moments that became the stock…."

Kaling also created an Indian-American character for the show, Kelly Kapoor, a role which she would also end up playing herself. As *Vanity Fair* wrote, "Kaling didn't rely on stereotypes about Indian-Americans in the workplace, but, with Kapoor, put forth a representation we hadn't seen before: an American-born desi who is ambivalent about her identity." The ditzy, but lovable, Kapoor character not only became a huge fan favorite, but also exposed Kaling as a talented actress to the world and broke stereotypes about Indian-American characters on television. Eventually, Kaling's success would lead to her to also become an executive producer on the show.

Kaling's stint on *The Office* was not all roses, as Kaling experienced discrimination during her tenure. As noted in *Elle*, "Early on in her tenure at *The Office*, the show was nominated for an Emmy for Outstanding

Comedy Series. Shortly after, the Television Academy, which puts on the awards show, told Kaling that because there were too many producers on *The Office*, they were going to cut her from the list. She, the only woman of color on the team, wouldn't be eligible for an Emmy like the rest of the staff." Despite these challenges, Kaling was determined that nothing would prevent her from pursuing her work and she set out to prove that *The Office* would not be her only achievement.

Kaling conceived a new television show which she would also produce and star in, called *The Mindy Project*, as her next vehicle. Given her popularity, getting the show off the ground was not difficult for Kaling. Fox, a major television network, purchased the show, which would tell the story of Mindy Lahiri (played by Kaling) and her experiences in New York City. The show became an instant success, and was hailed by *Vanity Fair* as "revolutionary". A lot of this success was attributed to Mindy presenting a non-ethnocentric viewpoint that was relatable to all, especially women. As *Vanity Fair* stated, "Kaling turned one of the most common tropes about Indian-Americans on its head: the aspiring, straight-A student who becomes a physician. Lahiri is a doctor, but she is not quiet or particularly geeky. She takes up space (sometimes to the point of narcissism), dresses in bright colors, subsists on rom-coms. She dates, and she likes sex. She is also sometimes offensive...." *The Mindy Project* would go on for six seasons, further embellishing the legend of Kaling. Due to the show, she became the first woman of color to produce, write, and lead an evening sitcom for a major network. Success continued to come for Mindy as she began to hit the big time with roles in blockbuster films such as the fantasy *A Wrinkle in Time* and *Ocean's 8*, a female-led heist film.

In 2020, Kaling produced and wrote Netflix's superhit series *Never Have I Ever*, a semi-autobiographical project based on her experiences of growing up as an Indian-American teen. The show proved to be a gigantic success for the streaming service, once again breaking barriers by focusing exclusively on the trials and tribulations of Indian-Americans in a universally accessible setting. Kaling admitted, however, that doing the show was not all that easy as she had found her childhood "incredibly embarrassing" and felt all of her negative emotions from that time would come back. However, it would be her interactions with fellow writers, who were Indian-American women, that would ultimately change her opinion, as she said, "...once they began sharing stories", her outlook changed. "It ended up being very cathartic, actually... it made me feel that all the stuff I was going through as a teenager, I was not alone."

With such a diverse career, Kaling continues to be a role model for South Asians in America. She was named as one of *People Magazine*'s Most Beautiful in 2011 and acknowledged the importance of what she has represented, most notably being a symbol of those young women who want to pursue careers in the arts.

Aziz Ansari: Funny Person

"Raaaaaaaaaaaandy" became a gigantic catchphrase when a young, bearded Indian-American comedian made a memorable cameo as a crazy stand-up comedian of the same name in *Funny People* in 2009. The film, starring big stars like Adam Sandler, Seth Rogen, and Leslie Mann, and directed by Judd Apatow, had such a strong pedigree to boost it, but audiences were enthralled by the short role done by comedian Aziz Ansari. Ansari's unique intonation, crazy delivery and cocky attitude in the role brought more attention to a comedian whose stock was already growing.

Ansari was born in 1983 in South Carolina and after a strong academic career in high school, enrolled at New York University, where he decided to study marketing at the prestigious Stern School of Business. Eventually, Ansari realized that this was not what he envisioned as his future and has since expressed that his only motivation to pursue marketing was because it would serve as a "practical" career decision. While he grew increasingly disillusioned with business, Ansari decided to continue to pursue his love for comedy and became a stand-up comedian. Unlike other South Asian comedians who were gaining popularity by focusing on racial humor and stereotypes, Ansari made his comedy more relatable, touching on topics such as relationships and popular culture, thus causing his stock as an amateur comedian to continue to grow.

Ansari's first step toward legitimate comedy came when he joined the Upright Citizens Brigade, a comedic institution in its own right. While there, he hosted a show entitled *Crash Test*, and made friends with two fellow comedians, Paul Scheer and Rob Huebel. Ansari's naturalistic and relatable comedy began to gain some further traction and in 2006, he was awarded the "Best Standup" jury award at the US Comedy Arts Festival from HBO. The win led Ansari, Scheer, Huebel, and comic filmmaker named Jason Woliner to sign a contract to produce their own sketch comedy show for MTV in 2007 entitled *Human Giant.* The show became an instant success, with Ansari standing out.

With *Human Giant* gaining popularity, Ansari caught the eye of writer-producer-director Judd Apatow, known for making films such as *The 40 Year Old Virgin* and *Knocked Up*. Apatow cast him in a small role as crazy comedian Randy in *Funny People,* which was a breakthrough role for Ansari. The character became so popular, that he received his own online short films. The effect of this character led Ansari to gain two significant landmarks for his career, a solo stand-up special *Intimate Moments for a Sensual Evening* in 2010 and as a regular on NBC's *Parks and Recreation*. The former became a huge success and set the foundation for Ansari's stand-up persona—a pop culture, food-loving, woke, and sarcastic young man navigating through daily situations that cause stress.

A dream came true for Ansari when in 2014 he starred in a stand-up special for Netflix, *Live at Madison Square Garden*, which he wrote, produced, starred in, and directed. For every stand-up comedian, performing at Madison Square Garden is a type of pinnacle, a validation of becoming an entertainer that appeals to thousands and can sell out a massive stadium. Very few comedians, let alone Indian-Americans, have become stand-up comedians with global appeal. This was a special moment not only for Ansari personally, but for the entire gamut of aspiring Indian-American comedians who saw someone like them achieve a dream that was previously thought of as unattainable.

In 2015, Netflix launched *Master of None*, a new comic-drama series co-created, written, produced by, and starring Ansari. Upon release, it was a blockbuster, bringing Ansari some of the best reviews ever in his career. The show, in some ways autobiographical, is both touching and humorous as Ansari's character is played with both pathos and confidence, and reflects common conflicts most young people go through in their late twenties to early thirties. Through the show, Ansari once again broke several stereotypes. Aside from being an Indian-American with complete creative control of the show, his character of Dev is also portrayed as an American, rather than as an Indian-American sans any stereotyping. He also pursues a career path in entertainment, subverting typical depictions of Indian-Americans as doctors or engaged in other common career paths, and is independent and self-sufficient.

The first season of *Master of None* was such a bona fide hit that Netflix renewed the show for a second season, which released in 2017. It was nominated for several prestigious awards in 2017 and 2018, and Ansari ended up winning a Primetime Emmy for Outstanding Writing in a Comedy Series and a Golden Globe Award for Best Actor in a Television Series—Musical or Comedy. Of note, Ansari became the first Asian to receive the latter honor, making history in the world of entertainment.

Since 2018, Ansari has laid low due to an upheaval in his personal life. An online portal, *Babe.net*, published an account of an unnamed woman who revealed uncomfortable information about a date she went on with Ansari. The story went viral and a fierce debate broke out among the public and entertainment industry about who was at fault. The incident was coupled into the #MeToo movement, and the once outspoken comedian retreated into a shell. In 2019, he surprised audiences with a Netflix special, *Right Now*, where he reflected on the controversial date and the realizations of the past year in his life. Only time will tell whether Ansari will make the comeback his fans want and restore his image to the glory of the older times, but his contributions to entertainment are undeniable.

Made in America: Nina Davuluri

The year was 2014 and something that no one anticipated happened—Nina Davuluri, a 25-year-old woman from New York, won the Miss America pageant. This was a moment of great pride for Indian-Americans and South Asians all across the US as Davuluri became the first Indian-American and South Asian to do so. The path toward achieving this dream was certainly not an easy one, but through hard work and determination, Davuluri achieved a feat that was considered impossible for South Asian women up until that key moment.

Davuluri, a native of New York, always had an interest in the field of science and believed that because her parents were involved in that realm, she would be pursuing a similar occupation, possibly as a doctor. However, as time went on, Nina exhibited excellence in a multitude of interests and by the time she was in her mid-teens, she started taking part in beauty pageants. During this phase, among the titles that she won were Miss Michigan Outstanding Teen, second place in Miss Teen America, Miss Syracuse, and Miss New York. After winning Miss New York, Nina entered into the Miss America competition and ultimately won the contest over 51 other contestants. While Davuluri's win was something to be celebrated, she would soon encounter a disturbing challenge.

Following her victory, Nina became the subject of hateful comments publicly and over social media over her ethnicity. However, she handled this situation with utmost grace by stating, "The biggest thing I realized is that many of these remarks aren't necessarily meant to be malicious but are simply a factor of ignorance."

Nina subsequently channeled all of her views, talents, and wins toward a myriad of social good causes, initiatives, and visual projects and is now a proud actor, producer, host, advocate, and entrepreneur. Among her many accomplishments, she has been the producer of a documentary, *#COMPLEXion*, focused on beauty and the skin lightening trade, a cause for which she has advocated tirelessly for diversity and embracing one's identity; she has been the host of a reality show, *Made in America,* on Zee TV Americas focused on helping young women understand their own beauty and break preexisting myths; launched a platform "Celebrating Diversity Through Cultural Competency"; spoken at 47 universities around the world; promoted women in STEM with the Departments of Energy and Education; and worked with former First Lady Michelle Obama on the "Let's Move" campaign, among other achievements.

Dancing into Our Hearts: Joya Kazi

While major successes in the arts get highlighted primarily on the acting and filmmaking front, what Indian-Americans have achieved in the arts beyond these fields cannot be disregarded. In particular, with dance and music being key staples of Indian culture and movies, it goes without saying that there are many who have established themselves as the gold standard in these art forms. On the dance front, one emerging talent who has won fans around the world through her excellent work is choreographer Joya Kazi.

Kazi was born in Mumbai but grew up in the Bay Area, and at a very early age, began to recognize her passion for dance. The earliest inspiration toward dance started for Kazi when she, at the age of three, saw Michael Jackson's chartbusting *Black or White* music video, where the presence of an Odissi dancer in the video caught her eye. Captivated by the thought of seeing someone like her on screen, Kazi immediately told her mother that she wanted to pursue something similar. Starting her training at the age of eight, Kazi would ultimately get trained in several different Indian dance forms such as Bharatanatyam, Odissi, and Kathak, setting a strong foundation for her future. It was officially at the age of 12, after seeing a concert choreographed by famous well-known Bollywood choreographer Shiamak Davar, that she openly expressed her desire to become a choreographer to her parents. From that point on, there would be no looking back for the ambitious young woman. When she turned 16, Kazi founded her very own dance company, Joya Kazi Unlimited, focusing primarily on Bollywood dancing and entertainment.

At the outset of her career, however, Kazi faced several challenges—the same ones many Indian-Americans face when they pursue a career in the arts—social stigma and heavy competition. The situation reached a point where she even decided that she would change her career path to the legal field, but during that time Kazi had an epiphany—that she was in charge of her own destiny and no outside source can or should influence her dreams.

Since that time, Kazi has built up an impressive reputation and résumé, making her a renowned choreographer across the world, working with names such as Hrithik Roshan, Madhuri Dixit, Jaqueline Fernandez, and Priyanka Chopra Jonas. Kazi has worked across international waters, in both the American and Indian film industries with television and film opportunities, music videos, and commercials for top companies like Disney and Dreamworks. She has also performed for prestigious events such as the Grammys and IIFA Awards and done music videos with talents such as Nick Cannon.

Kazi's latest accomplishment was her gig as the choreographer for Netflix's blockbuster show *Never Have I Ever*.

Other Entertainers of Prominence

There are so many other Indian-Americans who have continued to break barriers in the entertainment industry and have established a name for themselves, a trend that is here to stay.

One such name is actor-writer-filmmaker Jay Chandrasekhar, a member of the comedy troop Broken Lizard, who has written, directed, and acted in movies such as *Super Troopers*, *Super Troopers 2*, and *Beerfest*. He also directed the 2005 action comedy *The Dukes of Hazzard*, starring Jessica Simpson. While M Night Shyamalan is a very well-known Indian-American filmmaker, Chandrasekhar's filmography has proved that he is just as talented and prolific a filmmaker who has made his mark in Hollywood.

Comedians Russell Peters and Hasan Minhaj are also names to reckon with. Peters, originally from Canada, has been hailed as a pioneering comedian for South Asians and Indian-Americans, and is one of the highest-paid stand-up comedians in the world. His racial-focused humor has made millions around the world roll in the aisles with laughter and his stand-up specials *Outsourced*, *Notorious*, *Red White & Brown*, *Deported*, *Green Card* and *Almost Famous* are loved by international audiences.

Hasan Minhaj, also a stand-up comedian, achieved global fame with his stint as a correspondent on *The Daily Show*. Following a much-acclaimed appearance at the 2017 White House Correspondents Dinner, Minhaj garnered a critically acclaimed Netflix special, *Homecoming King*, followed by a successful Netflix series, *Patriot Act with Hasan Minhaj*. Minhaj was also named as one of the most influential people in the world by *Time* magazine in 2019.

It is also important to note that Indian-American actors have not only made waves in Hollywood, but have conquered Bollywood as well. A shining example of this achievement would be California-born and raised actor Omi Vaidya, who gained worldwide fame with his portrayal of Chatur "Silencer" Ramalingam in 2009's Hindi blockbuster *3 Idiots*. Following the success of the film, Vaidya won several awards for his acting from prominent Indian award programs such as IIFA, Screen and Lions Gold awards. Vaidya has continued to find success in both India and the US, acting in films such as *Dil Toh Baccha Hai Ji*, *Jodi Breakers*, *Desi Boyz*, *Players*, *For Here Or To Go*, *Blackmail* and *Mirror Game*. He also has received accolades for his role in the Indian-American series *Brown Nation* and *Metro Park*.

Among actors of Indian origin who have made a mark in Hollywood, most notable is Priyanka Chopra Jonas. The actress, who made a splash in Bollywood with a myriad of successful films, made a pathbreaking transition to Hollywood when she starred as the lead in ABC's *Quantico*. The success of *Quantico*, which lasted for three seasons, was followed by key roles in major Hollywood films for Chopra in projects such as *Baywatch*, *Isn't It Romantic?*, and *We Can Be Heroes*. Before Chopra, however, it is important to note that Indian actors such as Shashi Kapoor, Om Puri, Irrfan Khan, Shabana Azmi, Anupam Kher and Naseeruddin Shah all appeared in American films, some commercial and some independent. What defines Chopra's transition to Hollywood as important when compared to these prominent names is that she played a mainstream lead in major commercial projects, where only her character was important. There was no focus on her ethnicity, nor any attempt to formally define her as "Indian" or stereotype her. As society continues to globalize, where diversity and every ethnicity are a part of daily interactions and life, the success that Chopra has found in these roles means that being "Indian" and leading a project are a part of the norm. Everyone can identify with anyone, irrespective of race. In contrast, most of the roles portrayed by the Indian actors earlier were either supporting roles or blatantly trying to show the person as distinctly "Indian". The roles gave minor exposure to the actors, but typically begot similar types of roles for them in international projects.

Ashok Amritraj, youngest brother of tennis ace Vijay Amritraj, gained prominence as one of the most prolific producers in Hollywood with his production company Hyde Park Entertainment. He has produced successful films such as *Bringing Down the House* starring Steve Martin and Queen Latifah, *Ghost Rider: Spirit of Vengeance* starring Nicholas Cage, *Original Sin* starring Antonio Banderas and Angelina Jolie, *Battlefield Earth* starring John Travolta, *Get Carter* starring Sylvester Stallone, *Bandits* starring Bruce Willis and *Walking Tall* starring Dwayne "The Rock" Johnson, among countless other projects. All in all, he has produced over 100 films which have made over $2 billion at the box office.

Talent behind the scenes has not been limited to only producing and directing, but also technical areas such as cinematography. Andrij Parekh has made a mark for himself in cinematography and direction and, in 2020, won a Primetime Emmy for his directing work on an episode of HBO's *Succession.* Parekh, who was originally born in Boston and raised in Minneapolis, has several prominent film credits to his name that he has shot such as *Blue Valentine* and *The Zookeeper's Wife.* Due to his recent Emmy win and growing reputation as an excellent talent, Parekh has signed a one-year deal with HBO, where he will film an HBO limited series entitled *Scenes From a Marriage* and direct an episode of the next season of *Succession.*

On the music front, when one thinks of Indian-American achievers, immediately the name Norah Jones comes to mind. Daughter of the legendary doyen of sitar, Pandit Ravi Shankar, music was in Jones's blood. The 41-year-old has an astounding nine wins and 17 nominations from the Grammys, where for her first album (*Come Away with Me*) alone, she won five Grammys including Best Artist, Album of the Year, and Record of the Year. Aside from Jones, another name gaining recognition is composer-pianist Vijay Iyer, who received a Grammy nomination in 2011 for Best Jazz Instrumental Album, Individual or Group for *Historicity*.

When one thinks of an Indian-American that epitomizes the amalgamation of talent, beauty, glamor and achievement, the name of actress, author, model, entrepreneur and television host Padma Lakshmi comes to mind. Born in India, she was raised in New York and California. She followed modeling by pursuing her interests in acting by appearing in shows such as *Star Trek: Enterprise*, and films such as *Boom* and *The Mistress of Spices*. However, she would find her big break through her love for cooking, as since 2006, she has been a host of Food Network's popular show *Top Chef.* She is also an executive producer on the show and has written several cookbooks further displaying her culinary knowledge and talent.

In addition to these accolades, Lakshmi was named as one of *People Magazine*'s 100 Most Beautiful People in 2007 and was also on *Maxim*'s

Hot 100 of 2007 ranking. Lakshmi is also an Emmy nominee, runs several culinary and home decoration entrepreneurial ventures such as Padma's Easy Exotic and the Padma Collection, and has contributed to social causes as an ambassador for the ACLU and the United Nations Development Program. Her website also lists that she is a co-founder of the Endometriosis Foundation of America and is a visiting scholar at MIT.

The Rise of the Indian-American Entertainer

From the early days of Sabu, to today where Indian-Americans are winning major beauty pageants, starring in and producing their own projects for major studios and networks, and creating melodious music, the community has come a long way in the world of arts and entertainment. Kal Penn, Mindy Kaling, and Aziz Ansari's success marks a departure from anything seen before. Here were normal Indian-Americans who found success smoothly pursuing an unconventional path. The rise of these performers, among many others, is built on the foundation of the "normalcy" of their characters and this is a trend which will continue to give way to more Indian-American actors finding leading roles in Hollywood projects. What was believed to be unattainable and impossible is now seen as not only something viable, but also as a badge of honor and respect. Indian-Americans are all set to essay a larger role in the world of American entertainment.

References

AB Wire., 'Kal Penn's 90s audition scripts highlight racism in Hollywood' (*The American Bazaar*, 25 March 2017) <https://www.americanbazaaronline.com/2017/03/15/kal-penns-90s-audition-scripts-highlight-racism-in-hollywood423510/> accessed 2 November 2020

Bain, Jennifer 'Padma Lakshmi a global brand in the making' (*Toronto Star*, 22 December 2007) <https://www.thestar.com/life/food_wine/2007/12/22/padma_lakshmi_a_global_brand_in_the_making.html> accessed 6 January 2021

Brooke, Michael., 'BFI Screenonline: Sabu (1924-1963)' (*BFI Screenonline*, 2003-2014) <http://www.screenonline.org.uk/people/id/459165/index.html> accessed 25 October 2020

Czajkowski, Elise., 'The Evolution of Aziz Ansari' (*Vulture*, 6 November 2015) <https://www.vulture.com/2015/11/aziz-ansari-evolution.html> accessed 17 November 2020

Drummond, Charlotte., 'Interview with Joya Kazi' (*Overachiever Magazine*, Unknown) <https://www.overachievermagazine.com/interviews/interview-with-joya-kazi> accessed 22 December 2020

Freeman, Hadley., 'Mindy Kaling: 'I was so embarrassed about being a diversity hire' (*The Guardian*, 31 May 2019) <https://www.theguardian.com/film/2019/may/31/mindy-kaling-i-was-so-embarrassed-about-being-a-diversity-hire > accessed 16 November 2020

Gross, Terry., 'Mindy Kaling Brings A New Nerd To TV, And Finds She "Was Not Alone" As A Teen' (*NPR*, 27 April2020) <https://www.npr.org/2020/04/27/845440741/mindy-kaling-brings-a-new-nerd-to-tv-and-finds-she-was-not-alone-as-a-teen> accessed 16 November 2020

Hunt, Geoff and Pepe, T., 'More than pretty' (*ASBMB Today*, 2014 November 1) <https://www.asbmb.org/asbmb-today/people/110114/more-than-pretty#.VFpus_qPUUo.twitter> accessed 17 November 2020

King, Susan., "I Wasn't Bluffing": M Night Shyamalan Recalls 'Sixth Sense' Pitch and Frenzy That Followed' (*The Hollywood Reporter*, 2 August 2019) <https://www.hollywoodreporter.com/heat-vision/i-wasnt-bluffing-m-night-shyamalan-recalls-sixth-sense-pitch-frenzy-followed-1228534> accessed 2 November 2020

Lang, Brent., 'Mindy Kaling Created Her Own Opportunities (and Doesn't Plan on Stopping)' (*Variety*, 23 January 2019) <https://variety.com/2019/film/features/mindy-kaling-late-night-sundance-1203112400/> accessed 16 November 2020

Loosvelt, Derek., '"Parks and Recreation" Star Aziz Ansari Chose Comedy Over Go' (*Vault*, 19 April 2011) <https://www.vault.com/blogs/in-the-black-vaults-finance-careers-blog/parks-and-recreation-star-aziz-ansari-chose-comedy-over-goldman-sachs> accessed 17 November 2020

Mukhopadhyay, Samhita., 'Mindy Kaling in Full Bloom' (*Vanity Fair*, 30 May 2019) <https://www.vanityfair.com/hollywood/2019/05/mindy-kaling-in-full-bloom> accessed 16 November 2020

Nelson, Rebecca., 'Mindy Kaling Didn't Sign Up to Be a Role Model' (*Elle*, 9 October 2019) <https://www.elle.com/culture/a29340748/mindy-kaling-interview-2019/> accessed 16 November 2020

Nichols, Mackenzie., '"The Sixth Sense" Turns 20: M Night Shyamalan and Haley Joel Osment Tell All' (*Variety*, 2 August 2019) <https://variety.com/2019/film/news/the-sixth-sense-turns-20-m-night-shyamalan-haley-joel-osment-1203259434/> accessed 2 November 2020

Noah, Trevor., 'Hasan Minhaj' (*Time 100*, 2019) <https://time.com/collection/100-most-influential-people-2019/5567704/hasan-minhaj/> accessed 22 December 2020

Sims, David., 'How The Sixth Sense Conquered Hollywood in 1999' (*The Atlantic*, 6 August 2019) <https://www.theatlantic.com/entertainment/archive/2019/08/how-sixth-sense-conquered-hollywood-1999/595558/> accessed 2 November 2020

VoyageLA, 'Life and Work with Joya Kazi' (*VoyageLA*, April 15, 2019) <http://voyagela.com/interview/life-work-joya-kazi/?doing_wp_cron=1608644081.26153802871704101 56250> accessed 22 December 2020

Three Generations of Hoteliers: How Indian-Americans Reinvented the Hotel Industry

BIJAL PATEL

Like many Patels, I was born to be a hotelier. My parents brought me directly from the maternity ward to their roadside motel apartment in the Santa Cruz Mountains of California. I grew up playing baseball and riding bikes, while also pitching in with chores around our family's hotel property—sweeping outside, vacuuming inside, doing laundry, and changing sheets. In many ways, it was a classic American childhood, and it was certainly a motel home always filled with family and friends.

My story—and that of my family—is typical of the thousands of Indian-Americans who have invested decades of blood, sweat, and tears to reinvent the US hotel industry. As a result, today Asian-Americans own *half* of all hotels in the United States.

The hospitality business is a great fit for Indians because it allows us to proactively practice one of the fundamental principles of Hinduism: "*Atithi Devo Bhava* (the guest is god)".

My parents and grandparents lived that belief; so do I. As the third generation to run our family business and the youngest Indian-American to lead the California Hotel & Lodging Association, my work every day is guided by paying forward a spirit of service—a spirit that honors my family and that may inspire other young Indian-Americans to realize the rewards of hoteling as a way of life.

The First Generation: On the Road

Indian-American dominance of the US hotel industry began with individuals like my grandfather, Purushottambhai Vaghjibhai Patel. Aged 99 now, he grew up in India, then moved to Kenya with other compatriots who sought more opportunity in the 1930s and 1940s. He joined the East African Railway and started a family in Nairobi, where my father, Umesh, and his three brothers were born.

When the UK gave its African colonies independence in the 1960s, many Indians left the continent and returned to India. My grandfather tried to set up a printing business but realized he could be more enterprising abroad, so he again packed his bags, this time for England.

Grandfather returned to a job in transportation, working for the London Underground, and later, buying a newsagent—a shop that sold newspapers and magazines. Over the years, he was able to bring his family to England, one by one. But the reunion was frustrating. He worked such long hours that he rarely saw his family. He met the newspaper deliveries at 4 am, opened the shop at around 5 am, and worked until he shut the doors at 7 pm. Seven days a week.

And then there was the cold. No one moves to England for the weather but for my grandfather's family, the contrast with East Africa was dramatic. The freezing rain was biting; working at the newsagent shop, it seemed months would pass without warming up.

Going to San Francisco

Though the diaspora's presence in England was significant, Indians were busy putting down roots all over the world, including in the US. A visit from Jayantibhai (JC) Patel to my family home in London changed our lives forever. A colleague of my great-great uncle's from Uganda, JC had written my grandfather a letter. "I'm coming to visit England, may I stay with you?" In the 1960s and 1970s, that's how the Gujarati Indian diaspora worked: If you were a friend-of-a friend-of-a-relative, you were my brother.

JC talked excitedly about his new home in San Francisco. He had purchased one hotel in the dodgy Tenderloin section of the city and another in Santa Cruz, a coastal town 90 minutes south. Business was good—and the weather was great. He offered to return the hospitality if my grandfather wanted to visit California some day and check out the business.

The invitation piqued my grandfather's interest. He had previously flown to Chicago—to stay with friends-of-friends, of course—and then traveled around America with a one-month Greyhound bus pass. That's how Indians saw the US in those days. He decided to visit the US again, traveling this time to California, where JC gave him a tour of his properties and an orientation to the hotel business.

Grandfather was sold. He found a roadside motel for sale in a small mountain town called Ben Lomond, just twenty minutes above the surf of Santa Cruz. The mild weather reminded him of Kenya. He had to buy it—he just needed to get the money.

The Gujarati Effect

According to *National Geographic*, the first Gujarati-American hotelier began business in Sacramento in 1942. After arriving in California to work in the fields, many Gujaratis happily traded farm labor for budget-lodging proprietorship. Over the decades, the group's influence expanded to owning half of the nation's 54,000 motels and hotels. Today, 7,900 individuals of Indian descent work as lodging managers, according to the American Communities Survey.

The Indians who settled in America to open hotels during the 1960s and 1970s followed a different route than those who arrived back then. Instead of pursuing harvesting jobs or even master's degrees and professional jobs like today's immigrants, newcomers in those days came to buy small businesses. And considering my family's story, it is easy to see why, for Gujaratis, these enterprises were often hotels. A *New York Times* article estimates there were only about 60–70 Indian-American motel owner/operators in the 1960s and that most of these were in California.

Legally immigrating to the US wasn't that difficult in the 1970s. If you invested $40,000 in a business, you could get a visa, a green card, and a path to citizenship. But when grandfather sold his London shop, the proceeds still weren't enough to buy the motel.

Enter the Gujarati network. The same friends-of-friends who would serve you dinner or let you stay overnight were also happy to help you get on your feet in America. It was this "pay-it-forward" spirit that enabled many Indians to scrape together the funds to set up shop in the US.

My grandfather had helped plenty of Indian friends put down roots in London over the years so he knew the power of the network and how to leverage it. But first he had to clear an extra hurdle: England was in the midst of a moratorium on currency exchange. Only the equivalent of $300 could be taken out of the country at one time. The profit from selling his shop was trapped across the Atlantic.

Here's where the network came in: My grandfather and uncle set about calling and writing everyone they knew in the US—and then, everyone those people knew. The ask? I'll send you—a person I don't personally know—$300. Then you will buy me—a person you have never met—$300 worth of American Express Travelers Cheques. No guarantees. No paperwork. No signatures. Yet thousands of dollars were sent to America and all of the money found its way back to my grandfather.

To get the rest of the down payment? More legwork through the network. This time, contacting established Indian-American business owners. "You remember me/my uncle/my colleague from Kampala/London/Vadodara. Can you lend me $100/$1,000/$3,000 to buy a motel in California? I'll work hard and pay you back as soon as I can." Again, in flowed the cash. No promissory notes. No notaries. Just a line in my grandfather's ledger to repay the lender—which he did. Promptly, properly, and politely.

The network effect is why "Patels" and other Gujaratis are leaders in the US hotel industry today. Their success began with keeping their word and paying back all the private loans. As a newcomer, you were provided with a safety net for success—it was a powerful incentive to become a solid member of the community. As an old-timer, you were humbly grateful and wanted to "pay forward" the generosity that enabled your start.

Our First Hylton

Like thousands of other Indians who immigrated in the 1970s, my grandfather became a hotelier. He traded 15-hour days as a newsagent for 24-hour days as a motel owner-operator.

The difference? Family.

Gujaratis are an entrepreneurial group, not afraid of hard work, not afraid to accept risk, and most comfortable when earning a living while surrounded by loved ones. Motel owners could have their whole family live on-property in the manager's apartment. They could run the business and eat three meals a day with their kids. Financially, they saved considerably on living expenses: Housing and utilities were part of the business expenses. It was a compelling proposition.

A popular rule-of-thumb was "three times cash flow"—if a hotel could be acquired for no more than three times the amount of its annual revenue, then it could be profitable for a hard-working Indian-American family.

But the "immigrant mentality" was, and still is, about more than money—it's about security. It's about making a better life for yourself, for your children, and for future generations of the family.

The Ben Lomond Hylton hotel had 22 rooms in a setting of more than 100 towering redwoods right on tiny Highway 9 across from the San Lorenzo River. George Hylton had built the motel in 1956, admitting he couldn't resist the temptation to add his family name to the property.

Most Indian-American owner-operators ran their properties as a team, usually a married couple. The husband would run the front desk and do the finances; the wife would manage operations and housekeeping. They could not afford to hire staff so they did all the work themselves—checking in guests, cleaning rooms, and making improvements. They knew they had to pay back all the private loans before they could start to accumulate their own nest egg.

The Second Generation: Rooms to Grow

Word spread worldwide among the Indian diaspora that you could have a pretty good life in California. Over the years, more of our friends and relatives arrived to seek their fortunes in America. My father's eldest brother sold his business in England and bought a motel nearby. His other brother came a few years later. Not only was there an opportunity to have a successful business, but you could do it and still be near your extended family.

What drew Gujaratis to the hotel business? While it is unfair to generalize, many Gujaratis who landed to make their fortunes in lodging were not picky about their location. Many did not object to living in rural areas. The job didn't require perfect English so much as it required a willingness to work hard.

Another theory was that Indians arrived at the precise period that the postwar mom-and-pop hoteliers were reaching retirement age. Their kids didn't want to take over the family businesses and property prices became depressed. Indian immigrants were ready and willing to buy these distressed properties from the owners and usher them into the next era.

My father, Umesh, was the youngest of four sons. At 21, he was still struggling in London. My grandfather knew he would do better in California, and since he was under 25 years old, he was able to come to the US as a dependent in 1977 and jump directly into the motel business. By 1981, my parents were married and running the motel together.

A Motel to Call Home

Kids like me literally grew up on-property. I spent 16 years living in our motel apartment, with my grandfather, my parents, and my older sister and brother. For a child, it was a great multi-generational foundation of support. It was from this family environment that I gained invaluable character skills, cultural heritage, and a moral compass for life.

Meanwhile, our motel demonstrated how a family business can be the means to a better life—for me and for the local community. Our motel became one of the many small firms that made our area more vibrant, for example by sponsoring Little League baseball teams and by hosting all kinds of special events.

Our small town was quite white. In fact, we were the only Indian family in the community. Everyone knew us and respected us; we never felt any racism directed at us. I started an international fair at the local school—an annual spirit week where everyone shared food and customs from their culture. On holidays like Diwali, we would gather the three or four Indian families in the area and celebrate in someone's garage or hotel with food and dancing.

Modern American culture became the basis for our interactions outside the home and the family, but at home, we preserved our native Indian culture, religion, and values.

The hotel business was humming by the time President Bill Clinton came to office and raised the limit for Small Business Administration (SBA) loans to $5 million. These government-backed, low down payment, fixed-rate loans allowed small owner-operators like my parents to obtain financing for acquisition of additional properties.

Those loans created a boom in the hotel industry. Motel owners went from owning one property to owning two, three, four, or more. Rebranding became popular, with independent roadside motels signing on to the Day's Inn, Quality Inn or Econo Lodge chains as a way to increase rates and occupancies. While it might have been possible to run one or two hotels as a couple, it wasn't possible to run four or five. So my parents and other second-generation hoteliers began to put in a management structure and hire staff to grow their businesses.

One Bad "Patel"

Despite the many favorable trends, the life of an Indian-American hotelier in the US was not without challenges. The work was hard, especially during the busy summer vacation season—and it sometimes took 24 hours. A guest might ring the "night bell" and my father would have to jump from bed to help out regardless of what time of night.

Then there was the discrimination. In those days, most Americans relied on the American Automobile Association (AAA) guidebook of hotel and motel listings to find out where to stay as they traveled around the country. Trouble was, AAA would not send its inspectors to Indian-owned properties.

When my grandfather bought the Hylton, it had been listed in the AAA book and well-rated. As soon as my grandfather realized the guide may not list an Indian-American establishment, he would tell the AAA inspector, "I just work here; I don't own the motel,"—hoping that our Hylton would continue to be featured in the guidebook. Still, California hoteliers did not experience the racism that some other Indian-American owner-operators did in less tolerant parts of the US.

In the same way, the Gujarati network and the Patel name worked for my grandfather when he needed help to buy his first property but it worked against us when some bad apples started to pop up. Because when one Patel defaulted on a loan or another didn't pay his insurance premium on time, many banks and underwriters decided that no Indian-American was worth the risk.

AAHOA Checks in

In the late 1980s, as the hotel industry was poised for growth, discrimination in finance and insurance threatened to keep Indian-American hoteliers from taking part in this expansion. It was during this time that Day's Inn was expanding from a regional to a national brand. Its president, Michael Leven, was impressed by his Indian-American franchisees and wanted them to be a cornerstone for his company's growth. However, he soon realized the racism his owners from the diaspora were enduring.

As a Jew, Leven was no stranger to discrimination. He funded first-of-its-kind market research to prove Indian-American hotels were as well-managed and clean as those owned by other ethnic groups. Leven then helped bring together a group of about 100 Indian-American owners to found the Asian American Hotel Owners Association (AAHOA).

The goal of this new group was to share resources, to advocate for the industry, and to ensure Indians would be treated fairly by banks, insurance companies, and franchisors. Today, AAHOA has nearly 20,000 members, who together own about half of the hotels in America—it is among the most respected and most influential groups in the hotel industry. As of 2020, its members accounted for billions of dollars in property assets and hundreds of thousands of employees—not bad for a group that accounts for 1 percent of the US population.

Indian-American proprietors leveraged the support of AAHOA to improve their business even further. The group's political action committee (PAC) was founded in 2004 and grew to have significant influence in national elections and policies to be sure that the industry, its owners and its millions of employees were heard. The AAHOA PAC advocated for small businesses and laws to ensure growth and success.

It was around the same time in the 2000s, longtime owner/operator families expanded to build hotels from the ground up. Many contracted with mid-tier brands like Hampton Inn & Suites, Holiday Inn Express, Comfort Inn, and Best Western to construct properties of 80 or 100 rooms or more.

Soon, Indian-American owners were synonymous with the hotel business. The "outsiders" had become mainstream players.

A Spirit of Service

Compared to other professions, Indian-American women always played an important role in the US hotel business—if a mostly behind-the-scenes one. We were proud that our mother, Sandhya Patel, had stepped into the spotlight as a trailblazer for women in the hotel industry. She was proud to be the first woman elected to hold an executive leadership position in the entire hotel industry.

Mother convinced my father that they needed to sign a franchise agreement for our hotel with a brand, Econo Lodge. She then helped my father and grandfather to have our property become a "gold award" winner—a distinction bestowed upon lodges that cracked the top 20 percent nationwide for outstanding customer service and revenue earnings. Her success helped her work her way through the male-dominated Econo Lodge Franchisee Association (ELFA) leadership until she became its president in 2005.

AAHOA recognized her contributions by naming her 2005's Outstanding Woman Hotelier of the Year.

Unfortunately, it was also in 2005 that mother was diagnosed with pancreatic cancer. Recognizing the historic nature of her appointment, she fulfilled her service to the industry as she literally fought for her life. Though doctors had only given her three months to live, mother rallied to live fourteen months and complete her term as president before passing away at the age of 45.

The Third Generation: Next-Level Opportunities

The first generation of Indian-American hotel owners were "accidental hoteliers"—they didn't expect to be in hospitality as a career. They were educated in their mother country for a much different job path than they ultimately achieved in their adopted homeland. However, once they got started, they focused with dramatic success on their one or two small roadside operations.

The first generation of hoteliers created a solid, stable economic foundation on which the second generation of Indian-American owners could build. Often born in the United States and college-educated in business or hospitality, this new group of Indians expanded their family hotel portfolios and put in place sophisticated, data-driven management structure for improved profitability.

Now the third generation is moving to even higher levels of opportunity and success—for example, with larger properties and with international expansion.

Moving Forward and Giving Back

I was just 17 when my mother passed away. Suddenly, our family lost its matriarch, my father lost his life and business partner, and the hotel industry lost an influential leader. We were devastated.

When my mother's life ended, my life as a hotelier began. It wasn't what I had planned—and it wasn't what my parents had planned. They never envisioned for their children to take over their business; they intended to run it themselves. And for me, working in hospitality wasn't even on my radar as a teen. I, like my brothers and sisters, were set on going to college—my intended field of study was biotech.

Life plans had to be reevaluated. My sister and brother were already at university so it was just me at home. I was in my senior year of high school, so my classes ended right after lunch. When I got home, my father would need help with a few things around the hotel. "I'm having trouble with this reservation. Can you call the travel agent?" By pitching in to do the work my mother used to do, I realized I'd been training for a hotel career my whole life.

My father entrusted me with more and more responsibility as the months went by. I was charged with managing a $500,000 renovation of our hotel and with signing a new brand agreement. I decided to study business at Cal Poly University to learn more about the industry. I was fast becoming a real hotelier—and I loved it.

Becoming an "Actionpreneur"

My mother lived by the philosophy of *seva*—"giving back". She definitely put the spark in me to get involved in the industry and make sure my voice was being heard. I wanted to continue her trailblazing work, so while at Cal Poly, I attended my first AAHOA meeting in 2010. The association gave me a glimpse of how a group of owners can work together to drive change in the industry and to overcome obstacles we all face as hoteliers. I quickly learned how as a united group we could be a lot more effective than as unfocused, uncoordinated individuals.

I became an ambassador for AAHOA and a member of the group's Young Professional Hoteliers Committee. In 2017, I was honored with AAHOA's Outstanding Young Professional Hotelier Award.

I like to use the term "actionpreneur" to describe this process of donating time and energy to industry-wide initiatives. When hotel owners join together in trade associations, we can be smarter and quicker in overcoming the obstacles we all face at our respective properties. The group can be a catalyst for individual success.

Breaking Ground in California

I quickly felt at home in the AAHOA. The members were primarly family owners/operators. The discussions at meetings focused around operating efficiency and fundamentals. The meetings reinforced the learnings I had gathered growing up in the hotel business. When I attended an AAHOA conference, I found myself staring at my "Alabama me" or my "Midwest me"—third generation Indian-American hoteliers who had grown up in a very similar environment and now running a very similar proprietorship.

Through AAHOA, I was exposed to collaborating with California Hotel & Lodging Association (CH&LA). Even though I was just 24 at the time,

I was selected to visit Washington, DC, as part of a delegation of hoteliers. We met with senators Diane Feinstein and Barbara Boxer to advocate against certain excessively restrictive regulations in the industry.

Walking into the CH&LA was a very different scene. Where AAHOA proprietors might be managing a property with 100-200 rooms, a CH&LA member might be general manager, asset manager, or catering director of a hotel with 500 rooms—or even a 3,000-room convention hotel. This association was more focused on providing members with tools to expand their business, taking a much broader, 10,000-foot view of the industry, where it was going and how our company could fit in.

Ultimately, I was asked to join the CH&LA Executive Committee in 2017 and I gained the experience to become chairman in 2019. I was honored to be the youngest-ever chairman of the CH&LA since the group's founding in 1893.

Indian-Americans pushed another backer into national leadership when former AAHOA president Chip Rogers was named to the American Hotel & Lodging Association in 2018. Rogers brought several AAHOA members along with him to the national level, including past chairwoman, Jagruti Panwala.

A "Bomb" Hits the Industry

Leading up to 2020, the hotel industry was poised for another year of growth. But when the Covid-19 pandemic blindsided the global economy in March, Indian-American hoteliers were hit hard. The US government response of financial aid was only a little help to those who supported their entire families and staff with room revenue from an industry that was required by law to shut its doors immediately.

"Hotels are a signal industry. Hotel owners and their employees felt the impact of the Covid-19 pandemic at its onset as occupancy rates and revenue declined steeply," said AAHOA President & CEO Cecil P Staton in April.

Owners responded to the economic downturn by closing off floors or wings of their properties and laying off staff. Occupancy rates hovered in the single digits. Yet the US government never arrived with additional aid, taxing the family-owned hotel businesses around the country.

"The catastrophic declines in occupancy rates and revenues make it increasingly likely that the industry will not recover until 2023," Staton added and welcoming the appointment of AAHOA's vice chairman Vinay Patel to a two-year term on the United States Travel and Tourism Advisory Board, he said, "[Vinay's] experience and insight are a valuable addition to discussions about the role travel and tourism will play during the recovery and beyond."

I was humbled and honored when CH&LA chose me to serve a second term as chairman for the year 2021, again a first at CH&LA, and hope to contribute positively in my own way to help in the recovery phase of our sector.

Challenges will continue for our world and our industry, but hotels are important refuges of safety and comfort for travelers. We must protect guests from outside distractions and concerns—one person, one visit, one day at a time.

Inspiring the "Reluctant" Hoteliers

Our family's journey started with an independent, non-branded roadside motel, expanded as we bought branded hotels, and now is growing further as we build hotel properties from the ground up. For example, currently we are developing a Residence Inn by Marriott in Santa Cruz County.

My brother and sister will still tell you that they are not interested in the hotel industry. Granted, both are incredibly successful in their chosen fields. But they also remember how hard our parents worked, how it was tough to get a weekend off, how lousy it is to clean bathrooms, and how the buzz of that night bell still features prominently in their dreams.

I've definitely experienced some "career-ism" where friends question my decision to become a hotelier, asking, "Why do you want to run a motel with your dad?" Those questions are frustrating for me because I know that a career in hospitality is so much more than giving guests a room key when they check in and cleaning rooms after they leave. These days, being a successful hotelier requires extensive knowledge of various financial, technology, personnel, and legal issues.

Yes, I was lucky. After two years, my father entrusted me with major projects and took my ideas about which direction our business should go. With a combination of on-the-job learning and classroom education, I am proud to be taking our family business to higher levels.

Growing up in the hills above Silicon Valley, many of my friends and family have chosen more traditional paths in technology or law or other fields and have become very successful. They've got 401ks or stock options. I, on the other hand, might have to cover a night shift for a front-desk manager who is sick or pitch in changing sheets during the summer rush. I've rolled up my sleeves and cleaned a lot of hotel rooms, especially during the special circumstances brought on by Covid.

But I love that I'm my own boss; I've got all the flexibility I want, which will help me to have a great work-life balance when it's time to settle down and raise a family. I am enjoying myself, but more importantly, I am constantly looking for ways to do things better—for myself and for our industry. I have a whole new appreciation for how exciting, sophisticated, and rewarding the hotel business could be.

I'm hoping my career will inspire other third-generation kids who grew up on-property to join me in redefining the hotel industry for coming generations. We are all aware that the business world has changed dramatically since our parents and grandparents immigrated to the United States.

It's not just a mom-and-pop business anymore; today's hospitality industry is global, crowded, and competitive. It is more sophisticated, more expensive, moves faster, and requires more due diligence and legal protection. It is harder to assemble investment coalitions and almost unheard of to finalize deals with just a handshake—or a line in a ledger.

While doing business today is difficult, young Indian-Americans are well equipped to succeed in this environment—and succeed impressively. We are building on generations of knowledge and resources to take the hospitality business to the next level. The opportunities are almost endless.

Universities like Cornell and San Diego State now even offer business degrees in hospitality, which help get fledgling hoteliers off on the right foot. If we can get more young Indian-Americans to add "hotelier" to their list of career options, we can help ensure that Indian-Americans continue to be leaders and pioneers in the hotel industry.

Three Generations, One Way of Life

Like so many thousands of mid-century Indian-American immigrants, I don't think my grandfather envisioned that he would be the patriarch of a hotel business. And I don't think my mother ever envisioned her son would be building a Marriott. Nor would she have believed the combination of disasters that has hit our business in 2020. But having survived previous forest fires, floods, earthquakes and recessions, she would surely have believed our family and our business would emerge stronger. Like so many ethnic Indians of my generation, my parents and grandparents worked very hard to build a foundation for our family's business success.

Though my family no longer lives on-property, my father, grandfather and I still live together in a neighborhood nearby. Three generations of hotelier bachelors working from home in the same house—it sounds like the perfect setup for a TV sitcom, but actually it's the perfect environment to reflect with each other on the challenges ahead and to find ways that we can grow beyond, collectively as an industry and individually as owners.

And one thing's for sure: The hotel business is in our DNA. *Atithi Devo Bhava.*

Every day, my father, accompanied sometimes by my grandfather, still head over to our Ben Lomond hotel, to observe the operation and interact with our guests. One family has stayed with us every summer for decades. Now they bring their grandkids and great grandkids, as well. They can't go home until they've had a chance to see my grandfather and catch up.

That's the magic of *seva* at work: Sometimes it doesn't even seem like work.

Being a hotelier is indeed a great way to make a living, to build a family, and to give back to the communities where we do business. It's hard work, but it's simply an enriching way of life. And that's the credo that has been the guiding force for not just this three generations of Patel family—but hundreds of such Patel and other Indian-American hoteliers, most of whom owe their working traits and business acumen to the culture of their native Gujarat.

Millennials: Straddling Two Cultures Halfway Around the World

Laxmi Parthasarathy

In January 2020, Global Press launched in Mongolia, staffed by seven talented and rigorously trained journalists—all female and all hailing from local communities across the country in need of quality media coverage. Days later, the coronavirus pandemic hit, and Mongolia locked down faster than almost any country in the world. Other international media sources that relied on foreign correspondents could no longer access the country. Suddenly, our latest news bureau was one of the only sources of world-class journalism covering Mongolia for local and global audiences alike.

As chief operating officer of Global Press, I was confident our reporters would rise to the challenge—with good reason. I'd spent an entire year leading an exhaustive process to find those seven remarkable recruits. They came from the 700 applications we'd sought out from all over Mongolia—from the Gobi Desert in the south, to the city of Darkhan in the north. I'd crisscrossed the country to spread the word that Global Press was hiring, airing local and national radio ads in Mongolian and handing out information cards to dozens of local journalism associations and community groups.

After exploring a new country, it was time to go back to my roots. From Mongolia, I flew to India, where much of my extended family lives. In addition, my husband Varun—like me, a Western-born millennial of Indian descent—had moved to Delhi for a stint working in the Indian renewable energy sector. For both of us, our past, present, and future are scattered across continents. Our heritage is from India, we met and now live in the United States, and our hearts are set on changing the world well beyond the horizons our parents imagined when they left India to immigrate to North America.

Opportunity is the greatest gift my parents gave me. By raising me in their adopted country, they've given me a launchpad to spread my wings and pursue my convictions the world over. Now I've launched news bureaus from Puerto Rico to Nepal to Mexico to Mongolia. It's been a long personal journey over more than a decade since I held the first print copy of my own newspaper—my first venture in a career devoted to building diverse and representative newsrooms around the globe. The conviction that drives me is that journalism is failing communities around the world. It will take local, diverse reporters to reclaim the narrative about the communities they cover. In my role at Global Press—an international news organization that operates more than forty news bureaus from Mexico to Zimbabwe—I've reached a perch where I can offer this model of journalism around the world.

Three decades ago, if you told my parents that this would be their toddler's story, they'd have laughed you out of the room. But I'm not alone. A whole generation of millennials of Indian descent has taken the gift that our parents bestowed on us, a life on a new continent half a world away, and created a multitude of unique paths.

It's not all smooth sailing, to be sure. Along with great opportunity, my generation faces great confusion. The term "ABCD—American-born confused desi" is overused but apt. It's often challenging to straddle two cultures halfway around the world, serving as an intergenerational bridge in diaspora communities.

We've all responded to the opportunities—and the confusion—in different ways. Stereotypes notwithstanding, millennials of Indian descent are far more diverse than what many might realize.

And I want to tell you our stories.

Breaking Down the Millennial Stereotypes

The election of Vice President Kamala Harris was historic for many reasons, including that she's attained the highest elected office by any Indian-American. But what's particularly meaningful for me and many other millennials is that she was born in the United States to parents who had immigrated here. Her mother's immigration story begins in Chennai, India, while her father's story begins in Brownstown, Jamaica. She took advantage of the launchpad of opportunity from her parents, paved her own unique path, and remained proud of her heritage (in a viral campaign video, she cooked South Indian *dosa*s with Indian-American actor Mindy Kaling). Though Kamala Harris is one of relatively few US-born Indian-Americans of her generation, the majority of the millennial generation of Indian-Americans was born in the United States. As a result, her story resonates with, and is a shining example to, our generation.

In this chapter, I'd like to spotlight female Indian-American millennials who defy stereotypes. It's not that there aren't wonderfully successful male examples, but I'd like to showcase the accomplishments of women who are sometimes underrepresented in our culture. After all, Kamala Harris may be the first female vice president, but she won't be the last if the millennial generation of Indian-American women has anything to say about it.

Many Americans have a stereotype in mind when they think of Indian-Americans. That stereotype, known as the "model minority", paints us with a single brush as doctors, engineers, and lawyers who dutifully follow our parents' wishes, put our heads down, and work hard. Now, to be clear, that's actually one of the more thoughtful stereotypes. I am hopeful we've moved past the dangerous caricatures like the thick-accented convenience store owner Apu from *The Simpsons*—or even socially awkward Raj from *The Big Bang Theory*.

I've reflected a great deal on who we are, and I believe Indian-American millennials defy all of these stereotypes. We're a strikingly diverse lot, to which the "model minority" picture simply doesn't do justice. Here are some ways in which we break the mold:

- Some of us do end up becoming doctors, lawyers, or engineers. But quite often, Indian-American millennials in those careers stretch the boundaries of convention to have profound impacts in those fields.
- Others pursue entirely unconventional career paths, from public policy to the entertainment industry, in the process increasing the representation of Indian-Americans in those fields.
- Many Indian-American millennials focus on helping communities beyond just those of Indian descent, both within the United States and all around the world.

The perspectives of millennial women of Indian descent add another layer of nuance. Women tend to take on an outsize share of family responsibilities, and for many millennials, tough circumstances have pushed these women to focus on supporting their own parents who have worked hard to survive in their adopted homeland. In addition, women can find it particularly challenging to bridge some of the traditional elements of Indian culture with career and lifestyle pressures in the United States.

Of course, straddling two cultures also makes for rich life experiences. In my case, I invested two decades into learning the traditional Indian Odissi dance form and pursuing a professional dancing career for years. At the same time, I can break it down on the dance floor to Western hip-hop, or Trinidadian Soca, and anything else the DJ throws at me and my friends. Similarly, many of us were used to having cheese strings and bagels at school, but there were always fresh homemade chapatis ready to be devoured on weeknights and *masala dosa*s and *idli*s on the weekends.

My underlying point is that Indian-American millennial women are diverse and defy stereotypes, with stories worth exploring.

Fast Facts on the Millennial Generation

The idea of creating labels for generations is convenient but ridiculous. A "millennial" is defined as anyone born from 1981 to 1996—so in 2021, we're anywhere from 25 to 40 years old. Worldwide, I'm one of 1.8 billion people. Embarrassingly, I'll use the term throughout this chapter even though our Global Press Style Guide bans "millennial" for "forcing readers to make assumptions about the people so described".

We millennials of the Indian diaspora are a smaller group. Our parents still think of us as the thick talkers, the Facebook generation, the kids that the aunties sent to the other room to play video games during dinner parties. But the oldest millennials are now "aunties" themselves, fully twenty years into our careers—while our youngest are already five years out of university. We're now the Instagram generation, distinct from the edgier Gen Z types who frequent Tik Tok and Snapchat.

To be sure, some Indian-American millennials immigrated to the United States in recent decades and have been naturalized as citizens. But the majority were born in the United States to parents who immigrated from India. And although this chapter is about the diversity of Indian-American millennials, there is one dimension that is strikingly common across the cohort.

That dimension is political affiliation and voting behavior. All millennials have been old enough to vote for years, sometimes decades. And Indian-American millennials born in the United States vote together as a group even more strongly than our parents. According to research from the Carnegie Endowment, roughly two-thirds of US-born Indian-Americans identify as Democrats, compared with about half of foreign-born Indian-Americans. This split is consistent both when comparing US-born Indian-Americans under 40—mostly millennials—with older, immigrant Indian-Americans, as well as when comparing within the millennial generation between US- and foreign-born Indian-Americans. And more than twice the proportion of US-born Indian-Americans self-identify as "extremely liberal", compared with those born outside the country. Finally, US-born Indian-Americans under 40 voted at the highest rate among Indian-American subgroups for President Joe Biden and Vice President Kamala Harris—a whopping 72 percent.

Further study will be needed to discover why US-born Indian-American millennials tend to identify with liberal causes and support Democratic politicians. But in the meantime, I'll share my intuition. Having benefited from our parents making the dramatic move to the West, millennials of Indian descent now have the opportunity to help others and give back to the society in which we've grown up.

That opportunity has inspired a growing cadre of Indian-American millennials to enter public service and even run for elected office—at all levels of government. Just as we celebrate the historic achievement of electing Vice President Kamala Harris, we should also remember that 2020 marked the first year that an Indian-American woman—and a millennial to boot—won election to a state legislature. Jenifer Rajkumar, a civil rights lawyer and Democrat, won election to the New York State Assembly, blazing a trail that many others will surely follow. Other Indian-American changemakers like Steven Olikara are working across political parties on bipartisan efforts. Steven founded the Millennial Action Project to help leading young policymakers on both national and state level to spur bipartisan legislation and innovative policy solutions. He's working to ensure all young leaders have the resources and support to create, introduce, and pass legislation and forge productive partnerships on the issues affecting the youngest generation of Americans.

Still, a full understanding of the millennial generation requires understanding the immigration stories of our parents and the ways in which they've shaped us. Personally, I can trace my path back to the support I was lucky to get from my parents, who immigrated to Canada from India in 1976.

A Different Generation

First, a disclosure: I'm an Indian-Canadian in the process of becoming an Indian-American. Having spent my youth in Canada and my professional career in America, I'm adamant there is a significant difference between our identities as citizens of these North American neighbors. America is truly a melting pot, while Canada is a tossed salad. In the US you are first American, then Indian, Mexican, or Irish. In Canada, you are always Indian, Trinidadian, Guyanese, Tamil, or Punjabi first—and then you are Canadian. My husband doesn't buy it. He is an Indian-American who grew up in the San Francisco Bay Area and assures me that we are more similar than different. I don't argue too vehemently because he's sponsoring my transition to American citizenship.

One thing is surely common across Canada and the United States: Indian immigrants in our parents' generation almost uniformly tell their children the same story that they arrived in North America with only a few dollars in their pocket. They got married in their twenties, started a family, pursued a career, and overcame many rough times along the way. In order to ensure their children would become financially secure they advised us to choose a career in one of three skilled professions: doctors, lawyers, and engineers. I say this all tongue-in-cheek, particularly because my objective is to shatter stereotypes—but for so many of us, this immigration story does, in fact, resonate.

My parents met in India under comical circumstances. My mom was studying for a master's degree in mathematics. My father was an engineer visiting India on what we affectionately call, "The Most Eligible Bachelor Tour". He had been working in Germany for five years in the early 1970s and was making the rounds sporting an afro and bell-bottoms. Quite the catch!

He came for tea with my mom's family and a match was made. She packed her bags, left her studies, and moved to freezing Toronto with this guy she'd just met. It's tough to imagine how she managed to raise two girls in a foreign land and persevere through health issues to a successful career. Given our parents' conception of what it takes to achieve the "American [or Canadian] Dream", it only makes sense that they might want us to follow in their footsteps. For them, any other path to attending university, getting married, and starting a family just sounded illogical. Choosing a career other than that of a doctor, lawyer, or engineer was risky. Weird. Scary.

But breaking down stereotypes of my generation starts with better understanding our parents. Even though they might have a mental model of what the right path to career and personal success looks like, many of them are wonderfully supportive of the decisions we make—even if it causes them a lot of heartburn. In their own way, they understand that we think differently. For example, to many of the next generation of Indians, weddings and babies are not so much life goals as they are "icing on the cake". And many of us choose to pursue—and reinvent—careers that we're passionate about as ends in themselves, not means to surviving in a foreign land.

Indian-American millennials grow up hearing tales of our parents' lives in India and their immigration journeys. I am no exception. We're standing on the "leg up" that our parents gave us in order to see the world from a new vantage point. Thinking back to my mom's immigration story, it is easy to see why she did not have as much freedom to choose her own path.

To be sure, I probably owe a great deal of the freedom I've had to choose my own career path to my older sister, Priya. She had already checked all the "right" boxes: Becoming a doctor, *marrying* a doctor, and giving birth to a son—everything an Indian parent dreams of—all before the age of 35!

In all seriousness, my sister—now a naturalized American—is a great example of defying stereotypes. She's demonstrated how Indian-American millennial women sometimes do enter the traditional medical, law, or engineering professions but are now striving to reinvent not only their roles in these careers but entire industries as well.

Priya's decision to become a doctor arose from deeply personal reasons. When I was 12, our mom had a routine surgery that went horribly wrong. The entire right side of her lower body was paralyzed—an affliction that has never been fully resolved. As we visited her at the hospital over many months, we watched her work incredibly hard at physical therapy to regain control of her life. My mom was resilient, determined to bring normalcy back to her family's life, and grateful to be alive. She would eventually return to motherhood and her career several months after the accident, eventually becoming the deputy ombudsman of Canada's independent insurance complaint resolution body.

Priya was fascinated with my mother's experience. She's devoted herself not only to excelling as a surgeon, but to caring for her patients with empathy and making her profession better. Priya specialized in lower-limb surgery and now serves on the governing board of the American Board of Podiatric Medicine and is the spokeswoman and communications chair of the American Podiatric Medical Association. She's passionate about elevating the quality of care that patients receive—and the information they have access to guide healthier lifestyles. She loves writing for a broad audience to promote healthy habits.

Not everything she does is in the public spotlight. For example, one of her passion projects that she leads every year is "Operation Footprint". It's a surgical mission to Honduras in which Priya and her colleagues perform corrective surgery on children born with clubfoot, a congenital deformity that presents at birth. One simple surgery changes the lives of her patients forever.

Transforming the Legal Profession

Another fantastic example of an Indian-American millennial woman in a traditional "model minority" profession who is upending her field is Purvi Shah, a social entrepreneur who is challenging the US legal establishment. Though she followed a conventional career track in studying law, what she's done with her degree is strikingly unconventional and entrepreneurial. Her Movement Law Lab works to deploy law strategically to change culture, systems, and power. And after the Ferguson and Baltimore uprisings, she co-founded Law for Black Lives, a network of 3,400 lawyers to support the movement.

She traces her changemaker origins to her childhood in Miami and the values that her parents instilled in her. Her mother, a teacher at the same public high school that Purvi attended, was a strong advocate for those of Purvi's classmates who were socioeconomically disadvantaged. Those students didn't lack intellectual ability, her mother would tell her, never missing an opportunity to remind Purvi of the importance of being grateful and how much harder life could be. And having risen from working as a grocer to owning a bodega to selling health insurance policies, her father instilled in Purvi the importance of hard work.

But it was her sister, Palak, who most directly influenced the course of Purvi's career. Working alongside Palak, a community organizer in Miami, Purvi was captivated. The experience brought her shoulder to shoulder with low-wage workers, families of people in prison, and young people living on the margins.

Purvi devoured books by Aldon Morris and other civil rights scholars and began to think practically about how to dedicate her life to defending others. "I couldn't stand to witness something unjust," she told me.

So Purvi enrolled in law school at the University of California, Berkeley, after a year of community organizing. She went in with a clear sense of purpose: "To get a law degree to support new immigrants, defend labor movements, and empower those who are most marginalized." To be sure, when she passed on a lucrative corporate law career, her father was perplexed: "I worked 80 hours a week to give you the life you have. We struggled for you. Why are you struggling now?" In response, Purvi told her father, "Your sacrifice instilled in me a set of values and gave me the privilege to be able to care for others." When Purvi became a law professor after graduating, it gave her mother—a teacher—pride to know Purvi was fostering the development of others.

Today, Purvi can look back at a career already glittering with accomplishments. She's won a prestigious Ashoka Fellowship (I first met Purvi when I interviewed her for the award) as one of the nation's leading social entrepreneurs, along with various other honors such as a Soros Fellowship. But what really matters to Purvi is the impact she's had, particularly in transforming the legal profession. She's weaved litigation, education, media, policy, and protest into coordinated campaigns. Doing so makes it possible to accomplish far more than she "could have ever achieved alone in the courtroom". "I got hooked on this new style of lawyering. I've spent the last decade teaching other lawyers how to incorporate these approaches and work in partnership with community leaders and community movements to create social change," Purvi says.

She is proudest of how she has brought her parents along on her journey. In 2018, in response to President Trump's ban on immigration from Muslim-majority countries, Purvi went straight to Miami International Airport to offer legal assistance to travelers. There, she saw her parents holding up signs against the Muslim ban. "They were showing up—not just in support of me, but for others that needed it."

Blazing New Trails in the Entertainment Industry

Other Indian-American millennial women are shattering the model minority stereotype by skipping traditional professions altogether. The entertainment industry is notoriously inhospitable to minorities—witness the hashtag #OscarsSoWhite—and, until recently, virtually devoid of Indian-American representation. But the stories of two remarkable women, Richa Moorjani and Lilly Singh, demonstrate how Indian-American millennials have opened up new industries after surmounting steep obstacles to bridge Indian and American cultures.

In May 2020, a new TV show surged to become the most-watched show on Netflix. Fans across America fell in love with the immigrant Indian family in *Never Have I Ever*, including Kamala, a beautiful PhD student at Caltech with an accent and an impending arranged marriage. In her flawless execution of a somewhat stereotypical Indian immigrant (to be sure, her character serves up a twist!) actor Richa Moorjani succeeded in defying the stereotype of the Indian-American millennial, blazing her own arduous trail to stardom.

Reflecting on her childhood, Richa mused to me that acting was "a lifelong dream since before I can remember. But my dream was to be in Bollywood one day. I never saw myself in Hollywood. The only place where people looked like me was in Bollywood." The story of how she beat the odds and carved out a place in an industry where Indian-Americans have been severely underrepresented is an inspiration to young Indian-American women across the country.

That story starts in Silicon Valley, where Richa grew up. A perennial performer, she was an Indian classical dancer and starred in school plays all the way through high school. Though her parents have well-established careers, they are also musicians and surrounded Richa with art and music. So when she left for college, she had their support while enrolling as a theater major.

But her practical instincts soon kicked in. "I didn't know how to become an actor. I didn't know anybody who went into acting." So she switched to a communications major to keep her options open. Her first job was in marketing, and she pursued dance throughout college, but every time she tried something new, she felt a pull back toward acting.

She moved to Los Angeles (LA) to pursue her dream full time. It wasn't an easy road. "Ahead of the move, I knew going into this industry that I'd get a lot of rejections. But it's entirely different to actually face those rejections. I had to be so vulnerable." Over nine years, she endured thousands of auditions, "but you've only seen me in a handful of projects that I've actually booked." She learned to build a strong, robust sense of self and to not rely on anyone else's validation.

As she toiled to break into a Hollywood that rarely cast Indian-Americans, Richa retained her childhood dream to become a Bollywood actress. So at 24, she packed up and moved halfway around the world to Mumbai, India. Once more, she had to learn how to navigate a whole new industry. Yet Bollywood was less than welcoming. Ironically, she was stereotyped as a "non-resident Indian", an outsider, after leaving behind a Hollywood that also considered her an outsider.

After years of struggling to break into two different industries, she moved back to LA, determined to make it in Hollywood. It would take several more years, but she persisted and finally got her break. Out of 15,000 actors who auditioned to play Kamala in Mindy Kaling's debut series, *Never Have I Ever*, Richa won the role. And through her remarkable success, she's demonstrated that Indian-American women can make a lasting mark on the entertainment industry.

Another inspiring example is the NBC host Lilly Singh, who just so happens to be a fellow Canadian from my hometown, Malvern, a suburb of Toronto. The newspaper I founded, *My Roots*, featured her in the "Malvern Alumni" section about young people from our neighborhood who had become successful in their fields. One issue ran a large piece on Lilly Singh for starting her own professional Bhangra troop well before she had more than 15 million followers on YouTube. Of course, I remembered her as my best friend's cousin who was in my Brownie (Girl Scouts) troop.

Fast forward 15 years, and NBC chose Lilly to be the first female late-night host in more than 30 years. *A Little Late with Lilly Singh* garnered positive reviews and spent its debut season 2019–20 hosting dozens of personalities, from Natalie Portman to Snoop Dogg, Mindy Kaling to Jessica Alba.

Lilly's parents had immigrated from Punjab, India, and assumed their daughter would follow the conventional path like they did. But she did not identify as much with role models in the Indian community as much as she did with rapper Lil' Mo, actor Dwayne "The Rock" Johnson, and actress Priyanka Chopra.

After university, she struggled with depression and found an outlet for expression and support on YouTube. She had millions of followers before her parents even knew about her online stardom—but when they found out, they abandoned their dream for her to pursue a master's and gave their blessing for Lilly to pursue hers.

The rest is now Hollywood history. NBC renewed Lilly's contract for 2020-2021. Fellow hosts like Jimmy Fallon, Trevor Noah, and Amy Schumer have given Lilly their stamp of approval—and tips for survival. And Lilly's honesty in dealing with complex emotional issues like exhaustion, depression, and coming out as bisexual have truly established her as a trailblazer, impressing critics and winning new fans.

In a 2019 *Hollywood Reporter* interview she explains, "The very next meet-and-greet that I did after coming out was in India and I would say 50 percent of people in that line came out to me. To me, that is success."

Providing for a Family

The neighborhood where Lilly and I were born and raised was designated by the government as a priority neighborhood requiring special attention. Growing up in such a socioeconomically diverse community, I saw my peers take many paths. Although my own family did not go without, some of our Indian neighbors needed more help. A health issue, a failed business, a troubled child—these are the stories that can send any family spiraling into heartbreak and financial trouble. And for some families, these troubles are even more difficult to recover from.

Whereas I grappled with the choice to pursue a conventional or unconventional career, some of my peers didn't even have the luxury of that stress. Their family's financial struggles meant that getting a degree and a well-paying job to support the household were the first matters of business.

Hilori Kaloti exemplifies this story. Her mom raised her alone, all the while caring for her elderly grandmother as well. From childhood, Hilori learned to step up, dutifully taking her grandmother to the temple while her mom worked long hours to support their small family. Her mom's immigration story is nothing short of inspiring. She immigrated with Hilori—a toddler at the time—from India. She learned English, adapted to the lifestyle of her new country, and found a job to support her small family. That grit, resilience, and determination to provide for her family deeply imprinted on her daughter. When we were classmates in high school, I remember Hilori working year round as a counselor at a local children's activity center during the school year and at the zoo over summers. As Hilori grew older, she inherited an intense sense of responsibility to fund her own education and succeed in her career, considering carefully how any move she made would affect her ability to support her mom.

Against the odds, Hilori succeeded wildly. She graduated from college, studied abroad, and won admission to Cornell all on her own as she supported her mom and grandmother. Then, in less than a decade, she rose from a graduate student at Cornell University to climb the ranks and become head of human resources (HR) for The Hershey Company's international operations.

Her impressive success is a vivid illustration of the determination of many Indian-American millennial women. I don't know anyone who has worked harder or focused more intently on achieving her career goals—leading HR at a Fortune 500 company—and caring for her family at the same time.

Hilori's journey as a millennial contradicts the stereotypical story that our parents are always there to financially support us or review our university applications. The reality is that many people don't have a familial system to support their career path in a traditional way—and that the millennial herself must overcome many challenges to pave a path toward independence and professional success.

Making a Global Impact

"I'm going to work on a media development program in Swaziland!" After a moment, a response came from across the Atlantic. "Great! I'm so excited for you."

I'd called my mom from England, where I was studying at the London School of Economics (LSE). By this time, my long-suffering parents never knew what career move I'd come up with next—but they did know I was on a unique path. I'd missed the boat on medical school, law school, *and* an engineering degree. My parents' traditional senses made them more excited about me enrolling at LSE than about what I was studying or hoped to do with my life. They politely nodded whenever I resolutely informed that I planned to reimagine local and international news by creating more representative newsrooms to ensure that audiences are engaged, informed, and trust the news they consume.

No one else at Kannada Sangha had a daughter doing that.

Indeed, my projects were the source of many a narrowed eyebrow in their Indian diaspora community. Mine was not going to be a straight-and-narrow path toward financial security. Luckily, my parents always knew my enthusiasm was genuine. "I wanted to say 'Where on Earth is Swaziland?'" my mom confessed years later. "But I could hear the excitement in your voice. When you get a call like that from your daughter, you can't burst her bubble."

I'm glad she didn't. My own story is useful to tease out a common strand among many millennial women of Indian descent: the drive to make an impact on other communities at home and abroad. Because my parents immigrated to an extraordinarily diverse community filled with multiculturalism from all over the world, I had a chance to develop a lifelong conviction to build a more representative media industry to do justice to the diversity I saw all around me.

Growing up in Malvern, I was only dimly aware of the labels that defined our neighborhood. The stunning socioeconomic and cultural diversity all around me seemed like selling points rather than warning signs. My earliest memories are of carefully crossing the street to deliver freshly-cooked South Indian pilaf rice to Mrs Salvatore, our Italian neighbor. And of the Rajaratnams across the street, where on Friday evenings I'd gorge on Sri Lankan string hoppers and roti.

My first foray into journalism was inserting grocery store coupons into newspapers, stacking several hundred onto my red wagon, and delivering free copies of *The Scarborough Mirror* all over Malvern. I always found it strange that most prominent bylines were of white men sharing their perspectives, with ominous, grisly headlines about daily life in my neighborhood. These reporters weren't from Malvern, and their bland names were incongruous with the spicy, diverse mix of community members I knew and loved.

So, in 2007, I founded *My Roots*, a media start-up and community organization rolled into one. Our mission was to deliver news for the community through people living in it. *My Roots* was how I got started on answering the question: How do we build truly representative newsrooms that reflect the diversity of their audiences?

It was the beginning of what I wanted to be my life's work developing representative, community-led media. I had no obvious Indian role models to follow; nor did my parents have other friends with kids on this career path. I was on a new trail toward defining professional success.

Over the next several years, I moved across three continents to build on my vision. I worked on community-led radio programming in Rwanda, conducted media development research in rural South India, and organized media trainings in Swaziland to help journalists represent stories about gender-based violence with dignity and precision. Later, as director of media partnerships at Ashoka, I mined a treasure trove of data on media entrepreneurs around the world. Along with the business school at the University of Michigan, I published a report: "The Bottom-Up Media Revolution", which sifted through hundreds of such organizations to find the most transformative models. One in particular seemed perfectly aligned with my lifelong goal of building truly representative newsrooms: Global Press, an international news organization that trains and employs local female reporters in under-covered media markets, from Kirumba in the Democratic Republic of Congo to Jaffna in Sri Lanka. Its founder and CEO, Cristi Hegranes, was a former foreign correspondent in Nepal who'd pledged to make her job obsolete. It takes a rare and humble journalist to reflect on her own role in a systemic problem. But Cristi did just that and has continued inspiring the industry to reimagine international journalism for the last 15 years.

So in 2018, I took the plunge and joined Cristi as COO to lead our global expansion and hone our processes to reimagine international journalism. Ours is one of the most diverse newsrooms in the world. At Global Press, we go the extra mile—thousands of extra miles, actually—to cultivate our corps of 250 reporters that truly represent the communities they cover.

And that is why all our reporters are female. Diversity targets aren't some onerous constraint for us—they're the whole point of the enterprise. It's the storyteller who controls the narrative. And only local reporters who represent their diverse communities can reclaim that narrative.

Most women around the world face steep barriers to accessing a journalism job that provides financial security among a multitude of other barriers to entering the profession, which in turn creates a skewed and one-sided narrative. As I canvassed our local markets for recruits, I met women grateful that we brought an opportunity for employment to them, that the job application was available to communities without high internet penetration, and that the entire process was managed in the local language and not English, French, or German like so many other media development initiatives.

A Common Launchpad

It's hopefully clear by now that millennial Indian-American women are working hard to eradicate the "model minority" stereotype. To be sure, we are all traveling along different paths to reach our goals. And we are relying on hard work, grit, focus and a desire to leave the world better than we found it—a lesson we learned from watching our parents.

Like many millennial Indian-Americans, I'm thrilled that my parents are my biggest fans. They're happy that I was able to follow what I've been "on" about since I was a teen. They could not be more supportive or thrilled with what I've achieved—and they're proud that I blazed my own trail to do it.

For as much as we want to push boundaries and break away from stereotypes, most Indian-American millennials are indebted to our parents for enduring the immigrant struggle and creating a conducive launch environment for us—often leading by example. I knew my parents would always be there to provide a soft landing if my high-flying, risky efforts failed.

Thanks to them, I get to pursue my passion for transforming the media industry in ways they couldn't have imagined. Let me take you back to Mongolia, where Global Press launched our news bureau days before the coronavirus pandemic struck. One of our reporters, Odonchimeg, is the only epidemiologist in the entire province of Arkangai. After a successful medical career, she'd joined Global Press to follow her lifelong dream to be a journalist. But, when the pandemic surged, Odonchimeg penned a beautiful story about why her province and her hospital needed her. She went on leave to protect her community. And when she's ready to come back, we'll welcome her with open arms. Because Odonchimeg, and all of our reporters across 40 news bureaus all over the world, want what's best for their communities and to represent the unvarnished truth about them proudly to the world.

Now *that* is all I've ever wanted. And if you ask a hundred other Indian-American millennials what their standards of success are, you'll get a hundred unique answers. We don't fit neatly into a box, and we're proud to say so. Just don't tell our parents.

"Success" Through Lens of Women: Celebrating an Alternative Model of the Marginalized

Sujata Warrier and Shamita Das Dasgupta

The Asian Indian[1] (the authors prefer to use the term "Asian Indian" instead of "Indian-American" in this chapter) immigrant community in the US has become famous for its quick success in almost every arena of society. The culmination of this triumph is perhaps the election of Vice President Kamala Harris, who represents both the Asian Indian and African-American immigrant communities. Along with Harris, several Indian American CEOs in large IT companies, top-ranking physicians, and media experts have become the faces of accomplishment of the community. No doubt the community is currently enjoying the fruits of its struggles to achieve "success" in its adopted land.

Mapping the Contours

In this chapter, we argue that success as it is defined and celebrated in the diasporic community of Indians in the US—economic and individualistic—

is narrow and elitist. This limited version of success deliberately excludes activists and changemakers who work at the margins of the community. While individualistic successes have certainly brought fame and recognition to the community, they have not instigated internal changes or fundamental modifications to the community's inequitable culture. It is the marginalized, women, LGBTQ, and working class, who have redefined "success" in their own terms and pushed the community to do better. Here we are underlining these victories and offering an alternative model of success that is collective and at the margins.

Both of us authors write this chapter as immigrants from India who have participated in and witnessed the trajectory of development of the Asian Indian community in the US. Both of us have faced substantial animosity and resistance from the community when we decided to shape "success" differently than the majority of our mainstream compatriots. We collaborated to create successful leadership through Manavi (est. 1985),[2] the first organization in the US to focus on gender-based violence among Asian Indians.[3] It is this "success" at the margins that we nominate and celebrate in our essay.

To achieve this objective, we have briefly outlined the history of immigration of Indians to the US. Without this short historical sojourn, it would be difficult to comprehend the gendered nature of the community's resettlement in this country. Then we have characterized the power of labeling as it pertains to "success", and the pernicious effects of playing up to the stereotype of "model minority", a title that was bestowed on the community. The efforts of the community to present an unblemished face of a "model minority" to the larger "American" society has included masking the fissures within and reformulating the "home culture". We believe that the main casualties of this enterprise were women who were burdened with maintaining the often outdated and misogynist traditions. We end by discussing success through the lens of women and the marginalized. We contend that women are not helpless victims entreating attention, but energetic actors who have generated changes in the community and policies of the country to meet their needs.

Coming to America

In the early days of my (Shamita) being in this country, people frequently asked me, "Do you have only doctors and engineers in your country? How come this is all that we see?" A problematic question indeed. The Asian Indian community that was gradually crystallizing in those days did indeed overrepresent doctors and engineers. However, this was not the only Asian Indian community in the country; nor was the community homogenous.

The first wave of immigration that began its journey in the early 1800s migrated from the then undivided India under colonial rule. Within a hundred years, the group had nearly dissipated due to isolation, repatriation, and virulent racism it faced in the country (the Johnson–Reed Act). Among the early immigrants were only a handful of women. The Asian Indian women's community in those early days was minuscule as the US immigration services routinely denied visas to women, may they be wives, daughters, mothers, or sisters of men who were already in this country. The first woman who had applied for US citizenship was Kanta Chandra Gupta of Delhi who had entered the country at the age of nineteen. Kanta became a chiropractor and was part of the anti-colonial organizing in California that established the Gadar Party.[4] This initial community comprised of mainly farmers and laborers and was certainly not an abode of scholars. By early 1940s, the average education of the community had dwindled down to approximately fourth-grade level.

The late 1960s and '70s witnessed the second wave of immigration that arrived at the shores of the US from India. This second wave began after the relaxation of the national origin-based migration quotas integral to the amendment of the Immigration and Naturalization Act of 1965 (the Hart–Celler Act). Post space-race, the policies of the time privileged highly-educated individuals[5] and, thus, artificially congregated an Indian community of technically trained doctors, engineers, and scientists in the US. Due to the gendered nature of education in India and culturally permitted mobility, the primary immigrants were again, men. As women were not prohibited from entering the country as dependents of primary residents, they came as wives. Within a very short time, these men found occupational and financial success and solidly established themselves in their adopted home by creating a network of linguistically based community organizations, places of worship, and ways of educating the next generation in their parents' religions, traditions, and "cultures".

In light of their rapid and winning adaptation to the new society, mainstream America soon conferred the dubious title, "model minority", to this group. The label implied that Indians were a hardworking, family-oriented, problem-free lot that pulled themselves up by the bootstraps. The Indian community embraced this descriptor with delight and endeavored to live up to it. Consequently, the community became particularly cautious about the image it projected to outsiders and attempted to promote an immaculate and flawless façade. Accordingly, the community became adept at denying all social ills within its ranks—be it disease, crime, divorce, poverty, homelessness, under- and unemployment, delinquency, drug addiction, intergenerational conflict, and woman abuse.

For instance, in 1993, the mainstream organizers[6] of the India Day parade that celebrates India's independence in New York City, banned all organizations that worked with battered women, gays and lesbians, and taxi drivers. Obviously, the idea was to present a seamlessly monolithic appearance to the larger American community.

The epithet, "model minority", was replete with myths about the community. It celebrated some immigrant groups, mainly from India and some other Asian countries (notably the Japanese), that played within the rules of American functional systems. The successes of these communities were juxtaposed to black and Latino peoples to deny or minimize their histories of structural and systemic oppression. The veiled implication was that the latter groups were incapable of achieving success because they did not have "what it takes" to prosper in the US—wit, intelligence, skills, and industry. One (immigrant) community of color was being pitted against others to create divisions and discords, which effectively weakened the possibility of collective responses to various social ills and, thereby, absolved the ruling classes of their discriminatory practices.

However, Asian Indians were not the only ones to be used as wedges among communities of color. Within Asian-American communities, the use of the stereotype "model minority" created destructive divisions discouraging pan-Asian unity. For example, financial successes of Japanese Americans subsequent to World War II internment was held up as an "American Success Story", resulting in its isolation from other communities of color and negating the need for making amends for its mistreatment.[7] The continued use of the term, "model minority", has pushed the recipients of the title to mask painful problems and challenges, including the difficulty in acknowledging and challenging mainstream racism and xenophobia.

Recreating Traditions

As the new Asian Indian community grew confident with mounting economic security, it began to recreate the environment of the homeland it had left behind. The community became preoccupied with maintaining a distinct collective identity founded in its cultural roots. Temples and masjids, region-linguistic cultural institutions, Sunday schools for Vedic and Quranic educations, language classes for children began to be established wherever there was a concentration of immigrants from India. Women inhabited the religious and cultural spaces in throngs, but they seemed to be relegated to ancillary roles. A corollary to these efforts was the reinstallation of traditional tenets, e.g. gender inequity; prohibition against dating, particularly outside the community; promotion of arranged and semi-arranged marriage; son-preference; re-formation of joint family; casteism albeit subtle, etc. Even if these values may have helped to establish a distinct identity of the community, they disadvantaged girls and women to a great extent. Individuals who challenged this belief system of traditionality were quickly dubbed "inauthentic" and silenced, as well as dismissed as anomalies. Girls and women were burdened with the responsibility of maintaining these traditions that did not liberate them.

The demographics of this second wave of Indian community began to shift after 1980 when many post-1970 immigrants began to facilitate the passage of their kin to the US. These new immigrants, who migrated with the help of the family reunification policies, were frequently less educated than the earlier immigrants and filled blue-collar occupations such as taxi driving, shop keeping, and motel management. Indian business owners displaced from African countries also began to enter the US around the same time and establish their trade. The infusion of these non-technical workers increased the community's heterogeneity, but class differences based on education, occupation, and economics magnified the cracks in its purported internal harmony.

By now the Asian Indian women's community gathered in this country was educationally and financially quite different than its male counterpart. According to the 1990 US Census, although 59 percent of South Asian women over 16 years of age worked outside their families, they earned an average yearly salary of $11,746, an amount that was significantly lower than the average salary of men in the community[8] and below the federal poverty threshold.

In the 1990s, the Indian community experienced another wave of new immigration. This time, information technology (IT) professionals were invited in as workers of specialty occupations. This group was issued temporary work visas that were renewable for a particular period of time. With these migration inflows, the current community has become tri-modally distributed by socioeconomic status: the post-1970 technically trained immigrants constituting the first bump; the working-class immigrants of the 1980s making up the second; and the temporary specialty work visa holders comprising the third concentration.

Interestingly, Indian women continued not to reflect the same demographic patterns as men in the community. Whereas men entered the country as primary immigrants, most women came as dependents of their male relatives, that is, as wives and daughters, and less frequently, as fiancées, sisters, and mothers. In our experience we found that often, when single women migrated for education or work, it was to fulfill their families' ambitions rather than to realize their personal goals. Even highly-educated and working women who entered the country to live with their husbands on student (F1) or specialty worker visas (H1-B), were forced into dependency due to the requirements of the United States Citizenship and Immigration Services (USCIS). Dependents of non-immigrant working visa holders are still forbidden to hold any job legally regardless of their families' financial needs. The ensuing economic and emotional reliance on men continue to have tremendous consequences for women, particularly if the relationship is abusive.

Defining Success

Naming an event, action, experience, or idea is a powerful act.[9] "Naming" is to define and authenticate an action that provides the person or group that does it with the authority to say what something is, and what it is not. The capacity to name allows the person or group to categorically link the concept, which has been named, with the reality it is to represent. The power of naming comes with the power to delegitimize all other realities that do not fall within the boundaries already delineated. This special control, usually guarded carefully by people in power, is often related to the political contexts of the time. An easy example is the way undocumented immigrants of color in the US have turned overnight from laborers and refugees to criminals. While nothing in reality actually changed, it was the ability of the powerful that defined hitherto innocuous individuals as dangerous and, therefore, deserving of punishment.

This postulation about naming and defining reflects strongly on the characterization of "success" in the Asian Indian immigrant community. Embracing of the label "model minority" directed the community to work within the conventional boundaries of "success" demarcated by the dominant power structure. This "success" is regulated by patriarchy, capitalism, and individualism. The marginalized populations—the poor, LGBTQ, women, and educational nonconformists—had little role in shaping the contours of this "success" and were and continue to be routinely eliminated from owning it. Thus, it is mainly the heterosexual men in the community who claim success in financial, political, and cultural arenas and not the people inhabiting the fringes of the community.

Emergence of Women

Immigration placed Asian Indian women in paradoxical situations. Away from the restrictions of joint families and strict patriarchal diktat, women enjoyed a sense of unprecedented freedom. Yet they found themselves socially isolated and lonely at home and without appropriate role models at work.

By the early 1980s, women began to form organizations to find camaraderie and help in furthering their careers. Two pioneering organizations, Asian Indian Women in America (New York, est. 1980) and Sneha (Connecticut, est. 1983), emerged to provide sister-to-sister support to women and build their leadership capacities at work and community. While their focus and motivation were significant, but by following the socially accepted standards of success, they did not contest the myth of "model minority" that the Asian Indian immigrant society was adhering to strongly. No doubt, in a country built upon Anglo-European patriarchal ethos, these immigrant women were especially disadvantaged, not only due to their gender, skin color, and customary attire, but also the responsibilities of carrying out double shifts of work and home duties. This gender inequality was reflected in the wage disparity women experienced that has been mentioned earlier. Asian Indian women still earn $0.73 to every dollar their male counterparts with equal educational levels make.[10] Nonetheless, individual women began to arise in different arenas of work.

Asian Indian women began to make their mark in the academe quite early. Gayatri Chakravorty Spivak, Chandra Talpade Mohanty, Rajeswari Sunder Rajan, and Ketu H Katrak are well-known scholar–leaders in the US educational field. In contrast, women in the scientific world were less recognized, yet have occupied important positions in STEM disciplines.

Madhulika Guhathakurta, an astrophysicist with NASA, late Kalpana Chawla, an engineer and astronaut with NASA, and late Sujata Tewari, a neuroscientist researching alcoholism, are three such women. Despite such prominent individuals, gender disparity continues to plague STEM occupations. While exact statistics are not readily available, we can estimate gender distributions of Asian Indian women from the data on the Asian-American population: the percentage of women scientists and engineers with doctoral degrees employed in universities and four-year colleges is only half that of the men with equivalent education. The statistics on full professorship are even more dismal: approximately 9 percent of women to 29 percent men.

In business and industries, Asian Indians take great pride in the success of Indra Nooyi, CEO of PepsiCo. Other women leaders in business, Jayshree Ullal (CEO, Arista Networks, cloud networking firm), Padmasree Warrior

(CTO, Cisco Systems), and Neerja Sethi (co-founder and director, Syntel, IT firm) are less well-known. Of the two million Asian-American owned businesses in the US, 19.7 percent are owned by Asian Indians. Along with chains of motels and hotels, a large segment of this group owns small mom-and-pop family-owned businesses where, more often than not, women relatives of owners work without salary.

Asian Indian women's foray into the country's political realm began in New Jersey. In 1972, right after she became a US citizen, Kanak Dutta, a schoolteacher by profession, became engaged in Democratic Party politics. She was first elected to represent her New Jersey district and then, in 1981, ran unsuccessfully for the state assembly. She was elected as a state delegate in presidential elections in 1984, 1996, and in 2000. Kanak was the first Asian Indian woman who wore a sari throughout her political career.[11]

Although Kanak was the first, she was not the last Asian Indian woman to enrich the US political scene. Nimi Swamidoss McConigley served as a legislator in Wyoming from 1994 to 1996. Swati Dandekar was a legislator in Iowa Senate from 2009 to 2011, although belonging to the opposite political party of McConigley. A few other women from the immigrant- and second generations, such as Reshma Saujani, Manka Dhingra, Seema Verma, Aruna Miller, Rachel Paulose, Kshama Sawant, and Sara Gideon have played prominent roles in local and national politics. Among contemporary politicians, Nimrata Nikki Haley, Pramila Jayapal, and Kamala Harris are probably the most well-recognized names.

Nikki Haley, daughter of immigrant Sikh parents, was the first Asian Indian to win a seat in South Carolina's legislative assembly. She went on to become the governor of the state in 2011 for two terms, which would have ended in 2019. Haley resigned her position in 2017 to accept the position of US ambassador to the United Nations in the Trump administration. She resigned from this position in 2018. Unlike Haley, who belongs to the conservative Republican Party, Washington state's Pramila Jayapal represents the Democratic Party in the House of Representatives. A strong supporter of liberal social causes, Jayapal, an immigrant herself, has been a leader in the call to reform immigration laws and make them more case-sensitive and compassionate.

Among all the women of Indian heritage engaged in US politics, Kamala Devi Harris may be the one who has broken through the "bamboo" ceiling. She started her legal career as a county deputy district attorney, then district attorney of San Francisco, and then moving on to senatorship representing her state, California, in 2017. In August 2020 Joe Biden selected her as his running mate for his presidential candidacy. Harris celebrates her multiracial identity as a black and Indian-American.

The achievements of women above fall within the boundaries delineated by the definition of "model minority". While they certainly challenge race and gender-based ceilings, their successes do not necessarily dispute the patriarchally established and approved arenas.

However, there was another group of actors at the fringes of the Asian Indian community who balked at these norms and began to carve out an alternate space. These people highlighted and worked at the fault lines of the community and promoted a different model of success. Remarkably, the space they demanded emerged from the phenomenon of violence against women in the community. We are utilizing the trope of gender-based violence to discuss this alternate model.

Claiming a Singular Space

Challenging the idea of a problem-free "model minority", nearly two dozen anti-violence-against-women agencies work across the country today, offering myriad services to the Asian Indian community. These organizations hold awareness programs as well as strong social change agendas.[12] Several culturally specific shelters for female survivors of abuse have also been established in recognition of the distinct needs of immigrant Asian Indian women. Manavi is such an organization. It was the first organization in the US to focus on domestic violence and sexual assault in the Asian Indian community. In the 35 years of Manavi's existence, survivors of battering and sexual abuse and their advocates have indubitably created a collective force for community accountability and instigated change in various national and state policies that affect immigrant survivors.

The very presence of anti-violence-against-women organizations in the Asian Indian community dispute the notion of "model minority". These organizations have played a significant role in creating a progressive space. An early step in claiming this space was to enlarge the constituency. Although established mainly by immigrants from India, these organizations deliberately expanded their work to encompass immigrant survivors from all South Asian countries. There were two reasons behind this decision: (1) separate culturally appropriate and linguistically accessible agencies that could serve and support survivors from various South Asian countries did not exist, and (2) immigrant survivors from South Asia shared enough needs and common cultural and social practices to make distinct nation-based organizations unnecessary and duplication of work. This coming together of survivors from different South Asian countries also amplified the voices of women at the margins of these societies. Regardless of the political conflicts and relational tensions that afflict the countries of their origin, South Asian women in the US found commonalities among themselves to forge a cohesive sisterhood. As fundamentalist religious ideologies surfaced in immigrant communities, the "South Asian" identity provided ample opportunities to celebrate intra-group diversity as well as commonality. Nonetheless, the term "South Asian" remains contested, as it is often equated to Asian Indians, who tend to outnumber other diasporic immigrants from the region. Henceforth, in this chapter, we have replaced the term Asian Indian with South Asian, as the narrative we are about to recount cannot be parceled to smaller country-based groups.

An Alternate Success

South Asian anti-violence women's organizations have struggled in two fronts: (a) within the community, and (b) outside the community. From the inception, community leaders accused these organizations of being cultural traitors and airing dirty laundry in public. Their feminist principles were viewed as alien to the community's mainstream beliefs and, thereby, delegitimized. While "charity" work with "unfortunate" women could be tolerated, the agenda to change the community to a more gender- and class-equitable society that most such organizations promoted was viewed as impractical and destabilizing. Outside the community, the organizations were faced with complete incomprehension of cultural influences in types of abuse South Asian women experienced, including those related to the victim's immigration status. It took nearly a decade-long struggle to bring to policymakers' attention the distinct dynamics of intimate abuse that South Asian women experience in the US, such as economic control, coercion and threat, intimidation, public derogation, isolation, minimizing and denial, assertion of male privilege, and subjugation by cruel threats to residency. Even though these abuses overlap with intimate abuse in other communities, their scope is quite different. For instance, a batterer's threat of ruining his victim's reputation among her relatives might affect a South Asian woman differently. Also, a batterer could easily intimidate his wife by threatening her with deportation, taking away her children, and threats of violence to her family members back "home". Another esoteric threat that has enormous power over female victims is the indictment of being a traitor to their culture and community. It is due to the exertions of these women's organizations in the margins that the intersections of violence, gender, culture, immigration, and transnational laws have come to be recognized by state and national policymakers.

The progressive space that the women's agencies crafted have bred a number of other organizations that spanned class and sexuality. Sakhi for South Asian Women, an anti-domestic violence organization, initiated the first group to promote the labor rights of domestic workers—Domestic Workers Committee (est. 1994). This agency then, went on to form Workers' Awaaz (est. 1997) and Andolan (est. 1998) for domestic workers from South Asia. By forming domestic workers' unions, women's organizations were expressly supporting working class women who were hitherto invisible in a community dominated by the technologically educated and financially solvent upper classes. The domestic workers' movement has branched off to birth a number of Asian and Latina associations and have been highly successful in passing Domestic Workers' Bill of Rights legislations in a number of states.

In 1998, another organization headed by a South Asian woman emerged to demand rights for laborers, particularly taxi workers in New York—New York Taxi Workers Alliance (NYTWA). An alumna of Manavi, Bhairavi Desai, an Asian Indian, unionized NYTWA and led it within the folds of AFL-CIO. Currently, NYTWA's membership strength is over 180,000 licensed taxi and limousine drivers, of which immigrants constitute 94 percent.

The organization has been chartered to unionize taxi drivers in the rest of the country.

From this open corner in the edges of the community, began another progressive venture—a push to make visible South Asians who identified themselves as lesbian and gay. The mainstream South Asian community that includes immigrants from India, had long denied the existence of this group among its midst with the argument that same-sex love is a Western phenomenon. In 1986, Trikone was established in the California's Bay Area to support and disseminate information to South Asian lesbian, gay, bisexual, and queer communities. Later, Trikone also formed a women's group, Women of Trikone (WoT), to specifically support lesbian, bisexual, and queer women. Various other Trikone chapters in US states have been founded since then. In the East Coast, the South Asian Lesbian and Gay Association (SALGA) was established in 1991 and regularly held support groups as well as wellness clinics during the HIV/AIDS epidemic. The Asian Indian mainstream community's attitude toward SALGA was evident when between 1993 and 1997 when the Federation of Indian Associations (FIA) barred the group from participating in the India Day parade. SALGA was allowed in the parade from 1998 to 2000, and then barred again. Most women's organizations declared their solidarity with SALGA and were either banned or stayed away from the parade. Finally, from 2010 onward, the India Day parade organizers consistently permitted SALGA to join the parade after city officials intervened.

Success at the Margins

South Asian women in the US face both cultural and legal obstacles in their attempt to escape from family violence. In areas where there are no culture-specific agencies serving immigrant women, many South Asian survivors have complained of xenophobia and racism that dissuaded them from leaving abusive situations. Significant numbers of women have stated that their clothing, speaking accents, child-rearing practices, lack of fluency in English, food and toilet habits, etc. often make them targets of distressing curiosity and disdain. Frequently, their arranged marriages are perceived as "weird" and blamed for their abusers' actions. Furthermore, many mainstream shelters have limited experiences of dealing with immigration laws and are frequently unable to meet the legal needs of South Asian survivors. They are also at a disadvantage when women require language interpretation and translation. Thus, for South Asian women who are coping with abusive family relations, the support of a culture-specific agency and shelter becomes essential.

The issue of putting the entire culture on the stand came to the fore for advocates and activists when they needed to support battered women's residency petitions under immigration laws. Immigrants from Asia have historically been viewed by mainstream Americans as prisoners of violently misogynist and regressive cultures. Correspondingly, violence against women is seen as a marker of South Asian cultures. As battering among white people is seen as a product of individual bad behavior or predicament, culture escapes culpability. The perception that certain cultures are surfeit with vicious patriarchies and consequent brutalities toward women complicates the legal status of both batterers and victims in the US. Depending on the individual perspectives of law enforcement officers, judges, and attorneys, a battered South Asian woman may find her petition falls either on patronizing or disbelieving ears. Judges and attorneys may view South Asian batterers as vicious monsters or behaving in a culturally appropriate way. Rather than being complicit in vilifying the entire culture, South Asian activists relentlessly advocated to introduce nuanced explanations that go beyond cultural stereotypes to support survivors of abuse in courts of law. The work of these advocates nest at the complex intersections of race, class, nation, and individual ways of life to prevent cultures being reduced to the bizarre "other".

In addition to recognizing the influences of culture on how victims experience, react to, and ameliorate family violence, South Asian activists have collaborated with other immigration advocates to highlight the inequity of immigration policies and subsequently instigated changes in residency options for survivors of violence. Inclusion of options for hardship waiver, self-petition, U-Visa for women whose spouses might be using their dependent residency status to assert subjugation, were added in the Violence Against Women Act (VAWA, 1990, 1994, 2000).

A slight relaxation of restrictions to work for women, who came to the country on H4 visas and found themselves in abusive situations, was also introduced in 2015. Plights of financially dependent women who are abandoned in the home country or the US by their husbands have also been brought to the policymakers' attention by advocates. More than the individual women who have succeeded in academia and politics, South Asian activists acting collectively at the margins have brought significant social changes in the community and country.

Advocates working at the borders continue to challenge policy and practice responses within many of the systems designed to help survivors of abuse, blue-collar workers, and other marginalized groups. Collaborating with various culture-specific organizations, South Asian advocates have modified police and prosecutorial processes; required judicial officers to explore their own biases; mental health systems to understand the specificities of coercion in South Asian contexts; and the child welfare system to reimagine the nexus between domestic violence and child abuse. This collaborative work led to the creation of the first Asian American Pacific Islander Institute on Gender based Violence (APIGBV). Led by an Asian Indian, Firoza Chic Dabby, the institute has worked with grassroots organizations to instill changes at the federal level in the nation's responses to gender-based violence. Coordinating the efforts of many South Asian women's organizations, APIGBV advocated and brought changes to polices regarding language access for those with limited english proficiency (LEP); the impact of culture in gender-based asylum claims and women's responses to abuse; and the recognition of the needs of undocumented women, the elderly, domestic workers, and trafficked laborers.

As a result of the success of women advocates, the Asian Indian community has begun to acknowledge, with some resistance, the many issues it had hitherto ignored: domestic violence, LGBTQ concerns, elderly abuse, health consequences of long-term abuse, and the existential issues in second and third generations. Although some progress has been made, unfortunately, the issues of child physical abuse and neglect; incest; child sexual abuse; and sexual violence in the community remain shrouded in silence. Hidden in plain sight, issues of sexual violence across the life span continue to bedevil the community. While success gets defined as financial credits, those suffering from sexual violence find little solace and support from the community. Community leaders continue to uphold customary heteropatriarchal values to the detriment of confronting the present-day rape culture in the community.

However, more and more survivors of child sexual abuse, rape, incest, and sexual harassment have disclosed their experiences and valiantly challenged the community's "model minority" status.

Marching to a Different Drummer

The impetus to develop "successful" interventions for South Asian survivors of gender-based violence has meant the continuous interrogation of the community's heteropatriarchal values, particularly those pertaining to caste/class and misogyny. Resistance has entailed constant vigilance, the redefinition of success in collective terms, negotiating the role of the State in women's lives, and unpacking religion and "culture" to isolate misogyny. Simultaneously, activists at the margins have had to challenge traditions that blame and shame survivors while nurturing those that support perpetrators.

In this essay, we have utilized gender-based violence as a trope to exemplify the tenuous relationship the community has with the marginalized—women, working class, and sexual non-conformists. We have underscored the achievements of the marginalized to indicate how this group has redefined the notion of success and brought important changes in both the community and the nation. By deliberately eschewing conventional routes to "success", the advocates of the marginalized have played a significant role in shaping the South Asian/Asian Indian immigrant community. These activists' visions have been crucial in bringing the stories of the marginalized to the center, an essential step in guaranteeing equal membership and "success" to all.

Notes

1. We have used the term 'Asian Indian' instead of "Indian-American" throughout this essay. The United States Census Bureau uses the label "Indian-American" for people who trace their heritage back to India. The term distinguishes the group from "American Indians", the indigenous population of the country, who are also popularly known as "Indian/s". Activists prefer the label "Asian Indian" to indicate an identity based on the group's continent of origin, similar to "African-American" and "European American". Furthermore, the label "Asian Indian" allows for possibilities of coalition building with groups with similar histories of immigration, needs, and interests.
2. See https://www.manavi.org/

3. Shamita is a co-founder of Manavi, and Sujata has worked to shape its focus and agenda. Both of us have worked with the organization in various capacities for over 30 years.
4. Cheng and Bonacich, 1984
5. This second wave of migration was dubbed "brain drain" in India.
6. The NYC India Day parade was and continues to be organized by the powerful Federation of Indian Associations (FIA).
7. After decades-long agitation and organizing by Japanese American activists, President Ronald Reagan signed the Civil Liberties Act in 1988 and apologized for the internment. The Act provided $20,000 compensation to all the internees who were still living.
8. US Bureau of the Census, 1993
9. Pence and Dasgupta 2006; Mead, 1934
10. United States Census Bureau, 2012
11. Chatterjee, 2018
12. For a complete list of organizations working on ending violence against South Asian women in the US, see, http://www.manavi.org/south-asian-dv-agencies--by-state-.html
13. See, https://www.api-gbv.org/

References

Abraham, Margaret. *Speaking the Unspeakable: Marital Violence Among South Asian Immigrants in the United States*. New Brunswick, NJ: Rutgers University Press, 2000.

Abraham, Margaret. "Model Minority and Marital Violence: South Asian Immigrants in the United States." In *Cultural Psychology of Immigrants*, edited by Ramaswami Mahalingam, 197-216. Mahwah, NJ: Lawrence Erlbaum, 2006.

Ackerman, Donna. "A Matter of Interpretation: How the Language Barrier and the Trend of Criminalizing Illegal Immigration Caused a Deprivation of Due Process Following the Agroprocessors, Inc. Raids." *Columbia Journal of Law and Social Problems,* 43, no. 3 (2010, Spring): 363-398.

Agarwal, Priya. *Passage from India: Post 1965 Indian Immigrants and Their Children; Conflicts, Concerns, & Solutions.* Palos Verdes, CA: Yuvati, 1991.

Ahmed, Bipasha, Paula Reavey, and Anamika Majumdar. "Constructions of 'Culture' in Accounts of South Asian Women Survivors of Sexual Violence." *Feminism & Psychology*, 19, issue 1 (2009): 7-28.

Ahmad F, Riaz S, Barata P, Stewart DE. Patriarchal Beliefs and Perceptions of Abuse among South Asian Immigrant Women. *Violence Against Women.* 2004;10(3):262-282. doi:10.1177/1077801203256000

Balan, Sundari. *Being Asians, Good Moms and Great Workers: Investigating the Psychological Contours of Asian Indian Women's Model Minority Experience.* Doctoral Dissertation, University of Michigan, Ann Arbor, 2009.

Banerjee, Pallavi. *Constructing Dependence: Visa Regimes and Gendered Migration in Families of Indian Professional Workers.* Thesis, University of Illinois at Chicago (2013). https://hdl.handle.net/10027/9771

Banerjee, Payal. "Indian Information Technology Workers in the United States: The H-1B Visa, Flexible Production, and the Racialization of Labor." *Critical Sociology,* 32, issue 2-3 (2006): 425-445.

Bhattacharjee, Anannya. "The Habit of Ex-nomination: Nation, Woman, and the Indian Immigrant Bourgeoisie." *Public Culture* 5 (1992): 19-44.

Bhattacharjee, Anannya. "Woman, Nation and Identity in the Indian Immigrant Community." *SAMAR: South Asian Magazine for Action & Reflection,* no. 1 (1992, Winter): 6-10.

Bhattacharjee, Shikha, S. "Distant Silences and Default Judgments: Access to Justice for Transnationally Abandoned Women." *University of Pennsylvania Journal of Law and Social Change,* 16 (2013): 95-110.

Bhuyan, Rupaleem. "Navigating Gender, Immigration, and Domestic Violence: Advocacy with Work Visa Holders." In *Body Evidence: Intimate Violence Against South Asian Women in America,* edited by Shamita Das Dasgupta, 229-242. New Brunswick, NJ: Rutgers University Press, 2007.

Budiman, Abby, Christine Tamir, Lauren Mora, and Luis Noe-Bustamante, "Facts on U.S. immigrants, 2018." *Pew Research Center. Statistical portrait of the foreign-born population in the United States,* 2020, (August 20). https://www.pewresearch.org/hispanic/2020/08/20/facts-on-u-s-immigrants-current-data/

Burek, D. M. "National Federation of Indian American Associations." In *Encyclopedia of Associations in the United States* (26th ed. Part 2, Section 10), edited by D. M. Burek. Detroit, MI: Gale Research, Inc., 1992.

Burman, Erica, Sophie L. Smailes, and Khatidja Chantler. "'Culture' as a Barrier to Service Provision and Delivery: Domestic Violence Services for Minoritized Women." *Critical Social Policy,* 24, issue 3 (2004): 332-357.

Chang, Stewart. "Dreams of My Father, Prison for My Mother: The H-4 Nonimmigrant Visa Dilemma and the Need for an 'Immigration-Statius Spousal Support.'" *Asian Pacific American Law Journal,* 19, issue 1 (2014): 1-28.

Cheng, Lucie and Edna Bonacich. *Labor Immigration Under Capitalism: Asian Workers in the United States Before World War II.* Berkeley, CA: University of California Press, 1984.

Chatterjee, Jayashree. "Kanak Dutta: First Lady of Indo-American Politics," *The Statesman,* (2018, November 11). https://www.thestatesman.com/supplements/evolve/kanak-dutta-first-lady-of-indo-american-politics-%201502706905.html

Chaudhuri S, Morash M, Yingling J. Marriage Migration, Patriarchal Bargains, and Wife Abuse: A Study of South Asian Women. *Violence Against Women.* 2014;20(2):141-161. doi:10.1177/1077801214521326

Das Gupta, Monisha. *Unruly Immigrants: Rights Activism, and Transnational South Asian Politics in the United States*. Durham, NC: Duke University Press, 2006.

Dasgupta, Shamita Das. "Introduction." In *A Patchwork Shawl: Chronicles of South Asian Women in America,* edited by Shamita Das Dasgupta, 1-17. New Brunswick, NJ: Rutgers University Press, 1998.

Dasgupta, Shamita Das. "Women's Realities: Defining Violence Against Women by Immigration, Race, and Class." In *Issues in Intimate Violence*, edited by Raquel K. Bergen, 209-219. Thousand Oaks, CA: Sage, 1998.

Dasgupta, Shamita Das. "Is All Well with Domestic Violence Work in the United States?" *SAMAR: South Asian Magazine for Action & Reflection,* no. 1 (1999, Spring/Summer): 5-11.

Dasgupta, Shamita Das. "Charting the Course: An Overview of Domestic Violence in the South Asian Community in the United States," *Journal of Social Distress and the Homeless,* 9, no. 3 (2000): 173-184.

Dasgupta, Shamita Das. "Battered South Asian Women in U.S. Courts." In *Body Evidence: Intimate Violence Against South Asian Women in America,* edited by Shamita Das Dasgupta, 211-226. New Brunswick, NJ: Rutgers University Press, 2007.

DasGupta, Sayantani and Shamita Das Dasgupta, "Women in Exile: Gender Relations in the Asian Indian Community in the U.S." In *Contours of the Heart: South Asians Map America,* edited by Sunaina Maira and Rajini Srikanth, 381-400. New York, NY: Asian American Writers' Workshop, 1996.

DasGupta, Sayantani and Shamita Das Dasgupta. "Sex, Lies, and Women's Lives." In *A Patchwork Shawl: Chronicles of South Asian Women in America,* edited by Shamita Das Dasgupta, 111-128. New Brunswick, NJ: Rutgers University Press, 1998.

"Demographic Snapshot of South Asians in the United States." *saalt (Strengthening South Asian Communities in America,* (2019, April). https://saalt.org/wp-content/uploads/2019/04/SAALT-Demographic-Snapshot-2019.pdf

Deshpande, Anita A. *The Immigration Journey: Asian Indian Immigrant Women's Experiences of Gender and Acculturation*. PhD Dissertation, Dept. of Counseling, Developmental and Educational Psychology, Lynch School of Education, Boston College (2018, December), Boston: MA.

Devi, S. Uma. "Globalisation, Information Technology and Asian Indian women in US," *Economic and Political Weekly,* (2002, October 26): 4421-4428.

Gupte, Manisha. "The Role of 'Honor' in Violence Against South Asian Women in the United States." *Manavi Occasional Paper,* No. 11. New Brunswick, NJ: Manavi, 2015.

Hanna, Mary and Jeanne Batalova. "Indian Immigrants in the United States," *Migration Policy Institute,* (2020, October 16). https://www.migrationpolicy.org/article/indian-immigrants-united-states-2019

Hass, Giselle Aguilar, Nawal Ammar, and Leslye Orloff. "Battered Immigrants and U.S. Citizen Spouses." *Legal Momentum,* (2006, April 24): 1-10.

Helweg, Arthur W. and Usha M. Helweg. *An Immigrant Success Story: East Indians in America.* Philadelphia: University of Pennsylvania Press, 1990.

Hess, Gary R. "The Forgotten Asian Americans: The East Indian Community in the United States." In *Counterpoint: Perspectives on Asian America,* edited by Emma Gee, 413-422. Los Angeles, CA: University of California, 1976.

Hess, Gary R. "The Asian Indian Immigrants in the United States, 1900-1965." In *From India to America: A Brief History of Immigration; Problems of Discrimination; Admission and Assimilation,* edited by S. Chandrasekhar, 29-34. La Jolla, CA: A Population Review Book,

https://www.thehindu.com/news/national/most-online-content-on-child-sexual-abuse-from-india/article31377784.ece1982.

"Immigration and Nationality Act of 1965 (Hart-Celler Act)." *Immigration History, A Project of the Immigration and Ethnic History Society,* (2019). https://immigrationhistory.org/item/hart-celler-act/

"Immigrant Women and Girls in the United States: A Portrait of Demographic Diversity." *American Immigration Council* (ND). https://www.americanimmigrationcouncil.org/research/immigrant-women-and-girls-united-states

https://indiacurrents.com/beti-bachao-ask-south-asian-american-women-metoo/

Jensen, Joan M. *Passage from India: Asian Indian Immigrants in North America.* New Haven, CT: Yale University, 1988.

"Kanta Chandra Gupta." *Committee on South Asian Women Bulletin 5,* nos. 1-2, (1987): 7.

Kallivayalil D. Narratives of Suffering of South Asian Immigrant Survivors of Domestic Violence. *Violence Against Women.* 2010;16(7):789-811

Kwong, Deanna. "Removing Barriers for Battered Immigrant Women: A Comparison of Immigrant Protections Under VAWA I & II," *Berkeley Women's Law Journal,* 17, 2002: 137-152.

La Brack, Bruce. "Immigration Law and the Revitalization Process: The Case of the California Sikhs." In *From India to America: A Brief History of Immigration;*

Problems of Discrimination; Admission and Assimilation, edited by S. Chandrasekhar, 59-66. La Jolla, CA: A Population Review Book, 1982.

Leonard, Karen I. "Marriage and Family Life Among Early Asian Indian Immigrants." In *From India to America: A Brief History of Immigration; Problems of Discrimination; Admission and Assimilation,* edited by S. Chandrasekhar, 67-75. La Jolla, CA: A Population Review Book, 1982.

Leonard, Karen I. *The South Asian Americans.* Westport, CT: Greenwood Press, 1997.

https://www.thelily.com/the-silent-lives-of-childhood-sexual-abuse-survivors-in-americas-south-asian-diaspora/

Mani, Lata. "Gender, Class, and Cultural Conflict: Indu Krishnan's Knowing Her Place." *SAMAR: South Asian Magazine for Action & Reflection,* no. 1 (1992, Winter): 11-14.

Mead, George H. *Mind, Self, and Society.* Chicago: University of Chicago Press, 1934.

Mohanty, Chandra T. Feminism without Borders. Durham, NC: Duke University Press. 2003

Nadal, Kevin L. "The Brown Asian American Movement: Advocating for South Asian, Southeast Asian, and Filipino American Communities." *AARP: HKS Student Publication,* (2020, February 2). https://aapr.hkspublications.org/2020/02/02/the-brown-asian-american-movement-advocating-for-south-asian-southeast-asian-and-filipino-american-communities/

Office of the Historian. *The Immigration Act of 1924 (The Johnson-Reed Act).* (ND). https://history.state.gov/milestones/1921-1936/immigration-act

Pedraza, Silvia. "Assimilation or Transnationalism? Conceptual Models of the Immigrant Experience in America." In *Cultural Psychology of Immigrants,* edited by Ramaswami Mahalingam, 419-428. Mahwah, NJ: Lawrence Erlbaum, 2006.

Pence, Ellen and Shamita Das Dasgupta. *Re-examining 'battering': Are all acts of violence against intimate partners the same?* (2006). St. Paul, MN: Praxis International. https://praxisinternational.org/library/batterer- intervention/

Poore, Grace. *The Children We Sacrifice: A Resource Book.* Silver Spring, MD, 2000.

Prashad, Vijay. *The Karma of Brown Folk.* Minneapolis, MN: University of Minnesota Press, 2000.

Roberts, Lisa R., Semran K. Mann, and Susanne B. Montgomery. "Depression, a Hidden Mental Health Disparity in an Asian Indian Immigrant Community." *International Journal of Environmental Research and Public Health,* 13, no. 1 (2016): 27. doi: 10.3390/ijerph13010027

Robertson HA, Chaudhary Nagaraj N, Vyas AN. Family Violence and Child Sexual Abuse Among South Asians in the US. Journal of Immigrant and Minority Health. 2016 Aug;18(4):921-927. DOI: 10.1007/s10903-015-0227-8.

Roy A, Yalamarty H. Gender, Migration, and Exclusionary Citizenship Regimes: Conceptualizing Transnational Abandonment of Wives as a Form of Violence Against Women. *Violence Against Women.* 2018;24(7):747-774. doi:10.1177/1077801217720693

Rudra, Urjasi and Shamita Das Dasgupta. "Transnational Abandonment of South Asian Women: A New Face of Violence Against Women," *Manavi Occasional Paper 6,* New Brunswick, NJ: 2011.

Samar Collective. "One Big Happy Community? Class Issues within South Asian American Homes." *SAMAR: South Asian Magazine for Action & Reflection*, No. 4 (1994, Winter): 10-15.

Sabri B, Simonet M, Campbell JC. Risk and Protective Factors of IPV among South Asian immigrant women and perceived needs for services. Cultur. Divers. Ethnic Minor. Psychol. 2018; 24(3): 442-452.

Saran, Paramatma and E. Eames (eds.). *The New Ethnics: Asian Indians in the United States*. New York, NY: Praeger, 1980.

"Selected Characteristics of the Foreign-born Population by Period of Entry into the United States," TableID: S0502, *United States Census Bureau,* (2019). Available: https://data.census.gov/cedsci/table?q=immigration%20from%20India%20by%20gender&tid=ACSST1Y2019.S0502& hidePreview=false

Seth, Manju. "Asian Indian Americans." In *Asian Americans: Contemporary Trends and Issues*, Thousand Oaks, CA: Sage, 1995.

Shah, Shivali. "Middle Class, Documented, and Helpless: The H-4 Visa Bind." In *Body Evidence: Intimate Violence Against South Asian Women in America,* edited by Shamita Das Dasgupta, 195-210. New Brunswick, NJ: Rutgers University Press, 2007.

Singh AA, Hays DG, Chung YB, Watson L. South Asian Immigrant Women Who Have Survived Child Sexual Abuse: Resilience and Healing. *Violence Against Women*. 2010;16(4):444-458. doi:10.1177/1077801210363976

Spivak, G. "Can the Subaltern Speak?" I*n Reflections of an Idea, edited by Rosalind Morris,* 21-78. New York, NY: Columbia University Press. 1983.

Tewary, Sweta. "Asian Indian Immigrant Women." *Journal of Human Behavior in the Social Environment,* 11, no. 1 (2005): 1-22.

Pratyusha Tummala-Narra, Anmol Satiani, Neha Patel. "Sexual Violence in an Immigrant Context: South Asian Women in the United States." In Gendered Journeys: Women, Migration and Feminist Psychology, 2015

U.S. Bureau of the Census. *1990 census of population: Social and economic characteristics, United States.* Washington, DC: U.S. Government Printing Office, 1993.

United States Census Bureau. *The Asian population: 2010, 2010 Census briefs.* Washington, DC: U.S. Department of Commerce, Economics and Statistics Administration, (2012, March).

Venugopal, Arun. "The Truth Behind Indian American Exceptionalism." *The Atlantic*, (January/February, 2021). https://amp-theatlantic-com.cdn.ampproject.org/c/s/amp.theatlantic.com/amp/article/617258/

Warren, Sherry. "The U Visa for Immigrant Victims of Violent Crime: What Social Workers Need to Know." *Journal of Ethnic & Cultural Diversity in Social Work*, 25, issue 4 (2016): 320-324.

Whatley, Monica and Jeanne Batalova. "Indian immigrants in the United States in 2011." *Migration Policy Institute*, (2013, August 21). https://www.immigrationresearch.org/system/files/Indian%20Immigrants%20in%20the%20United%20States.pdf

Epilogue

ARUN K SINGH

Joe Biden selected Kamala Harris, of Indian origin through her mother, as his vice-presidential running mate on August 11, 2020. After the election, he nominated Neera Tanden to a cabinet-level position as director of the crucial Office of Management and Budget. More than twenty Indian-Americans were appointed to key positions in the White House, National Security Council, and other departments in the first phase of post-inauguration appointments in January 2021.

All this drew attention to the growing presence of Indian-Americans in US politics, administration, and in the Capitol, going beyond the traditional image of the community as focused more on its economic stabilization in the country of adoption.

The shift was noticeable first as the Obama administration came into office in 2009. A large number of Indian-Americans were inducted into the administration, with Raj Shah at a sub-cabinet position as director of USAID. Several key assignments—surgeon general, ambassador to India, assistant secretary of state for South and Central Asia, chief information officer, chief technology officer, chief data scientist, among others—went to Indian-Americans. In the Trump administration, Nikki Haley, as the permanent representative to the UN, was a cabinet-level appointee, with several others in important positions, including Seema Verma as administrator for Medicare and Medicaid Services.

Till 2012, only two Indian-Americans, Dalip Singh Saund and Bobby Jindal, had been elected to the US Congress. That year saw the election of the third, Ami Bera, from California. Since 2017, five have been present simultaneously, through several election cycles. They are present in or head important committees, such as the Asia-Pacific Subcommittee of the House Foreign Relations Committee. Pramila Jayapal heads the Progressive Caucus of the House Democrats.

The political profile now supplements the significant presence in key economic sectors: more than 100,000 doctors, caring for one out of seven patients; 40 percent of all hotel rooms; highest median income ethnic group, with income level of $120,000 annually; highest in educational achievements.

In September 2015, I had the occasion to travel to California to prepare for the visit of Prime Minister Narendra Modi. I could see for myself that Indian-origin tech entrepreneurs, high-skilled workers, and CEOs were an integral part of the US global leadership in technology and innovation, including in IT. At a public event with the Indian PM, CEOs of five leading US technology companies—Google, Microsoft, Adobe, Cisco, and Qualcomm—were present. Three of the five were of Indian origin.

This visible presence, across sectors, has occurred in the backdrop of an overall increase in numbers. The size of the community is now estimated to be over 4 million, with 1.8 million eligible electors. In some states, their numbers are larger than the margins of victory in the 2016 and 2020 presidential elections. The community is now wooed actively by both parties. Donald Trump, as president, had attended a 50,000-strong rally in Houston, in September 2019, organized in honor of PM Modi. He visited India in February 2020, the election year, and attached importance to his welcome by a 100,000-strong crowd in Ahmedabad, for which many Indian-Americans had flown in. Both Biden and Harris issued special messages on the occasion of India's Independence Day in August 2020, pledging support for India's concerns, including cross-border terrorism and the situation along the line of actual control with China.

As ambassador, I was often invited by congressmen and senators to attend events where their Indian-American constituents were present. The community has, at times, played a useful role in advancing India–US relations. Its advocacy during the process of the Civil Nuclear Cooperation Agreement from 2006 to 2008 had been noticed. Finalization of this agreement in 2008 led to higher-level technology releases from the US, and more defense cooperation. Before 2008, India hardly bought any defense supplies from the US. Now it has contracted for $20 billion worth of military purchases. The US has declared India a "major defense partner". Cooperation is being explored in defense technology partnerships, and deepening involvement of Indian companies in global supply chain of US defense companies. The US and India now do more military exercises with each other bilaterally than with any other country. They have signed agreements for reciprocal logistics support, communications security and sharing of geospatial data, and are working to enhance interoperability. The US has declared support for India's permanent membership of the United Nations Security Council.

There is now bipartisan support in the US for consolidating the India relationship. The new phase was started by Democratic President Bill Clinton when he visited India in 2000, putting behind him the period of sanctions against India in the wake of our 1998 nuclear tests. Republican President George W Bush transformed it through the landmark Civil Nuclear Cooperation Agreement, in the process modifying US law and Nuclear Suppliers' Group (NSG) commitments. Democrat Barack Obama was the first US president to visit India twice in his tenure, the first as chief guest on our Republic Day, when the two countries also declared a Joint Strategic Vision for the Indian Ocean and the Pacific. Republican Donald Trump placed India on Strategic Trade Authorization Level (STA-1) for highest-level technology releases (for closest allies and partners); launched a 2+2 dialogue of foreign and defense ministers; recognized key role for India in US strategy for the Indo-Pacific (to shape the environment around the rise of China); and revitalized the Quad with Japan and Australia and raised it to ministerial-level meetings.

The spokesman of the US State Department, following Secretary of State Antony Blinken's first call with India's external affairs minister on January 29, said, "The secretary underscored India's role as a pre-eminent US partner in the Indo-Pacific and the importance of working together to expand regional cooperation, including through the Quad." Similar support for the India relationship was expressed by Secretary of Defense Lloyd Austin at his confirmation hearing on January 19.

As the relationship with India strengthens, there will be greater welcome in the US for Indian students and H1B workers. Growing numbers of the Indian-origin community in the US would incentivize US elected representatives to be sensitive also to India's concerns.

No doubt, there will be challenges. India is a diverse country, which is among its strengths. However, at times, sections of the community may disagree with aspects of the Indian government's policies. Some have, in the past, done advocacy in US Congress and elsewhere, critical of India.

Despite this, amidst the current flux in the international system, the India–US relationship is headed for further consolidation, with their convergence of interests, particularly in the Indo-Pacific. The Indian-origin community in the US, with its economic, technological, and societal presence, is well placed to deepen further interest in and cooperation with India.

Various chapters in the book give us a sense of the community's diversity and its all-round presence. They enable us to have a better understanding of a phenomenon, still at a nascent stage, yet rapidly evolving.

Contributors

Aziz Haniffa is a Sri Lanka-born, Washington-based journalist of four decades who Indian Ambassador Taranjit Singh Sandhu called "one of the best-known names among the Indian-American community in the United States". From President Joe Biden to Vice President Kamala Harris, Barack Obama to George W Bush, he has interviewed them all for *India Abroad* where he rose to become its executive editor. He was the only South Asian print journalist who was part of the White House press delegation that accompanied President Bill Clinton to India, Pakistan, and Bangladesh in 2000. Last year, subjects of his countless stories gathered over a unique virtual event to honor and pay tributes to his journalism.

Shashi Tharoor, a third-term member of parliament for Thiruvananthapuram, India, is the best-selling author of 22 books, both fiction and nonfiction, besides being a former under-secretary-general of the United Nations and a former minister of state for human resource development and for external affairs in the Government of India. He has won numerous awards, including the Pravasi Bharatiya Samman, a Commonwealth Writers' Prize and the Crossword Lifetime Achievement Award. In 2019, Tharoor was also awarded the Sahitya Akademi Award in the category of "English Non-Fiction" for his book *An Era of Darkness*. He chairs Parliament's Standing Committee on Information Technology.

TP Sreenivasan, former ambassador, has spent 10 years in the US in different diplomatic assignments, including ambassador/deputy chief of mission in Washington. He has also served in Japan, Bhutan, Russia, Myanmar, Fiji, and Austria. He was a member of the National Security Advisory Board, Government of India. At present, he is the director general of the Kerala International Centre and a freelance columnist. He has authored seven books on international affairs.

Maina Chawla Singh is a scholar-professor focusing on gender, identity, and Indian diaspora. She has taught at premier universities in India, Israel, and mostly at Georgetown and American University, Washington, DC. She has lived in Russia, Japan, Ethiopia, France, and the United States, and speaks multiple languages.

MR Rangaswami is an entrepreneur, investor, corporate eco-strategy expert, community builder, and philanthropist. Recognized as a software business expert, he participated in the rapid expansion of Silicon Valley. He was named to the Forbes "Midas" list of investors and also recognized by CRN as one of the "top 25 technology executives". He is also the founder of Indiaspora, a nonprofit to unite the Indian diaspora and transform their success into meaningful impact in India and on the global stage.

Pradeep K Khosla is chancellor, UC San Diego, recognized as one of the top 15 research universities in the world. An internationally renowned electrical and computer engineer, he is an elected member of the American Academy of Arts and Sciences, National Academy of Engineering, and the American Society for Engineering Education. In 2012, he was named one of the 50 most influential Indian-Americans by *SiliconIndia*.

Suman Guha Mozumder has worked as a journalist, both in India and in the US, for more than 30 years, chronicling stories of the four-million-strong Indian-American community while working, first for IANS and then *India Abroad* weekly, the oldest and the most reputed newspaper for the Indian-American community. He was recognized by the New Jersey state assembly in 2011 for his contribution to journalism.

Raj L Gupta, chairman of APTIV PLC since March 2015, was formerly chairman and CEO of Rohm and Haas. He was chairman of the American Chemistry Council and the Society of Chemical Industry, America Section. He is a member of the DuPont board and is the chairman of Avantor Inc. He has also served on the boards of Arconic (Howmet Aerospace Inc), HP, IRI, the Vanguard Group and Tyco International, among other companies.

Deepak Raj is the chairman of Pratham USA and also the chairman of the India Philanthropy Alliance. He is the founder of the Neera and Deepak Raj Center on Indian Economic Policies at Columbia University's School of International and Public Affairs and is a co-founder of Indian-American IMPACT, an initiative to build a nationwide network of Indian-American leaders in policy, politics, and government.

Ashish Shah is the senior director of philanthropy and community engagement at Indiaspora, focused on philanthropy and diaspora engagement. He is focused on understanding giving habits and patterns of the Indian diaspora in the United States in order to help elevate its level of giving. Prior to Indiaspora, Shah co-founded GivingRise, an online giving platform focused on making giving to India from the United States simple, transparent, and highly impactful.

Arun Kumar is a veteran journalist and foreign correspondent who has reported on all things concerning India and Indians from three vantage points—Islamabad, Beijing, and Washington—for nearly two decades. Returning to India after 11 years as IANS correspondent in Washington, DC, he continues to track the Indian-American story.

Mayank Chhaya has been a journalist for the last 40 years with a reporting career out of India, Pakistan, Sri Lanka, and the United States. He is the author of an authorized biography of the Dalai Lama, *The Dénouement*, *Vikram Lunar Lander: Dead or Alive?*, and *Sam Pitroda: A Biography*. He is also writer-director of the documentary *Gandhi's Song*.

Ajay Ghosh, veteran journalist and social worker, is media consultant of the American Association of Physicians of Indian Origin (AAPI). He is the founder-president of the Indo-American Press Club and served as adjunct faculty at the Graduate School of Social Work, Fordham University and Bridgeport University.

Vikrum Mathur is a Washington, DC, area resident with deep interest in entertainment, film, pop culture, media, theater, and politics. He has served as a film critic for *The American Bazaar* since 2016 and has interviewed various prominent cinema personalities. He has also been an actor-performer, having performed in plays at the Kennedy Center and DC Capital Fringe Theater Festival, and his short films have been screened at the Tribeca Film Festival and DC South Asian Film Festival. He has also worked as legislative director in the Maryland general assembly.

Bijal Patel is chairman of the California Hotel & Lodging Association (CHLA), the largest state hospitality group in the US whose members operate almost a quarter-million hotel rooms, besides also being the CEO of Coast Redwood Hospitality. A third-generation hotelier, he is the youngest person to head CHLA in the association's 128-year history.

Laxmi Parthasarathy is the chief operating officer of Global Press, an international news organization that trains and employs local female reporters with more than 40 bureaus around the world. She has been a media innovator for more than a decade, working across Africa, Asia, Europe, and North America, and most recently was the director of Global Media at Ashoka, the world's leading association of social entrepreneurs.

Sujata Warrier is the chief strategy officer for the Battered Women's Justice Project. She has worked at local, national, and international levels on issues of violence against women, culture, and intersectionality. During the Obama administration, she served, after being appointed by the attorney general, to the Federal Department of Justice, Office on Violence against Women's Advisory Board.

Shamita Das Dasgupta is a co-founder of Manavi, an organization in the United States that focuses on violence against women in the South Asian community. She has taught at Rutgers University and in the clinical law program at NYU Law School. She specializes in the study of ethnicity, gender, immigration, and violence against women.

Arun K Singh is a former ambassador of India to the US, France, and Israel. He is currently a Halle Institute distinguished fellow at Emory University, Atlanta, US, visiting professor at Ashoka University, India, and a distinguished non-resident senior fellow in the Asia Program at the Washington, DC-based German Marshall Fund. He was also a distinguished visiting professor at Center for Advanced Study of India at the University of Pennsylvania, US.

Index

AAM Foundation 140
Abraham, Thomas 55, 63, 64, 69, 157, 158, 161
Ackerman, Gary 25
Adalja, Amesh 197
Adiga, Mala 156
Adobe 46, 94, 122
Advanced Research Projects Agency-Energy (ARPA-E) 106, 154
Adve, Sarita V 117
Affleck, Ben 208
Affordable Care Act 150, 152
Afghanistan 4, 23
AFL-CIO 266
Africa/African 6, 53, 58, 62, 73, 151, 222, 225, 260
Agarwal, Vandana 197
Agarwal, Vivek 175
Aggarwal, Dinesh 28
Agnihotri, Bhishma 28
Agrawal, Durga 68
Ahmedabad 43, 104
Ahuja, Kiran 156
Akanksha Fund 137
Alabama 186, 231
Alba, Jessica 248
Albright, Madeleine 26
Allen, George 53
Alphabet Inc 94, 116, 122
Ambedkar, BR 30
American Academy of Arts and Sciences 108, 117
American Association of Physicians of Indian Origin (AAPI) 40, 41, 54, 62, 69, 102, 185, 186, 187, 189, 190, 191, 192, 193, 194, 195, 196
American Automobile Association (AAA) 227, 228
American Board of Podiatric Medicine 244
American College of International Physicians 189
American College of Rheumatology (ACR) 198
American Council on Education 105, 113
American Hotel & Lodging Association 232
American India Foundation (AIF) 137
American Jewish Committee (AJC) 69
American Medical Association (AMA) 186, 188, 189, 190, 192
American Physical Society (APS) 167
American Podiatric Medical Association 244

American University 37
Amritraj, Ashok 216
Amritraj, Vijay 216
Amritsar 150
Amsterdam 82
Amway 128
Anand, Rajen 159
Andhra Pradesh 61, 184, 194
Andolan 266
Ansari, Aziz 201, 210, 211, 212, 218
Antani, Niraj 43, 73
Antrim, Doron K 184
Apatow, Judd 210, 211
Apple 80, 81, 92
Arab 7
Arabella Advisors 141
Arista Networks 94, 262
Arizona State University (ASU) 106
Arkangai 253
Arlington 113
Arogya World 137
Arora, Nikesh 94, 122
Asava, Anna 143
Asava, Aradhana 143
Asava, Raj 143
Ashoka Fellowship 246
Ashtekar, Abhay 167, 168, 169, 176
Asia/Asian 1, 2, 26, 27, 35, 36, 37, 41, 43, 54, 56, 57, 59, 61, 62, 65, 67, 74, 77, 105, 129, 148, 149, 150, 156, 157, 158, 161, 185, 210, 212, 221, 228, 255, 256, 257, 258, 259, 260, 261, 262, 263, 264, 265, 266, 267, 268, 269, 270
Asian American Hotel/Motel Operators Association (AAHOA) 62, 69, 102, 228, 229, 231, 232, 233
Asian American Pacific Islander Institute on Gender based Violence (APIGBV) 269
Asian Americans/Pacific Islanders in Philanthropy (AAPIP) 157
Asian Indian Women in America 262
Asian-American Heritage Month 61
Aspect Development 93
Assam 107
Association of American Physicians of Indian Origin 40
Association of Indians in America (AIA) 56, 59
Association of Pakistan and Islamic Physicians 189
Atlanta 62, 192
Atlantic 206, 224, 250
Atreya 182
Australia/Australian 108, 128
Austria 21
Ayer, Ramani 122
Ayushman Bharat 195
Azmi, Shabana 216

Baan 82
Bahl, Gaurav 175
Bains, Didar Singh 9
Bajwa, Jashan 146
Baltimore 50, 245
Bandaranaike, Sirimavo 2
Banderas, Antonio 216
Banerjee, Abhijit Vinayak 104
Banga, Ajay 46, 120, 122
Bangladesh 2, 4
Bansal, Preeta 12, 45
BAPS Swaminarayan Sanstha 136
Barve, Kumar 41
Basu, Sanjay 175
Bates, Jim 189, 190
Batra, Dhruv 175
Battle Creek 186
Bedi, Kabir 203
Belmont 79
Ben Lomond Hylton 223, 225
Bendapudi, Neeli 113
Bengaluru 8, 9, 85, 96
Benioff, Marc 88, 92
Bera, Ami 48, 49
Bereuter, Douglas K 26
Berkeley 109, 154
Berkshire Hathaway 119
Berry, Halle 12
Best Western 229
Bezos, Jeff 86
Bhagavad Gita 48

Bhagwati, Jagdish Natwarlal 103
Bharadia, Dinesh 126
Bharat Bazar 77
Bhargava, Bharat 158
Bhargava, Manoj 142
Bharucha, Jamshed 113
Bhatia, Karan Krishna 160
Bhatia, Sabeer 28, 65
Bhatia, Sangeeta 178
Bhatnagar Prize 110
Bhatt, Ajay 123
Bhattacharya, Sharmila 177
Bhusri, Allison 142
Bhusri, Aneel 88, 94, 142
Bhutan 4
Bhutto, Benazir 2
Biden Foundation 156
Biden Victory Fund 14
Biden, Joe 1, 14, 15, 16, 33, 34, 35, 50, 54, 55, 70, 73, 74, 147, 151, 152, 153, 154, 155, 156, 157, 161, 194, 241, 264
Big Blue 94
Bill and Melinda Gates Foundation 141, 149
Biswal, Nisha Desai 149
Blackwill, Robert 68
Bloomington 40, 182
Boeing 82
Bombay University 159
Bose Corporation 103, 114, 125
Bose, Amar Gopal 103, 114, 125, 126
Boston 39, 62, 184, 186, 197, 217
Boston Hospital 184
Boulder 40
Boxer, Barbara 32, 232
Britain/British/Britons 4, 5, 6, 9, 10, 16, 17, 59, 104, 183
British Academy 108
British Columbia 6
Brookhaven National Laboratory 104
Brookings Institution 32, 197
Brooklyn 112, 196
Brown Book 2.0 161
Brown University 108, 112, 160, 175, 178
Brown University School of Public Health 112
Brownback, Sam 27
Brownstown 239
Buffett, Warren 142
BUILD 92
Burma 21
Burns, Ken 199
Burns, Nicholas 71
Burton amendment 25, 26
Burton, Dan 25
Bush, George HW 57, 80, 158
Bush, George W 31, 67, 68, 69, 71, 159, 160, 161, 191, 198

Cage, Nicholas 216
Cal Poly University 231
Calcutta 103, 183
California 6, 14, 32, 35, 38, 39, 40, 48, 49, 58, 60, 61, 62, 76, 78, 83, 86, 97, 109, 154, 158, 160, 173, 175, 197, 199, 215, 217, 221, 222, 223, 224, 226, 228, 231, 257, 264, 267
California Hotel & Lodging Association (CH&LA) 231, 232, 233
California Institute of Technology (Caltech) 9, 158, 247
California State University, Long Beach 159
Cambridge 104, 105, 110, 165, 176
Canada/Canadian 6, 21, 148, 151, 166, 168, 215, 242, 243, 244, 248
Cannon, Nick 214
Capitol Hill 12, 42, 156
Caribbean 2, 7
Carnegie Endowment for International Peace 159, 241
Carnegie Mellon University 101, 105, 106
Carter, Jimmy 61
Center for American Progress 152
Center for Cognitive Ubiquitous Computing (CUbiC) 151
Center for Nutrition Policy and Promotion 159
Center for Nutrition Policy and Promotion (CNPP) 159
Centers for Medicare & Medicaid Services 150
Chadha, Gurinder 203

Chakrabarty, Ananda Mohan 169, 170
Chalil, Joseph M 181, 199
ChaloGive 138, 139, 145
Chandigarh 43, 45
Chandra, Naresh 28
Chandrasekhar, Jay 215
Chandrasekhar, Subrahmanyan/ Chandra 9, 13, 65, 105, 164, 165, 166
Chari, PR 32
Chary, Ranga-Ram 173, 174
Chatterjee, Swadesh 54, 69, 70, 71, 73
Chaturvedi, Jagdish 126
Chaudhary, Satveer 47
Chawla, Kalpana 13, 28, 65, 177, 262
Chennai 2, 14, 33, 76, 147, 151, 239
Chennai University 151
Cherian, Joy 63, 157
Cheryan, Sapna 110
Chetty, Raj 108
Chicago 49, 61, 62, 150, 159, 165, 168, 186, 192, 195, 223
China Europe International Business School 103
China/Chinese 4, 8, 31, 34, 37, 58, 69, 83, 128, 130, 163, 168
Cho, John 204
Chopra Center for Wellbeing 199
Chopra, Aneesh Paul 45, 123
Chopra, Deepak 9, 28, 140, 192, 199
Chopra, Rohit 154
Christ Church College 161
Chu, Steven 179
Cipher State Inc 115
Cisco 80, 81, 94, 122, 263
Citigroup 122
Citizenship Amendment Act (CAA) 15
City University of New York 112
Clear Shape Inc 115
Cleopatra 20
Cleveland 50, 61, 186
Clinton, Bill 24, 26, 27, 28, 29, 33, 47, 67, 175, 227
Clinton, Hillary Rodham 32, 66, 148, 153, 158, 192
CMP Technology 92
CNN 197
Cognizant Technology Solutions 122
Coimbatore 177
Cold War 121
Colorado 40
Columbia University 42, 64, 103, 104
Columbia University Medical Center 199
Columbus 61
Comfort Inn 229
Commission for Religious Freedom 12
Commonwealth 22
Communications Act of 1934 151
Comprehensive Test Ban Treaty (CTBT) 31
Concord 40
Connecticut 60, 181, 262
Consumer Financial Protection Bureau 154
Cooper Union for the Advancement of Science and Art 113
Cornell India Law Center 102
Cornell University 102, 103, 104, 109, 113, 125, 199, 234, 250
Cornyn, John 66
Cosmos Club 69
Council for Aid to Education 144
Coury, John 189
CRY America 137
Cupertino 80, 95
CyLab 101

D'Souza, Francisco 122
Daan Utsav 139
Dabby, Firoza Chic 269
Dalberg 134
Dallas 62, 68, 198
Damon, Matt 208
Dandekar, Swati 47, 263
Daniels, Greg 208
Darkhan 237
Das, Riva Ganguly 195
Dasra 137
Dastagir, Sabu 202, 218
Datar, Srikant M 111
Davar, Shiamak 214
Davuluri, Nina 201, 212, 213
Day's Inn 227, 228

Dayton 43
DBS Bank 131
Defense Advanced Research Projects Agency (DARPA) 100, 101, 158
Delhi 4, 8, 16, 22, 27, 32, 54, 62, 96, 108, 148, 173, 238, 257
Deloitte 77, 125
Democratic National Committee's Indo-American Council 47
Democratic National Convention 14
Democratic Republic of Congo 252
Department of Agriculture 159
Department of Defense (DoD) 175
Department of Justice 45, 157
Department of Transportation 158
Desai Sethi Foundation 140
Desai, Bhairavi 12, 266
Desai, Bharat 140
Detroit 58, 73, 186, 187, 192
Dewji, Mohammed 142
Dham, Vinod 40, 122, 130
Dhillon, Neil 158
Dhingra, Manka 263
Digital Equipment Corporation 78
Disney 206, 214
District of Columbia 45
Dixit, Madhuri 214
Doctors for America 154
Dole, Bob 56, 157
Domestic Workers Committee 266
Dow Chemical Company 128
Drexel University 125
Druva 97
Dublin 95
Duke, David 12
DuPont 120
Dutch 82
Dutta, Kanak 263
Dutta, Soumitra 113

East Africa 6, 62, 151, 222
East African Railway 222
Econo Lodge 227, 229
Econo Lodge Franchisee Association (ELFA) 229
Eddington, Arthur 165
Edison 43
Ekal USA 137
El Camino Real 77
Ellison, Larry 79, 93
Embarcadero Center 77
Emory University 104
Endometriosis Foundation of America 218
Equal Employment Opportunity Council (EEOC) 157
Esper, Mark 151
Ettan 95
Europe 101, 129
European Union 130
Excess Bandwidth Corporation 115

Facebook 76
Fallon, Jimmy 248
Federal Bureau of Investigation (FBI) 151
Federal Communications Commission (FCC) 150, 151
Federal Energy Regulatory Commission (FERC) 57, 157
Federation of Indian Associations (FIA) 60, 61, 69, 267
Federation of Kerala Associations of North America (FOKANA) 62
Federation of State Medical Boards (FSMB) 190
Feeding America 143
Feinstein, Diane 232
Ferguson 245
Fernandez, Jaqueline 214
FIA Northern California 61
Fiji/Fijian 3, 10, 17, 21, 22, 23
Filipino Medical Association 189
Fiske, Cyrus 184
Flaherty, Robert J 202
Flint 179, 186
Florida 38
Foundation for Excellence (FFE) 137
Fowler, William 164
France 168
Freedom Employability Academy (FEA) 140
Fremont 95
Freshworks 97

Gabbard, Tulsi 48, 49
Gadar movement 56, 57
Gadar Party 257
Gandhi, Indira 2, 23
Gandhi, Mahatma 28, 58, 60, 70, 137, 138
Gandhi, Rajiv 21, 22
Ganguli, Sampriti 141
Gates, Bill 94, 122, 142
Gates, Melinda 142
Gauba, Gary 95
Gawande, Atul 154
Gaylord Restaurant 77
General Electric 161
General Electric Research and Development Center 169
Georgetown University 37
Georgetown University Law School 45
Georgia Institute of Technology 175
German/Germany 82, 83, 243, 252
Ghana 5
Gibson, Mel 206
Gideon, Sara 263
Gill Foundation 156
Gilman, Benjamin 26
Gingrich, Newt 192
Giving Tuesday 139
Giving USA 134
Glenn amendment 26
Global Association of Physicians of Indian Origin (GAPIO) 194, 195
Global Healthcare Summit (GHS) 194, 195
Global Organization of People of Indian Origin (GOPIO) 55, 69, 73, 157, 161
Global Press 237, 238, 240, 252, 253
Gobi Desert 237
Goel, Anita 178, 179
Goel, Prabhu 81
Goizueta Business School 104
Golden Gate Bridge 80
Golden Temple 13
Goldman Sachs 82, 160
Goodman, Barak 199
Google 46, 94, 99, 122, 154, 161
Googleplex 95
Gopalan, Shyamala 2, 19, 33, 36, 108, 109, 147
Gopinath, Gita 104
Gopinathan, Srijith 95
Gounder, Celine 154
Government Accounting Office (GAO) 190, 191
Government of India Act, 1935 4
Goyal, Jay 42, 47
Goyle, Raj 47, 48, 74
Gramm, Phil 57
Grand Rapids 186
Greene, Brian 177
Greens 80
Grossman School of Medicine 154
Guggenheim Fellowship 104
Guhathakurta, Madhulika 177, 262
Gujarat/Gujarati 14, 45, 121, 149, 151, 155, 171, 194, 223, 224, 228, 235
Gulf 3, 7, 29
Gupta Rahul 156
Gupta Software 78
Gupta, Jagdish 196, 197
Gupta, Kanta Chandra 257
Gupta, Rajat 122
Gupta, Sanjay 197
Gupta, Umang 78
Gupta, Vanita 11
Gurugram 8
Guwahati University 107
Guyana/Guyanese 5, 10, 242

Haley, Nikki/Randhawa, Nimrata 10, 13, 46, 148, 150, 160, 161, 263
Hampton Inn & Suites 229
Haniffa, Aziz 42
Harlem 58
Harman International Industries 122
Hart–Celler Act 38, 185, 257
Hartke, Vance 189
Harvard University 55, 74, 103, 104, 108, 111, 112, 127, 150, 153, 155, 165, 178, 179, 184, 185, 198
Harvard Business School (HBS) 103, 111
Harvard Global Health Institute (HGHI) 112

Harvard Kennedy School 55, 74
Harvard Medical School 184, 198
Harvard School of Tropical Medicine 184
Harvard–MIT Joint Division of Health Sciences and Technology 178
Hastings, Reed 86
Hegranes, Cristi 252
Herschbach, Dudley R 179
Hewlett Packard/HP 78, 80, 120
Hippocrates 182
Holiday Inn Express 229
Holley, Robert W 105, 166
Honduras 244
Hong Kong 3
Hotmail 28, 65
House Intelligence Committee 151
House of Commons 10
House of Delegates 41, 189
House of Lords 10
House of Representative India Caucus 66
Houston 33, 43, 45, 68, 76, 80, 195
Howdy Modi 14, 33
Huddersfield, Yorkshire 153
Huebel, Rob 211
HungerMitao 143
Hutchins, Robert Maynard 165
Hyde Act/Henry J Hyde US–India Peaceful Atomic Energy Cooperation Act 32, 46
Hyderabad 43, 122, 195
Hylton, George 225

IBM 78, 79, 80, 94, 119, 122
Idaho National Laboratory 175
Idli Caucus 73
Immigration and Naturalization Act of 1965 7, 35, 56, 58, 102, 121, 185, 257
IMPACT Fund 44, 48, 73, 161
India Abroad 42, 63, 64, 187
India Abroad Fellowship Program 42
India Caucus 12, 32, 46, 65, 66
India Chamber of Commerce of America 58
India Club 64
India Interest Group Lobby 46
India League of Americas 28, 57, 58
India Medical Association of Illinois (IMA, IL) 186
India Philanthropy Alliance (IPA) 137
Indian American Center for Political Awareness (IACPA) 42, 64, 65
Indian American Forum for Political Education (IAFPE) 28, 63, 69
Indian American Foundation (IAF) 42
Indian American Friendship Council 42
Indian Institute of Management (IIM), Ahmedabad 103, 104
Indian Institute of Science 151
Indian Institute of Technology (IIT) 9, 40, 59, 69, 78, 121, 124, 151, 154
Indian Medical Association of America Inc (AMAI) 186
Indian Medical Association of New England (IMANE) 186
Indiana 25, 38, 182, 189, 203
Indian-American Issues Conference 57
Indian-American Leadership Initiative (IALI) 47, 48
Indiaspora 48, 72, 96, 130, 134, 136, 137, 138, 144, 145
Indiaspora Monitor of University Giving 144
India–US Civil Nuclear Agreement 46
Infosys 85, 110
Infosys Prize 110
Innovaccer 97
Inside HigherEd 105, 113, 114
Institute for Enzyme Research 104, 105, 166
Integrated Systems 115
Intel 122
Inter University Centre for Astronomy and Astrophysics 168
International Association of American Physicians (IAAP) 188, 189, 190, 191
International Monetary Fund (IMF) 104
Iowa 47, 186, 263
Iran 4, 54
Ireland/Irish 10, 242
Israel/Israeli 25, 49, 50, 83
ITC 161
Iyer, Vijay 217

Jackson, Samuel L 206
Jaffna 252
Jain, Ajit 119
Jain, Dipak 103, 107
Jain, Prashant 175
Jaishankar, Dhruva 32
Jalan, Bharat 175
Jamaica 19, 36, 239
Jammu and Kashmir 68
Janssen Pharmaceuticals Companies 198
Japan/Japanese 8, 31, 37, 168, 258, 259
Japanese-Americans 8
Jayapal, Pramila 15, 48, 49, 155, 156, 263
Jet Propulsion Laboratory 171
JFK Airport 22
Jha, Ashish K 112, 197
Jha, Sanjay 122
Jindal, Bobby (Piyush) 10, 11, 12, 13, 15, 46, 150, 160, 161, 162
John F Kennedy Center for the Performing Arts 155
Johns Hopkins Center for Health Security 197
Johns Hopkins School of Public Health 150
Johns Hopkins University 112, 146
Johnson, Dwayne "The Rock" 217, 248
Johnson, Lyndon B 38, 102, 121, 185
Johnson–Reed Act 257
Jolie, Angelina 180, 216
Jonas, Priyanka Chopra 214, 216
Jones, Norah 217
Jonnalagadda, Sudhakar 191
Joshi, Anandibai 183
JSS Medical College, Mysuru 181
Justice Department 12, 151

Kailath, Thomas 102, 115, 116
Kakarala, Jagan 187
Kalantry, Sital 102, 109
Kaling, Mindy/Chokalingam, Vera Mindy 201, 207, 208, 209, 210, 218, 239, 248
Kallivayalil, Nitya 175
Kaloti, Hilori 249, 250
Kampala 224
Kansas 39, 40, 45, 47, 48, 74
Kapoor, Shashi 216
Kapur, Devesh 146
Kapuria, Samir 127
Karbhari, Vistasp 113
Kargil 67
Karnataka 153, 156
Kashkari, Neel Tushar 160
Kashmir 15, 25, 45, 66, 67, 68, 154, 155
Katrak, Ketu H 262
Katyal, Neal Kumar 45
Kazi, Joya 201, 213, 214, 215
Kellogg School 103, 107
Kendrick, John Fox 184
Kennedy administration 189
Kennedy, Edward 32, 61
Kent State University 76, 97
Kentucky 73, 186
Kenya 21, 23, 222, 223
Kerala 7, 24, 62, 64, 149, 157
Khan, Irrfan 204, 216
Khanna, Gopal 161
Khanna, Ro 15, 47, 49, 96
Khator, Renu 112, 113, 117
Khatri 56
Kher, Anupam 216
Khorana, Har Gobind 9, 13, 65, 104, 165, 166
Khosla, Neeru 142
Khosla, Pradeep 100, 105, 111, 112, 116
Khosla, Vinod 40, 78, 130, 142
Kingsborough Community College 112
Kingsley, Ben 9
Kini, Ratnakar 187
Kirumba 252
Kiva 141
Kleiner Perkins 90
Kocherlakota, Narayana 160
Kolkata 54, 183, 195
Kolli, Ravi 188
Korean 37, 204
Kothari, Ujamlal 186, 187
Kovind, Ram Nath 195
KPMG India 149
Krishna, Arvind 94, 119, 122
Krishnamoorthi, Raja 49, 73
Kulkarni, Nima 73

Kumar, Sunil 112, 122
Kumar, Vijay 113, 116
Kumaratunga, Chandrika 2
Kunda, Maithilee 126
Kurian, George 94, 122
Kurup, Deepika 177, 178

Lacy, Mark 176
Lady Davis Institute for Medical Research 109
Lahiri, Jhumpa 13, 204
Lahore 166
Lakhanpal, Sharad 198
Lakhanpur 68
Lakshmi, Padma 217
Lane, Ray 91
Las Vegas 92
Latifah, Queen 216
Law for Black Lives 245
Lawrence Expressway 77, 92
Lederle Laboratories 184, 185
Leiner, Danny 204
Leonard N Stern School of Business 104
Leske, Lucy Apthorp 114
Leven, Michael 228
Lieberman, Joe 190
LIGO-India 168
LinkedIn 76
Liveris, Andrew 128
Livermore 95
LivingMyPromise 142, 143
London 7, 222, 224, 226
London School of Economics (LSE) 109, 250
London Underground 222
Loop Quantum Gravity program 168
Los Angeles 50
Los Angeles Times 57
Louis, Arul 66
Louisiana 10, 11, 12, 46, 48, 150, 160
Louisiana Department of Health and Hospitals 160
Luce–Celler Act 56, 58
LyondellBasell 123

Madhur, Meenakshi 175
Madhusudana, Uma 181
Madison Square Garden 33, 211
Madras 43, 184
Magic Bus USA 137
Mago, Ashok 62, 66, 70, 72
Maitra, Anuradha Luther 107
Majumdar, Arun 106, 116, 154
Makhija, Neil 44
Malaya 5
Malaysian 3, 17
Mallipattu, Sandeep 175
Malvern 248, 251
Mammen, Mathai 198
Management and Business Review 127
Manavi 256, 264, 266
Mandarin Oriental Hotel 48
Mangipudi, Latha 73
Mann, Leslie 210
March of Dimes 156
Mars Science Laboratory (MSL) 171
Martin, Steve 216
Maryland 41, 47
Massachusetts 28, 32, 103, 125, 155, 165, 175, 207
Massachusetts Avenue 28
Massachusetts Institute of Technology (MIT) 9, 103, 104, 106, 109, 111, 114, 126, 149, 177, 178, 180, 218
Mastercard 46, 120, 122
Mathrani Sandeep 122
Mauritius 3, 5, 10
Mayfield 90
Mayo Medical Center 198
Mazda 83
Mazumdar-Shaw, Kiran 142
McAvoy, James 207
McConigley, Nimi Swamidoss 263
McConnell, Mitch 150, 153
McGill University Faculty of Medicine 109
McKinsey & Company 122
McMahon, Shawn 191
McNamee, Roger 91
Mehrotra, Sanjay 94, 122
Memorial Sloane Kettering Cancer Center 198
Menlo Park 82

Menon, PNC 142
Menon, Sobha 142
Mexico 238
Miami 39, 50, 151, 153, 155, 245
Miami International Airport 246
Michigan 14, 62, 73, 103, 179, 186, 213, 252
Michigan Association of Physicians of Indian Origin (MAPI) 186
Microchip Technology 126, 128
Micron 94, 122
Microsoft 46, 80, 91, 92, 94, 122
Midas List 84, 93
Mike Mansfield Room 56
Millennial Action Project 242
Miller, Aruna 47, 263
Miller, Chris 151
Milpitas 95
Minhaj, Hasan 215
Ministry for Overseas Indian Affairs (MOIA) 3, 5
Ministry of External Affairs (MEA) 6, 8
Minneapolis 160, 161, 217
Minneapolis Federal Reserve 160
Minnesota 38, 39, 40, 47
Minority Business Development Authority (MBDA) 158
Mishra, Brajesh 27, 28
Mississippi 15, 40
Mo, Lil' 248
Modi, Narendra 6, 14, 15, 16, 33, 34, 97, 195
Moghe, Prabhas 112
Mohanty, Chandra Talpade 262
Mongolia/Mongolian 237, 238, 253
Moorjani, Richa 246, 247
Morgan Stanley 82
Morris, Aldon 245
Motorola 92, 94, 122
Movement Law Lab 245
Moynihan 189, 190
Mt Sharp 171
Mukherjee, Siddhartha 65. 199
Mukkamala, Apparao 194
Mukunda, Gautam 74
Mumbai 3, 159, 166, 195, 214, 247
Murali, Geetha 141
Murthy, Vivek 45, 153, 154, 193, 194
Myanmar 21
Mysore 73, 202

Nadella, Satya 46, 94, 115, 122
Nagel, Ilene H 113
Nair, Mira 15, 203, 204
Nair, Sree 29
Nairobi 222
Namaste Trump 14
Nanda, Navin C 199
Narasimhan, Laxman 129
Narasimhan, Shekar 47, 48, 53, 54
Narasimhan, Vasant "Vas" 119, 122
Narayan, Jayaprakash 9
Narayen, Shantanu 46, 94, 122
Nashua 177
Nasscom Product Conclave (NPC) 93
Natarajan, Priyamvada 109, 110, 176, 177
National Academy of Engineering (NAE) 116, 117
National Academy of Medicine (NAM) 116
National Academy of Sciences (NAS) 116, 154, 168
National Aeronautics and Space Administration (NASA) 40, 171, 177, 262
National Asian Pacific American Women's Forum 157
National Association of Americans of Asian Indian Descent (NAAAID) 56, 57, 157
National Association of Inventors 151
National Center for Emerging and Zoonotic Infectious Diseases 175
National Convention of Asian Indians in North America 56
National Economic Council (NEC) 155
National Federation of Indian American Associations (NFIA) 56, 61, 62, 63
National Institute of Standards and Technology (NIST) 158
National Radio Astronomy Observatory 176

National Republican Senatorial Committee 57
National Science Foundation (NSF) 101, 106, 151, 175, 176
National Security Council 151, 159
Nebraska 12
Nehru, Jawaharlal 9, 21, 58
Nepal 4, 238, 252
NetApp 94, 122
Network of Indian Professionals 11
Network of South Asian Professionals (NETSAP) 27
Nevada 70
New Delhi 4, 8, 16, 54, 62, 108, 148, 158, 159
New England 186, 191
New Hampshire 73, 178
New Jersey 39, 43, 47, 60, 192, 203, 263
New Jersey Restart and Recovery Commission 152
New York 7, 12, 20, 22, 28, 33, 38, 39, 46, 48, 50, 56, 58, 60, 61, 64, 82, 112, 125, 154, 183, 185, 192, 195, 199, 208, 209, 210, 212, 213, 217, 223, 242, 258, 262, 266
New York Taxi Workers Alliance (NYTWA) 266
New York University (NYU) 104, 144, 154, 210
New York-Presbyterian Hospital/Weill Cornell Medical College 199
Nilekani, Nandan 142
Nilekani, Rohini 142
NIO USA 94
Nirenberg, Marshall W 105, 166
Noah, Trevor 248
Nobel Prize 9, 103, 104, 105, 164, 165, 166, 167, 176, 184
Nohria, Nitin 111
Nooyi, Indra 46, 65, 122, 262
Nori, Dattatreyudu 199
North America 6, 56, 61, 62, 136, 238, 242
North Carolina 54, 69
Northwestern University 103, 117
NortonLifeLock 127
Novartis 119
NRI Academy of Medical Science 194
Nuclear Liability Act 32
Nuclear Nonproliferation Treaty (NPT) 31, 32, 71
Nuclear Suppliers Group 32
Numerical Technologies, Inc 115
Nunes Memo 151
Nunes, Devin 151

Oakland 95
Obama, Barack 12, 14, 20, 44, 45, 47, 106, 121, 122, 148, 149, 150, 151, 152, 153, 154, 155, 156, 157, 158, 159, 193, 198
Obama, Michelle 213
Odonchimeg 253
Office of General Counsel 150
Office of Management and Budget 45
Office of National Drug Policy 156
Office of Social Innovation and Civic Participation 45
Ohio 39, 42, 43, 47, 73, 76, 155, 166, 186
Olikara, Steven 242
Omidyar, Pierre 86
Oracle 79, 81, 88, 91, 92, 93
Overseas Friends of the BJP 28
Overseas Indians' Day 3
Owens, Major R 25

Pai, Ajit Varadaraj 150, 151
Pakistan/Pakistani 2, 4, 15, 25, 63, 67, 166
Pal, Piya 175
Paliwal, Dinesh C 122
Pallone, Frank 26, 66, 192
Palo Alto Networks 81, 94, 122
Panayampalli, Subbian 175
Panchal, Haresh 62
Panchanathan, Sethuraman "Panch" 106, 114, 115, 151, 176
Pandit, Farah 45
Pandit, Vikram 122
PANIIT 40, 69
Pant, Milind 128
Panwala, Jagruti 232
Parekh, Andrij 217

Pasadena 171, 173
Pasand 77
Patel, Bob 123
Patel, Jayantibhai (JC) 222
Patel, Kashyap "Kash" 151
Patel, Kavita 197
Patel, Purushottambhai Vaghjibhai 222
Patel, Ramesh 41
Patel, Sandhya 229
Patel, Vedant 155
Patel, Vinay 233
Patil, Pratibha 2
Patil, Suhas 81
Paul, Lord Swraj 9
Paulose, Rachel 263
Peace Corps 161
Pebble Beach 91
Pelosi, Nancy 70
Penn, Kal/Modi, Kalpen Suresh 13, 201, 203, 204, 205, 218
Pennsylvania 14, 39, 44, 48, 109, 167, 188, 205
Penrose, Roger 167
PepsiCo 46, 122, 262
Perth 108
Peters, Russell 215
Peterson, Patti McGill 113
Philadelphia 120, 125
Philadelphia Chemical Company 120
Philanthropy Northwest 156
Philippines 56, 58
Phillips, Charles 92
Phoenix, Joaquin 206
Pichai, Sundar 46, 94, 115, 116, 122
Pillai, Jan 57, 63, 157
Pillai, Parthasarathi 20
Pittsburgh 188
Planning Commission 26
Plattner, Hasso 92
Pokhran 158
Pomona 197
Portman, Natalie 248
Portugal 10
Prabhakar, Arati 158
Prabhu, RD 70
Prahalad, CK 103
Pratham USA 137
Pravasi Bharatiya Divas (PBD) 3
Pravasi Bharatiya Samman 20
Precourt Institute of Energy 154
Premji, Azim 142
Presidency College 165
Presidential Commission on Mental Retardation 158
Pressler amendment 63
Preventive Detention Act 31
Princeton University 104
Pritzker, Penny 149
Project Impact for South-Asian-Americans 149
Puerto Rico 238
Pune 168
Punjab 158, 194, 248
Punjab Engineering College 177
Puri, Amrish 203
Puri, Om 216
Puri, Sanjay 69, 161

Quality Inn 227
Quayle, Dan 192
Quest Labs 122

Raghavan, Gautam 156
Rajan, Raghuram Govinda 104
Rajan, Rajeswari Sunder 262
Rajasethupathy, Priya 175
Rajasthan 194
Rajkumar, Jenifer 73, 242
Raju, Gopal 42, 63, 64
Raju, VK 198
Ramachandran, Sohini 175
Ramakrishnan, Venkatraman "Venki" 104, 166, 167
Ramamurti, Bharat 155
Raman Scattering 165
Raman, Chandrasekhara Venkata (CV Raman) 165
Raman, Indira M 117
Ramchand, Latha 113
RAND Corporation 159
RAND Graduate School 159
Rangamani, Padmini 175

Rangaswami, MR 48, 72, 75, 130
Rao, Bhimsen 187
Rao, Gitanjali 179, 180
Rao, Neelam 41
Rao, PV Narasimha 25
Rao, Sanku 194
Raphael, Robin 67
Raymer, Steve 182
Reagan, Ronald 63, 147, 157, 158
Reckitt Benckiser 129
Red Baraat 49
Reddy, Raj 105, 116
Reddy, Ranga 185, 186, 192, 199
Reddy, Vinay 154
Redpoint 90
Reid, Harry 70, 148
Rekhi, Kanwal 81, 130
Renjen, Punit 125
Reserve Bank of India 104
Reynolds, Ryan 204
Rockefeller Foundation 141, 150
Rockefeller University 175
Rogen, Seth 210
Rogers, Chip 232
Rogers, Harrison L 192
Rohm and Haas 119, 125, 126, 127, 128, 129
Rohrabacher, Dana 25
Rolodex 90
Room to Read 91, 141
Roosevelt Institute 155
Roshan, Hrithik 214
Rushdie, Salman 9, 17
Russell Reynolds Associates 113
Russia/Russian 83, 151
Rutgers University 112

Sachdev, Rakesh 122
Sacramento 223
Saison 95
Sakhi for South Asian Women 266
Salesforce 88, 92
SALGA 267
Salt Lake City 82
Samosa Caucus 10, 49, 73
San Antonio 195
San Diego 101, 111, 166, 175, 234
San Francisco 56, 57, 61, 76, 77, 80, 84, 92, 95, 141, 222, 223, 242, 264
San Jose 62, 76, 94, 95, 97
San Lorenzo River 225
Sand Hill 81, 84, 89, 90
Sandhu, Taranjit 26
Sandler, Adam 210
Sanghi, Steve 126, 128
Sangisetty, Ravi 48
Santa Clara 77, 83, 95
Santa Clara Convention Center 92
Santa Cruz 107, 221, 223, 233
SAP 79, 82, 88, 92
Saujani, Reshma 48, 263
Saund, Dalip Singh/Dalip Singh "Judge" 10, 35, 56
Sawant, Kshama 263
Scheer, Paul 211
Schumer, Amy 248
Scott Paper Company 125
Scottish 82
Scroll 110
Seattle 43, 49, 110
Sellers, Peter 203
Sen, Amartya 103
Sen, Ronen 68, 69, 71
Sengupta, Anita 177
Sequoia 90
Sethi, Neerja 140, 263
Sethna, Beheruz Nariman 102
Shah, Aisha 155
Shah, Bhanu 187
Shah, Jayesh 193
Shah, Naseeruddin 216
Shah, Navin C 186, 190, 199
Shah, Niraj S 122
Shah, Premal 141
Shah, Purvi 245
Shah, Rajiv 45, 141, 149
Shah, Sonal 45
Shankar, Ravi 65, 217
Shapley, Harlow 165
Sharif, Nawaz 67
Sharma, Deven 122
Shenoy, Sachi 141

Sheth, Jagdish 104
Sheth, Manju 197
Shetty, BR 142
Shetty, CR 142
SHG Foundation 91, 92
Shiva Murugan Temple 40
Shivangi, Sampat 193
Shriram, Ram 94
Shukla, Venktesh 130
Shyamalan, M Night 27, 28, 201, 205, 206, 207 215
Sidharth, SR 53
Sigma-Aldrich 122
Silicon Canyon 68
Silicon Valley 8, 28, 36, 38, 40, 48, 49, 65, 75, 76, 77, 78, 79, 80, 81, 82, 83, 84, 85, 86, 87, 88, 89, 90, 91, 92, 93, 94, 95, 96, 97, 101, 115, 116, 121, 130, 139, 163, 233, 247
Simpson, Jessica 215
Singapore 5
Singer, Bryan 204
Singh, Arun Kumar 195
Singh, Jagjit 58
Singh, Jaswant 26, 27, 32
Singh, Lilly 246, 248
Singh, Manmohan 3, 31, 32, 148
Singh, Nirvikar 107
Sinha, Manisha 109
Sloan School of Management 104
Slovenian 177
Smith, Kern 189
Smithsonian Institution 155, 170
Sneha 262
Sobha Group 142
Solarz, S 65, 66, 189, 190
Solarz, Stephen 65, 190
Solomon 2
Soros Fellowship 246
South Africa/South African 83, 127
South American Physician Association 189
South Asia Americans Leading Together (SAALT) 74
South Asia/South Asian 2, 27, 37, 57, 65, 74, 77, 149, 161, 185, 203, 210, 212, 260, 265, 266, 267, 268, 269, 270
South Asian Lesbian and Gay Association (SALGA) 267
South Carolina 10, 13, 46, 150, 160, 210, 263
South Jordan 40
South Pacific 22
South Virginia 53
South Windsor Hospital 181
Southwest Asia 159
Soviet 23
Spacey, Kevin 204
Spielberg, Steven 205, 207
Spivak, Gayatri Chakravorty 103, 109, 262
Sreenivasan, TP 19, 66
Sri Ganesha Hindu Temple 40
Sri Lanka/Sri Lankan 2, 4, 251, 252
Srinivasa, Krishna 57
Srinivasan, Sri 45
St Lawrence University 113
St Regis Hotel 54
Stallone, Sylvester 216
Standard & Poor 122
Stanford University 94, 102, 103, 106, 107, 108, 115, 116, 154, 156, 175, 198
State Department 65, 66, 148, 154
Staton, Cecil P 232
Statue of Liberty 38
Steitz, Thomas A 166
Stony Brook School of Medicine 175
Struve, Otto 165
Subbarow, Yellapragada 183, 184, 185
Subbaswamy, Kumble R 113
Subrahmanyam, Sanjay 108
Sudarshan, ECG 17
Sun Microsystems 40, 78
SUNY-Buffalo 113
Surendranath, Yogesh 175
Suresh, Subra 106, 151
Suriname 3, 5
Sushruta 182
SVC Inc 150
Swasthya Community Health Partnership 153
Swaziland 250, 251, 252
Swiss 29

Symphony Technology Group 40, 94
Syntel 263

Tabu 204
Taj Campton Place 95
Tak, Mahinder 47, 48
Talbott, Strobe 26, 27
Tanden, Neera 152, 153, 162
Tandon, Chandrika 144
Tanzanians 16
Tata Chair for Strategic Affairs 159
Tata Consultancy 85
Tata Institute of Fundamental Research 166
Tebbit, Norman 17
Television Academy 209
Tellis, Ashley J 68, 159
Telugu Association of North America (TANA) 62
Temple University 57, 157
Tenderloin 223
Tewari, Sujata 262
Texas 11, 14, 39, 43, 45, 60, 62, 66, 68, 71, 72, 76, 77, 143, 195, 198
Thailand 127
Thanedar, Shri 73
The Center for Public Leadership 74
The Economist 29, 115
The Enterprise 90
The Giving Pledge 142
The Hartford 122
The Hershey Company 250
The Hindu 14, 45, 110
The Indus Entrepreneurs (TiE) 81
The Post-American 159
The Rockefeller Foundation 141
The Wall Street Journal 84
The Washington Leadership Program (WLP) 42
The We Company 122
Thind, Bhagat Singh 56, 57
Thiruvalla 157
Thiruvananthapuram 29
Thrifty Food Plan 159
Toronto 218, 243, 248
Travolta, John 216
TrialNetworks 153
Trichy 173
Trikone 267
Trinidad and Tobago/Trinidadian 3, 10, 240, 242
Trinity College 110, 165
Tripathi, Satish K 109, 113, 114
Trivedi, Manan 48
Troubled Asset Relief Program (TARP) 160
Truman, Harry 56, 58
Trump, Donald 14, 15, 16, 33, 34, 50, 148, 150, 151, 154, 158, 163, 195, 246, 263
Tulia 11
Tyco 120

UC Davis 107
UC Santa Cruz 107
Uganda 223
Ullal, Jayshree 94, 262
UMass Amherst 113
Union City 95
Uniphore 97
United Nations Development Program 218
United States Citizenship and Immigration Services (USCIS) 260
United States Travel and Tourism Advisory Board 233
University at Buffalo 109, 113, 114
University of Alabama 199
University of Calcutta 108
University of Califonia-Riverside 155
University of California 101, 105, 154, 166, 173, 175
University of California (UC), Berkeley 109, 154, 245
University of California, Los Angeles (UCLA) 105, 108, 171, 173, 203
University of California-San Diego 101, 111, 175
University of Chicago 104, 105, 165, 168
University of Chicago Booth School of Business 104, 112, 115

University of Chicago Law School 156
University of Colorado 177
University of Connecticut 109
University of Delhi 108
University of Florida 155
University of Houston 68, 113
University of Illinois, Chicago (UIC) 170
University of Illinois-Urbana-Champaign 109, 117, 175
University of Iowa 103
University of Liverpool 104, 166
University of Louisiana System 160
University of Louisville 113
University of Madras 104
University of Michigan 103, 252
University of Michigan, Ann Arbor 108
University of Minnesota 156, 175
University of Minnesota School of Public Health 156
University of Missouri (MU) 113
University of Pennsylvania Law School 109
University of Pittsburgh 104
University of Punjab 166
University of Texas 113, 177
University of Virginia 149, 175
University of Washington 110
University of West Georgia 102
University of Wisconsin 105, 109, 166
University of Wisconsin-Milwaukee 115
Upaya Social Ventures 141
UPenn 113
Upright Citizens Brigade 210
US Agency for International Development (USAID) 45, 149
US Air Force 148
US Airways Group 122
US and Foreign Commercial Service (USFCS) 149
US Comedy Arts Festival 211
US Court of Appeals 45
US Department of Defense 156
US Department of Health and Human Services 152
US Federal Communications Commission (FCC) 150
US Food and Drug Administration (FDA) 184
US Planck Data Center 173
US Public Health Service Commissioned Corps 193
US–India Business Council (USIBC) 32, 69, 149
US–India CEO Forum 149
US–India Chamber of Commerce 198
US–India Civil Nuclear Agreement 71
US–India Friendship Council 69
US–India Innovation Forum 149
US–India Political Action Committee (USINPAC) 69, 161
US–India Strategic & Commercial Dialogue (S&CD) 149
US–India Strategic Partnership Forum 148
Utah 38, 40, 104
Uttar Pradesh (UP) 123, 160

Vadodara 224
Vaidya, Omi 215, 216
Vajpayee, Atal Bihari 27, 28, 29, 30
Vallabh, Sonia 126
Vancouver 166
Vanderbilt University 175
Vanguard Group 120
Varghese, Maju 157
Varkey, Sherly 142
Varkey, Sunny 142
Varshney, Ashutosh 108
Vasavada, Ashwin 171
Vayali, Shamsheer 142
Vayali, Shabeena 142
Venkatesh, Akshay 108
Verma, Richard Rahul 148
Verma, Seema 150, 263
Vijay and Marie Goradia Foundation 140
Vijayawada 194
Virata Corporation 115
Virginia 53, 149, 156, 175, 176
VISIONS Worldwide 153
VisionSpring 137
Vogel, David 206
Vora, Ankur 141

Wadhwani Foundation 139, 140
Wadhwani, Romesh 40, 93, 139, 142
Walt, Stephen 55
Warren, Elizabeth 155
Warrior, Padmasree 94, 122, 262
Washington 6, 20, 23, 24, 25, 27, 28, 29, 37, 42, 43, 46, 48, 49, 53, 54, 58, 61, 63, 65, 66, 67, 69, 70, 110, 148, 149, 156, 160, 161, 170, 186, 189, 192, 193, 232, 263
Washington, DC 37, 42, 46, 47, 48, 49, 53, 54, 61, 63, 66, 69, 70, 148, 156, 170, 186, 189, 232
Washington, George 58
Wayfair 122
Wazed, Sheikh Hasina 2
Wells College 113
West Godavari 184
West Virginia 156
West Virginia Ophthalmology Foundation 198
West Virginia University 156
Wharton School 115, 154, 160
White House 2, 10, 14, 15, 27, 33, 44, 45, 58, 61, 67, 71, 96, 147, 155, 156, 157, 159, 198, 215
White House Office of Digital Strategy 155
White House Office of Management and Budget 152
Whole Foods 95
Williams, Sunita 13, 177
Willis, Bruce 206, 216
Win, Ne 21
WindRiver Systems 115
Wipro 85
WISH Foundation 140
Witt/Kieffer 114
WLP 42, 65
Woliner, Jason 211
Woman's Medical College of Pennsylvania 183
Wood, John 91
World Bank 136
Wulf, Norman A 71
Wycliffe, Sunny 20
Wyoming 263

Yale Law School 152
Yale University 109, 152, 153, 155, 176, 182
Yang, Jerry 86
Yangon 21
Yonath, Ada E 166
YouGov 14
Yuba City 35

Zachariah, Zach 57
Zakaria, Fareed 83, 159
Zander, Edward 92
Zeya, Uzra 154
Zia, Khaleda 2
Zimbabwe 238